Clíona Ní Ríordáin, Stephanie Schwerter (eds.)

Speaking Like a Spanish Cow:
Cultural Errors in Translation
With a foreword by Michael Cronin

The editors of this book would like to thank the
Université Polytechnique Hauts-de-France (UPHF) and the
Université franco-allemande (UFA) for their kind and
generous support for this publication.

Clíona Ní Ríordáin, Stephanie Schwerter (eds.)

SPEAKING LIKE A SPANISH COW: CULTURAL ERRORS IN TRANSLATION

With a foreword by Michael Cronin

Bibliografische Information der Deutschen Nationalbibliothek
Die Deutsche Nationalbibliothek verzeichnet diese Publikation in der Deutschen Nationalbibliografie; detaillierte bibliografische Daten sind im Internet über http://dnb.d-nb.de abrufbar.

Bibliographic information published by the Deutsche Nationalbibliothek
Die Deutsche Nationalbibliothek lists this publication in the Deutsche Nationalbibliografie; detailed bibliographic data are available in the Internet at http://dnb.d-nb.de.

ISBN-13: 978-3-8382-1256-2
© *ibidem*-Verlag, Stuttgart 2019
Alle Rechte vorbehalten

Das Werk einschließlich aller seiner Teile ist urheberrechtlich geschützt. Jede Verwertung außerhalb der engen Grenzen des Urheberrechtsgesetzes ist ohne Zustimmung des Verlages unzulässig und strafbar. Dies gilt insbesondere für Vervielfältigungen, Übersetzungen, Mikroverfilmungen und elektronische Speicherformen sowie die Einspeicherung und Verarbeitung in elektronischen Systemen.

All rights reserved. No part of this publication may be reproduced, stored in or introduced into a retrieval system, or transmitted, in any form, or by any means (electronic, mechanical, photocopying, recording or otherwise) without the prior written permission of the publisher. Any person who does any unauthorized act in relation to this publication may be liable to criminal prosecution and civil claims for damages.

Printed in the EU

Table of Contents

Foreword
Michael Cronin IX

Introduction
Clíona Ní Ríordáin, Stephanie Schwerter XVII

Errors or Manipulation?

From Incongruence to Inhospitality, and Back Again:
Conceptualizing Cultural Error with Ricœur
Terence Holden 1

On the Websites of Others
Katja Grupp 21

"The Echo We Hear is Not the Echo of Our Own Words and Even
the Best Translation is Something Alien": On the Translation
of German Exile Literature
Angela Vaupel 49

On the Translation of Bulgakov's *A Young Doctor's Notebooks* into
the Language of the Cinema
Marina Tsvetkova 69

Tom Paulin's Destabilising Translations: Misunderstandings,
Errors, Manipulations
Stephanie Schwerter 91

(Mis-)reading Cultural References

How Khayyám Got Lost in Translation: Cultural Errors and
the Translators of the *Rubáiyát*
  Bentolhoda Nakhaei 113

Too Graphic a Novel?! *Charlie Hebdo*, Cultural Connotations, and
Change of Register in the German Translation of Luz' *Catharsis*
  Marie Schröer 135

The End of Eddy, The End of France?
  Clíona Ní Ríordáin 163

Translation Errors in Higher Education
  Gundula Gwenn Hiller 181

Blind Rice for Lunch? Cultural Errors and Their Impact on Tourism
  Ana Isabel Foulquié-Rubio, Paula Cifuentes-Férez 205

Creative Errors

Cultural Errors and Creativity: How Visual and Textual Triggers
Create New Meanings
  Costas Mantzalos, Vicky Pericleous 227

Translation and Tragic Error: Culture, Conflict and Northern Irish
Translations of Sophocles' *Antigone*
  Charles Ivan Armstrong 251

The Farmer, the French Translator and the Traveling Salesman:
Cultural Errors in Bob Dylan's Satirical Songs
  Jean-Charles Meunier 269

The Vanishing of Verlaine: Cultural Error in Translations of
Gainsbourg's "Je suis venu te dire que je m'en vais"
    Paul Grundy..289

Edward's Filmer's French Court Airs Englished
    Chantal Schütz...315

Authors 339

Foreword

Blaise Pascal in his *Pensées* was not particularly hopeful about the constancy of affection. One day you wake up and the other is no longer the beloved but a complete stranger:

> Il n'aime plus cette personne qu'il aimait il y a dix ans. Je crois bien : elle n'est plus la même, ni lui non plus. Il était jeune et elle aussi ; elle est tout autre. Il l'aimerait peut-être encore, telle qu'elle était alors. (II, 123)

> [He no longer loves the person he loved ten years ago. I believe: she is not the same nor is he. He was young and so was she; she is completely different. Perhaps, he would love her still as she was then.]

For the French philosopher, the fickleness of human affections demands the durability of divine love. Underlying Pascal's description of the hapless lovers is a particular way of viewing events, which is central to Western ontology. One moment the couple are in love, the next they are not. I am sitting or I am standing but I cannot be doing both at the same time. Otherwise, I am in the realm of the paradoxical. The work of *logos* is to determine. The more the object is determined, the greater the sensation of the object's existence. Hence, the great movement in Western art in the early and late Renaissance, as EH Gombrich has pointed out, to give weight, heft and substance to the world through the determinations of the artist's brush. The more vivid the sense of the world on canvas, the more it could be said to properly exist. The difficulty is what to do with or how to think about transitional states, that position between one state, one language and another.

Aristotle in his *Physics* tries to offer a definition of the colour grey and claims that it is black with the respect to white and white with respect to black (67). There is a distinct uneasiness here about what is neither black nor white but something in between. The ontological fixation makes thinking about certain phenomena difficult or problematic. Can we say there is an exact moment when people fall out of love? Is there a precise minute or hour or day when I begin to grow old? Am I young at 11.55 am and middle-aged at 12? Can we specify the hour, the day, the year, when the Soviet Union entered irreversible decline?

Answering any or all of these questions is not easy and suggests that our own specific conceptual traditions may not always be adequate to the experiences that are the lot of humans. The French sinologist François Jullien advocates the usefulness of looking at other traditions as a way of both revealing blind spots in how we interpret the world and locating repertoires of thinking that allow us to capture important dimensions to subjective and social experience. In his case, he draws on the Chinese term, biàntōng, which can be variously translated as "to accommodate to circumstances", "flexible", "to act differently in different situations" (26-27) as a way of thinking about transition in a way that is not beholden to Western ontological assumptions. The two characters that make up the word refer to "modification" and "continuation". At one level, these are opposites but at another, each is the precondition of the other. It is thanks to "modification" that a process engaged in does not exhaust itself but is renewed and can "continue" and it is thanks to "continuation" that modification can communicate itself, can make sense in the context of the overall process. By way of illustrating what he means by "silent transformations", Jullien selects one of the abiding themes of classical Chinese art, the passage of the seasons:

> La « modification » intervient de l'hiver au printemps, ou de l'été à l'automne, quand le froid s'inverse et tend vers le chaud, ou le chaud vers le froid; la « continuation », quant à elle, se manifeste du printemps à l'été, ou de l'automne à l'hiver, quand le chaud devient plus chaud ou le froid plus froid. L'un et l'autre moment alternent, de modification ou

de continuation, mais même celui de la modification, en réparant par l'autre le facteur qui s'épuise, opère au profit de son autre et sert à la continuation d'ensemble du procès. (27)

[The "modification" comes in the passage from winter to spring, or from summer to autumn when the cold changes to warm or the warm changes to cold; the "continuation" is apparent in the passage from spring to summer or from autumn to winter when the warm becomes warmer or the cold colder. Each moment of modification or communication alternates, but even modification, by repairing through the other the factor that is exhausting itself, operates to the benefit of the other and allows the whole process to continue.]

From this standpoint, it is not defining Being or substance (offering precise definitions of what constitutes winter, spring, summer or autumn) that matters but rather the actual process of change itself. What the binomial term with its polar opposites attempts to account for is the nature and coherence of the transition just as each word I am writing is new (modification) but I am still (I hope) making sense (continuation). Thus, to return to Pascal's example the focus is not on the subject, the lover who no longer loves or is loved, but on the process that leads to this state of affairs. The process itself becomes the true subject of enquiry. This enduring Western ontological prejudice is powerfully reinforced in the contemporary moment by the binary logic of the digital - one/zero, on/off.

The focus on epochal moments of rupture – *Ten Days that Shook the World* – is inimical to the ontological status of translation which is infinitely more akin to Jullien's paradigm of silent transformations – the gradual shift from one state to another through the cumulative effects of a multiplicity of minor changes. This makes the relationship between translation and social change often difficult to account for as translation does not lend itself easily to the schismatic ontological drama of the Great Turning Point or the Revolutionary Event (Meylaerts and Gonne 133-151). On the other hand, in offering a more credible pointer as to how change actually occurs – whether this involves the dissemination of Buddhist teachings in China or the spread of Reformation thinking in Western Christendom – translation can help us to think through implications of changes in knowledge organisation in our culture.

Errare humanum est. The Latin tag suggests the only error is to be believed we do not err. If the error is conscious, we call it manipulation, if unconscious, creativity. *Errare*, of course, also means to wander or to stray and here we have to be mindful of the nomadic logic of translation, the wandering between languages and cultures, the straying between disciplines and beliefs. If translation through the paradigm of silent transformation is so resistant to the dichotomous ontology of on/off, yes/no, us/them, it is because it inevitably involves a straying away from the essentialist comforts of partisan identification. We see an example of this errant behaviour in the fortunes of Alexis-François Rio's *De la poésie chrétienne* (1836) translated into English in 1854.

The translation is read by John Ruskin who is particularly taken by what Rio has to say about the Sistine frescoes and the English critic begins for the first time to take an interest in a largely neglected Italian painter, Sandro Botticelli (Levey 291-306). Botticelli is subsequently championed by the pre-Raphaelite disciples of Ruskin and the rest is art history (Kermode 3-31). The translation strays back into the language of the source text in the prominence of Botticelli in Proust's *À la recherche du temps perdu*, the French translator of Ruskin indirectly acknowledging the artistic benefaction of his English master (Karpeles 122-125). To err on the side of caution may be the preferred option of the censor or the self-censor of the translator in contested circumstances. However, even the most anodyne of translations can end up throwing caution to winds. Who would have expected a translation of a book on Christian poetry in the 1830s to change the course of Western art history and profoundly shape the iconographic outreach of one of the most important writers in the French language in the 20th century? It is indeed this spirit of nomadic enquiry, this desire to treat all comfort zones as potential exclusion zones, which informs the essays in this collection. In particular, the essays challenge the prescriptivist terror of what might be termed "errorism", the use of translation "mistakes" as a way of punitively getting students to subscribe to the disciplinary regime of the fair copy. This version of the linguistic superego, which has dogged translation from the hazing rituals of instruction in classical languages to the Darwinian logic of elimination in *thème* and *version* tests for State competitive examinations in France and elsewhere, means that to err is to be consigned to the sub-human. This pedagogic war on error rarely has happy outcomes. For many, translation becomes forever after associated with the generalised anxiety of the language classroom, the *forts en thème* like the successful candidates in *The Apprentice* or *The Weakest Link* strutting forward into the rising sun of fame and fortune under the humiliated gaze of their more linguistically challenged peers. Another casualty of the war on error is translation practice itself which comes to seen as an arid form of substitutionism, finding the "right" word (preferably in a dictionary) or phrase (preferably on the internet) to avoid being outed in red ink. What the present volume demonstrates is the poverty of this legacy, the extent to which translation offers a way into thinking about language, culture and society that resists the summary logic of the "errorists".

  Maggie Berg and Barbara Seeber in *The Slow Professor* have detailed the consequences of cultures of accelerated productivity for universities and the continual erosion of the spaces and possibilities of deep thought. As the impending ecological crisis demands decelerationist, long-term, non-extractivist thinking and practice it suggests that we look to translation as an activity which potentially offers careful, attentive, time-rich attention to language and text. The French translator Mireille Gansel describes how she initially retranslated "Sensible Wege", the title of a poem by Reiner Kunze, as "Fragile Paths" and then, thirty years later, retranslated it as "Sensitive Paths". A change in one word reflected three decades of reading and experience and she notes that at the moment of making the change she "understood translation both as risk taking and continual re-examination, of even a single word – a delicate seismograph at the heart of time" (36).

This concern for time and the requirement to respect the time necessary for translation expressed by certain translators (Schwartz) is easily mocked by the pragmatico-realists of the translation industry but it is the intrinsic temporal logic of the latter that will precipitate ecological mayhem not the thoughtful deliberateness of the former. The championing of a different kind of translation kinetics – a one that values an investment in the long now – should no longer be seen as a quaint throwback to a world of unearned privilege but as the only feasible way of creating a world based on long-term sustainability. Reflecting on and discussing what are perceived or construed as errors is part of that careful, painstaking attention to the consequences of translated language. For translation to have a future it must reflect on how it might contribute to that future. Challenging fundamental ontological prejudices, helping to elaborate new forms of knowledge organisation and focusing on the development of non-reductionist approaches to translation analysis and pedagogy are part of this potential brief to which the present volume contributes. If Frank Wynne has argued that "translators are the beating heart that make it possible for stories to flow beyond borders and across oceans" (np.), translation must not only be about beating hearts but about thinking heads.

Michael Cronin
Dublin, 28 February 2019

Works cited

Aristotle. *Physics*. Oxford University Press, 2008.

Berg, Maggie; Seeber, Barbara. *The Slow Professor: Challenging the Culture of Speed in the Academy*. University of Toronto Press, 2016.

Gombrich, Ernest H. *The Story of Art*. Phaidon, 2007.

Jullien, François. *Les transformations silencieuses: Chantiers, I*. Livre de Poche, 2009.

Karpeles, Eric. *Paintings in Proust: A Visual Companion to in Search of Lost Time*. Thames and Hudson, 2008.

Kermode, Frank. *Forms of Attention*. University of Chicago Press, 2011.

Levey, Michael. "Botticelli and Nineteenth-Century England". *Journal of the Warburg and Courtauld Institutes*, no. 23, 1960, pp. 291-306.

Meylaerts, Reine and Gonne, Maud. "Transferring the city – transgressing borders: cultural mediators in Antwerp (1850-1930)". *Translation Studies*, vol. 7 no. 2, 2014, pp. 133-151.

Pascal, Blaise. *Pensées*. Livre de Poche, 2000 [1670].

Wynne, Frank (ed.). *Found in Translation*. Head of Zeus, 2018.

Webography

Schwartz, Ros. "How Long Will It Take You to Type This in English?", *ATA Chronicle*. http://www.atanetorg/ chronicle-online/featured/how-long-will-it-take-you-to-type-this-in-english, 2017. Accessed 1 February 2019.

Introduction

> Ever tried. Ever failed. No matter.
> Try again. Fail again. Fail better.
> Samuel Beckett (7)

The central tension that has wracked Translation Studies since its inception has been that of fidelity/infidelity to the source text. This paradigm is premised on linguistic fidelity, and as such is typified by the French vein in translation studies, which focusses on comparative micro-analyses of source and target text, as outlined by Jean-Pierre Vinay and Jean Darbelnet in their pioneering volume *Stylistique comparée du français et de l'anglais*. The authors establish a typology of translation procedures ["procédés de traduction"], which are often transformed into a compendium of errors by those who engage in pedagogical translation exercises.

Our volume adopts a different angle – its approach seeks to focus on cultural errors, often determined by an incomprehension of underlying cultural references in the source texts and the source culture, and it veers away from purely linguistic considerations to examine translation problems via the wide-angled lens of intercultural contact zones (Mary Louise Pratt 33-40). The scope of the different chapters is resolutely interdisciplinary, and a macro-analytical viewpoint is adopted by many of the contributors, who discuss a broad range of topics from cinema to visual art, from literature to music and politics.

How does one define the notion of cultural error? Cultural errors may take various shapes and forms and may generate completely different readings of the source text in translation. They occur when the translator ignores or misunderstands one or several connotations that underpin a term, which is unique to the source culture. In this instance, the cultural error is due to an insufficient knowledge of the cultural environment from which the source text emerges. As Robert C. Sprung underlines: "Effective translation bridges the gap between cultures, not merely words" (xiv). Elsewhere, a translator may be conscious of the cultural implications of a term but is unable to transfer it appropriately into the target culture. This type of cultural error may generate ambiguous or inconsistent translations, which can lead readers of the target text astray. An instance of this can be seen when one examines the term "male nurse" – time and time again it is wrongly translated into German as "männliche Krankenschwester". While it is correct from a linguistic perspective, any native German speaker would probably associate the term with transvestism, as verbatim it suggests the image of a male dressed up as a female nurse. The culturally correct term in German is "Krankenpfleger" [literally "carer for the sick"].

Translators can also ignore or overlook a cultural element in an effort to simplify a complicated cultural notion. This may lead to the elimination of a key aspect of the cultural notion that impedes the comprehension of the source text's message. Some translators also choose to omit certain cultural connotations in a deliberate attempt to attribute another meaning to the source text. This can be viewed as an effort on the part of the translator to reinvent the concept in the target culture in order to influence those who engage with the target text. In this case, the question arises as to whether the translator has made a cultural error or is attempting to manipulate unsuspecting readers.

All of these definitions view the error in terms of loss or even manipulation, however, it is important also to acknowledge the positive dimension of the error. Errors can be the source of serendipitous discoveries, in science for instance, or can be the source of inspiration. Errors can also reveal modes of thought, which can in turn be typical of a particular cultural mindset. For theorist André Lefevere, in *Translating, Rewriting and the Manipulation of Literary Fame*, or for Clive Scott in *Translating Rimbaud's Illuminations*, the divergences between source text and target text are not to be viewed as errors, rather they are to be considered as deliberate acts of rewriting or re-creation, where the notion of error is evacuated in favour of the creative impulse.

Multiple volumes devoted to the notion of errors in translation have been published to date in the field of Translation studies. Umberto Eco's *Dire quasi la stessa cosa. Esperienze di traduzione* and David Bellos' *Is that A Fish in Your Ear* outline the many pitfalls that await unsuspecting translators. Jörn Albrecht in *Literarische Übersetzung* pays particular attention to literary translation from an historical angle but does not devote any space to the question of cultural errors. Mona Baker in *Translation and Conflict* argues that translation is a form of narration, and she outlines the disastrous consequences that errors in translation can have in relationships between warring nations. Maria Tymoczko and Edwin Genztler explore the thematics of the error from a sociological perspective in *Translation and Power*. The cultural aspect of the translation error is addressed in *Translating Cultures* by David Katan and in *Translation, Power, Subversion* by Román Álvarez and Carmen-África Vidal. However, only one or two chapters of these volumes are devoted to the notion of cultural errors, an entire volume on the topic has not been published to date.

  This volume is divided into three complimentary sections. Part One examines the controversial topic of the relationship between error and manipulation. The first essay examines the notion of cultural error through the prism of Paul Ricœur's key themes of incongruence and inhospitality. Katja Grupp's chapter on the Russian website *InoSMI.ru* leaves us in no doubt as to the important role translation and cultural errors play in international relations. The distinctly Russian flavour persists in the other essays in the section, which draw on the BBC's production of Mikhail Bulgakov's *A Young Doctor's Notebooks*, while Stephanie Schwerter's article explores the "Irishing" of poems by Vladimir Mayakovsky, Alexander Pushkin and Anna Akhmatova. Part Two is devoted to the (mis-)reading of cultural references. These essays address controversial topics like the reception of comics in the wake of the *Charlie Hebdo* attacks, and cultural errors that influenced the reception of the work of Omar Khayyám. The final section focusses on the serendipitous nature of the error by turning its attention to the creative dimension that emerges from cultural errors, and has a distinctly lyrical feeling, with articles that examine the work of Bob Dylan, Serge Gainsbourg, and the court airs of Edward Filmer. In this section, the authors address questions related to art, music, and literature (notably for the adaptations of Sophocles). In each case, they highlight the innovative impulse that is created by perceived cultural errors.

The title of our volume seeks to highlight the incomeprehension fostered by a literal translation as a result of inadequate cultural information. The expression "parler comme une vache espagnole" can be traced back to Honoré de Balzac, where in *Splendeurs et misères des courtisanes*, the character Jacques Collin is described as "speaking like a Spanish cow": "Jacques Collin parlait le français comme une vache espagnole en baragouinant de manière à rendre ses réponses presque inintelligibles et à s'en faire demander la repetition" (Balzac 419) [Jacques Collin spoke French like a Spanish cow, jabbering so much that he made his replies almost incomprehensible and was constantly asked to repeat himself]. However the expression, if nineteenth century etymologists are to be believed, makes reference not to a "vache" but to a "Basque" (Roznan 236; Quitard 676), in other words someone speaks French badly because s/he speaks with the accent of a native of the Spanish Basque province. In translating this idiomatic expression, one has to resort to paraphrase as a corresponding image does not exist in English.

In conclusion, we hope this volume will provide food for thought for all of those who attempt to bridge cultural barriers via translation. We have demonstrated that translators are more than mere wordsmiths; they also are also vital actors who decode cultural contexts in order to act as worthy intermediaries in the area of linguistic exchanges on the world stage.

Clíona Ní Ríordáin, Stephanie Schwerter
Paris, 15 February 2019

Works cited

Albrecht, Jörn. *Literarische Übersetzung. Geschichte. Theorie. Kulturelle Wirkung*. Wissenschaftliche Buchgesellschaft, 2006.

Álvarez, Román; Vidal, Carmen-África. *Translation, Power, Subersion*. Multilingual Matters, 1996.

Baker, Mona. *Translation and Conflict. A Narrative Account*. Routledge, 2006.

Balzac, Honoré. *Splendeurs et misères des courtisanes*. Fourne et Dubochet, 1847.

Beckett, Samuel. *Worstward Ho!* John Chandler, 1983.

Bellos, David. *Is That a Fish in Your Ear?* Allen Lane, 2011.

Eco, Umberto. *Dire quasi la stessa cosa. Esperienze di traduzione*. Bompiani, 2003.

Lefevere, André. *Translation, Rewriting and the Manipulation of Literary Fame*. Routledge, 1992.

Pratt, Mary Louise. "Arts of the Contact Zone". *Profession*. MLA, 1991, pp. 33-40.

Quitard, Pierre Marie. *Études historiques, littéraires et morales sur les provebes français et le langage proverbial*. Techener, 1860.

Roznan, Charles. *Petites ignorances de la conversation*. Lacroix–Comon, 1857.

Scott, Clive. *Translating Rimbaud's "Illuminations"*. University of Exeter Press, 2006.

Sprung, Robert C. "Introduction". *Translating into Success: Cutting-edge Strategies for Going Multilingual in a Global Age*, edited by Robert C. Sprung. John Benjamins, 2000, pp. ix-xxii.

Tymoczko, Maria; Gentzler, Edwin (eds.). *Translation and Power*. University of Massachusetts Press, 2002.

Vinlay, Jean-Pierre; Darbelnet, Jean. *Stylistique comparée du français et de l'anglais*. Didier, 1958.

Errors or Manipulation?

From Incongruence to Inhospitality, and Back Again: Conceptualizing Cultural Error with Ricœur

Terence Holden

Introduction

If we are to engage with Ricœur's late work on translation, we must first look through it. *On Translation* appears initially to present us with a somewhat sketchy theoretical framework cobbled together from a series of guest lectures; and yet it is one of the final products of a long and rich intellectual career. In seeking to gauge the value of this text for arriving at a deepened understanding of cultural error, I will treat it as the uppermost layer of a palimpsest. Ricœur proposes a dialogical theory of translation, which draws upon the dialogical model of self-identity which he develops in *Oneself as Another*. However, little of the ambiguity of the latter text, in what concerns notably the relation between universal and particular, finds its way into his text on translation. Accordingly, I will here seek to explore the consequences for our conceptualizing of cultural error of a more sustained confrontation between these two works.

I will first reconstruct the guiding trajectory of *On Translation*, which leads from the abandonment of the standard of correspondence underpinned by a metaphysics of the "perfect language" towards the standard of hospitality on which Ricœur founds his ethics of translation. I will then seek to bring out the particularity of the idea of cultural error, which thus emerges by considering what Ricœur contributes to Berman's dialogical model of the "experience of the foreign". I will ultimately argue that the true contribution of Ricœur lies in the unintended consequences which accompany his attempt to transpose his dialogical model of self-identity into the sphere of translation, and that a return to *Oneself as Another* requires us to revisit much of what Ricœur rejects in arriving at his ethics of hospitality.

1. From correspondence to hospitality

The idea of cultural error which emerges from Ricœur's short work on translation is the culmination of a transition. Ricœur's point of departure is a rejection of the standard of correspondence from the perspective of which cultural error would amount to incongruence between the translation and its original. The problem with this standard, Ricœur tells us, is that it comes with metaphysical baggage and, in this first section, I will detail how the dialogical standard of hospitality is to emerge from a jettisoning of this baggage.

The first element of this baggage is the notion of a "perfect language" which has nourished the utopian vision of many across the centuries. In the foreground is Walter Benjamin's model of the "pure language" which does not suffer estrangement from the "creative word" as all historical languages do. In accomplishing his or her task, Benjamin insists, the translator is to bring the latter into greater proximity to the former (261). The messianic horizon of a pure language which Benjamin seeks is of course biblical in origin, although strongly influenced by the meditations on language by the German Romantics. A more explicitly secular refraction of the biblical notion of an Edenic language, Ricœur informs us, is the Enlightenment dream of "building up the complete library, which would be, by accumulation, the Book, the infinitely ramified network of the translations of all the works in all the languages, crystallizing into a sort of universal library from which the untranslatabilities would have been erased" (*On Translation* 9).

It is this desire to transcend the limitations of lingua-cultural conventions, which represents for Ricœur the most regrettable aspect of both models. It is a desire, however, which is as old as Europe itself. Europe was obliged "at the very moment of its birth to confront the drama of linguistic fragmentation", we discover from Eco, and a natural response to this fragmentation was the search for a remedy whereby "some looked backwards, trying to rediscover the language spoken by Adam. Others looked ahead, aiming to fabricate a rational language possessing the perfections of the lost speech of Eden" (19). Into such retrospective and prospective projections of this same goal we may integrate the discussion surrounding the possibility of a universal grammar prominent in medieval culture, Lull's meditations on a universal mathematics of combination, Dante's hunt for a proto-vernacular, Bohme's sensual speech and Leibniz's *lingua genera*. Eco detects the traces of this perennial dream in the generative grammar of Chomsky (45).

Ricœur insists that the horizon of a "perfect language" transcending lingua-cultural limitations is also projected whenever the ideal of the "perfect translation" is brought into play, either implicitly or explicitly. In essence, it is brought into play whenever the standard by which a translation is judged is that of "correspondence" or "faithfulness" to the original. Any espousal or mere practical investment in this standard presupposes the ideal of a third language, which overarches the original and target language, as a position from which the level of correspondence can be established. More emphatically, the notion of a perfect language is one possible response to the recognition that something more complex is taking place in translation than the mere "duplication" of the original. According to the model of the "perfect" translation, the translator should do more than create a double of the original: the act of translation should at least partially free the text from the limitations of the source language (*On Translation* 6). Benjamin expresses most clearly how such a dynamic brings into play the horizon of a perfect language. The translator is not to imitate the original but to awaken the pure language from within the original, the "ultimate, decisive element" which "remains beyond all communication – quite close and yet infinitely remote" (261). In pursuit of this element, Benjamin exhorts the translator to follow a trajectory, tangential to both source and target languages, which leads towards the pure language.

Ricœur's principal objection to this ideal of a perfect translation, informed by the vision of a perfect language, is that the epistemic confidence it proffers comes at too high a price. The correspondence which this ideal installs as standard is impossible for any historically situated language to satisfy: only the "pure language" itself, within which the "totality" of the partial "intentions" of each language "supplement one another", would be able to ensure that what is gained across the process of translation is not outmatched by what is lost (Benjamin 257). Translation is thereby inscribed within a horizon of pathological mourning, and it is to free translation from this horizon that Ricœur seeks to replace the standard of correspondence with that of hospitality. It is worth citing Ricœur in full:

> When the translator acknowledges and assumes the irreducibility of the pair, the peculiar and the foreign, he finds his reward in the recognition of the impassable status reasonable horizon of the desire to translate. In spite of the agonistics that make a drama of the translator's task, he can find his happiness in what I would like to call linguistic hospitality. (*On Translation* 9)

Gone is the "kinship" between languages presupposed by Benjamin, we are instead confronted with their "irreducibility". No longer may we entertain the standard of faithfulness invoked across the reconstitution of the original within the target language; we are rather called to welcome within the "same" that which could never be reduced to it: the distance between languages is no longer to be overcome; rather a certain "distance in proximity" is to be preserved in an act of self-alienation performed by the translator on behalf of the target language. The provisional status of this hospitality, of the welcoming the other within the same, establishes a correlation between translation and conversation, hence the "dialogical" character which Ricœur seeks to attribute to translation: translation is envisioned as the product of a conversation between languages, and like all conversations remains unfinished, culminating at most in a "fragile" consensus (*On Translation* 10).

We might refer to the resonance of Eco's exegesis of the myth of Babel within Ricœur's work when seeking to understand what is at stake in his turn towards hospitality. Genesis 11 presents us with a familiar myth: a plurality of languages is imposed as a curse upon humanity, who in its hubris seeks to build a tower to the heavens to rival God. Genesis 10, in its listing of the descendants of Noah, provides a different reading of this plurality. It is presented merely as the product of the natural progression of one generation to the next, and as such it represents "a chink in the armour of the myth of Babel. If languages were differentiated not as a punishment but simply as a result of a natural process, why must the confusion of tongues constitute a curse at all?" (Eco 10)

What for Ricœur secures passage from a paradigm of translation dominated by Genesis 11, a domination to which Benjamin's work on translation clearly attests, towards Genesis 10 is the adoption of the dialogical model of translation orientated towards the standard of hospitality. "Translation is definitely a task", Ricœur tells us, "not in the sense of a restricting obligation, but in the sense of the thing to be done so that human action can simply continue" (*On Translation* 19): the plurality of languages with which translation negotiates is not to be mourned; it is intrinsic to being human. The most human of actions is speech, and speech would be neither possible nor necessary from the perspective of a language purified of all heterogeneity. Such a language would be capable of no more than continuous monologue. Likewise, no standard of hospitality would be possible from the perspective of translation viewed in terms of correspondence underpinned by a perfect language to the extent that we cannot be hospitable towards ourselves.

Ricœur's model of translation, underpinned by the standard of hospitality where "the pleasure of dwelling in the other's language is balanced by the pleasure of receiving the foreign word at home", is certainly liberating in that it dispels any air of excessive mourning through its invocation of a "happiness" brought about through such an exchange (10). In what follows, I will pose two interlinked questions. Is this transition from correspondence to hospitality fully realizable? How in practice does Ricœur's ethics of hospitality, in its unmooring from the perspective of a perfect language, change our understanding of cultural error? I will argue ultimately that an adequate response to the second question is contingent upon arriving at a negative response to the first.

2. Ricœur and the dialogical model of translation

By re-orientating the exercise of translation away from correspondence and toward the standard of hospitality, Ricœur's model of translation strongly echoes the ethical turn in translation studies, or as Drugan and Tipton put it: "the well-documented shift in the past 20 years away from deontologically oriented approaches to translator ethics towards differentiated approaches in which the whole communicative situation is brought to bear (Drugan, Tipton 119)". Ricœur is notably influenced by Berman's model of translation orientated towards the "experience of the foreign" as a criterion for identifying cultural errors in translation, and it is Berman who first calls for a reorientation towards a "dialogical relation between foreign language and native language" (9). I will enquire here into how Ricœur transforms our understanding of cultural error by seeking a more precise understanding of how he advances this dialogical model initially proposed by Berman.

Berman inscribes the act of translation within an overarching relation between domestic and foreign cultures which endows translation with two vying impulses. On the one hand, translation is infiltrated by the "reductive drive of culture" which seeks to "domesticate" the foreign text or carry out a "systematic negation" of its "strangeness". On the other hand, there is a "desire" for the foreign which impels the translator to reach beyond the confines of his or her domestic culture towards the very strangeness, which the foreign culture embodies (5). The extent to which translation allows itself to be animated by one or the other impulse may serve as a criterion for the identification of an errant translation. However, this would be a criterion which implies a shift in emphasis away from an understanding from "good" and "bad" translation in terms of more or less faithful reconstitution of the original. We are instead directed towards the type of "discursive strategies", as Venuti puts it in his engagement with Berman, which are harnessed across the process of translation itself (23): the "trumpery" which conceals the "manipulations" of the foreign text, or the "respect" which strives for such correspondence, as Berman tells us (92). It is this respect which in the work of Ricœur will assume the form of hospitality towards the foreign.

Ricœur responds to the uncertainty which Berman expresses concerning how exactly we are to conceptualize the relation to the foreign within a dialogical model of translation. Berman arrives at his "experience of the foreign" through an engagement with German romantic theories of translation through which such a dialogical model may be glimpsed only imperfectly. The romantic framework is limited, Berman tells us, in that it formulates the relation to the foreign within the parameters of the model of *Bildung* which projects a "cyclical" dynamic of exodus and odyssey whereby the individual arrives at an authentic form of self-relation through confrontation with the foreign. However important a contribution, this model of *Bildung* makes towards the valorization of engagement with the foreign, it proposes a model of selfhood which entails that, however far the self departs from its point of origin, it is only ever ultimately in search of itself (136).

Berman underlines the need to advance beyond the initial steps made by the model of *Bildung* towards a more authentically dialogical conceptualizing of this desire through which the foreign is sought as an end itself, no longer within a cyclical dynamic but one of reciprocal exchange. Within the confines of his work on German Romanticism, however, Berman does no more than evoke the need for such a model and show how it is foreshadowed in later figures such as Schleiermacher and Hölderlin. We may understand Ricœur's work on translation as an attempt to proceed further along this path on which Berman sets out. A deepening of the dialogical model of translation proposed by Berman is thus the implicit goal, which animates Ricœur's project of leaving behind the standard of correspondence and the horizon of a perfect language.

We should also appreciate the extent to which the rejection of this standard and the dispelling of this horizon occur under the aegis of the dialogical model proposed in the earlier work *Oneself as Another*. This work presents us essentially with a meditation on the dialogical roots of self-identity. Self-identity is dialogical in character, Ricœur tells us, to the extent that otherness is constitutive of it. It is across dialogue that we become in a fundamental sense who we are. "It is first for the other that I am irreplaceable", Ricœur tells us; and it is equally first for me that the other is irreplaceable: individuality is not a property which we possess, it is rather a status to which we accede and which is bestowed upon us across everyday communication; it is thus derived from a capacity for speech and an ethics which is always implicitly in action across speech (*Oneself as Another* 193).

This ethics can only be imperfectly codified since it is spontaneous and inherently dynamic in nature. In essence, it stipulates the following: we can arrive at a positive understanding of ourselves as autonomous, responsible individuals worthy of esteem only within relations of mutual affirmation with others; we cannot attribute selfhood to ourselves without simultaneous attributing it to others and all the dignity that it confers. This dialogical model remains in the background and silently directs the transition, which Ricœur plots from the rejection of perfect language towards his dialogical model of translation.

What does this extension of the dialogical model of Berman, brought into contact with the dialogical model proposed by Ricœur in *Oneself as Another*, contribute in practical terms? Whether it be in his philosophical engagement with time, memory, communication or action, in his later work Ricœur is especially fond of establishing *aporia*: essentially lines of fracture which no philosophical discourse may heal in its inherent drive to arrive at a systematic whole. The fragments which assemble around this fracture nevertheless expose their own incompleteness from the inside, impelling the search for a means to overcome their division. Ricœur invariably proceeds to demonstrate that, while no theoretical solutions to such *aporia* may be found, we may find a means of negotiating with them by appealing to a "practical" or "ethical" form of exchange. If we are to understand how the notion of hospitality advances the dialogical paradigm of the experience of the foreign, and thereby provides us with an enriched model of cultural error, we must identify the central *aporia*, which animates Ricœur's thinking on translation. We must follow the consequences of this *aporia* beyond those explicitly registered within the confines of Ricœur's brief engagement with the theme of translation.

The *aporia* in question is that, as Ricœur puts it, translation is "theoretically incomprehensible" but "actually practicable" (*On Translation* 14). This *aporia* arises from the following consideration:

> either the diversity of languages gives expression to a radical heterogeneity – and in that case translation is theoretically impossible; one language is untranslatable a priori into another. Or else, taken as a fact, translation is explained by a common fund that renders the fact of translation possible; but then we must be able ... to find this common fund, and this is the original language track. (*On Translation* 13)

Either a basic kinship exists between languages, to the extent that they all draw in some way upon an "original language", or there is a basic incommensurability between languages which cannot be overcome. We have seen that Ricœur rejects any notion of an original language, and to this extent accepts the "theoretical impossibility" of translation; however, we are prevented from settling upon this extreme, "we are thrown back upon the other bank", by the simple fact that "since there is such a thing as translation, it certainly has to be possible" (*On Translation* 15). Ricœur is ultimately content to oscillate between these alternatives of the theoretical impossibility of translation, which emerges upon abandoning the presupposition of a perfect or original language, and the practical reality of translation. This is because the problem of this "impossibility" is not in fact his primary concern: his real concern, to recall, is with deepening the dialogical aspect of Berman's model of the experience of the foreign. To this end, the dramatizing of this *aporia* serves as something of a pretext for or means of exalting this dialogical dimension by exposing the theoretical groundlessness of the practical gesture of communication.

This groundlessness allows Ricœur to highlight all the more that translation is "set in motion by the fact of human plurality" alone: not, that is, fundamentally by any standard of truth orientated towards the search for a perfect language (*On Translation* 29). By the mere establishing of the *aporia*, Ricœur has already arrived at his overarching objective which is to reinforce the engagement with the foreign as an end in itself beyond the limited horizon of the cyclical model of *Bildung* as Berman reconstructs it.

In practice, what this means is that Ricœur accentuates the "heterogeneity" which exists between languages in order to further exalt the dialogical dimension in the experience of the foreign. Ricœur's fundamental preoccupations are evinced by a further displacement relative to Berman's modelling of the "experience of the foreign". Berman certainly raises the thematic of "untranslatability" on a number of occasions over the course of his survey of the romantic theory of translation. He evokes the romantic "will" for their work to become "untranslatable" (38). Yet the untranslatable element of any text, he argues, is never what is most essential to the work:

> Languages are translatable, even though the space of translatability is loaded with the untranslatable. Linguistic untranslatability lies in the fact that all languages are different from each other. Linguistic translatability in the fact that they are all languages. (127)

The dimension of untranslatability, the referential nexus idiomatic to each language, represents a hurdle to be crossed: translatability constitutes the more fundamental reality which both enables and directs this overcoming. Berman, in short, would strongly protest against Ricœur's raising of the dimension of the untranslatable into an absolute under the guise of the "impossibility of translation".

It is not my objective here to take sides in this debate over the relative or absolute status of untranslatability; in any case, I hope ultimately to make clear that Berman and Ricœur are brought in different ways before the same composite standard: it suffices here merely to emphasize how much Ricœur's dialogical theory of translation needs this dimension of impossibility. The "impossible" act of translation is one which must rely exclusively on the dynamic which Ricœur outlines in *Oneself as Another*: to recall, we become who we are, an individual worthy of esteem, through a dialogue which serves simultaneously to confirm the other as an individual worthy of esteem. This desire for mutual confirmation across dialogue can be the end of translation only if it is also the condition of possibility for a translation which would otherwise be "impossible".

If translation is rendered possible rather on the basis of a pre-existing dynamic, then this dialogue reverts once again to becoming a means. This reversion can in fact be observed within Berman's work, however much he seeks to enhance the dialogical dimension. Language is fundamentally translatable, he argues, since the literary work is already a form of "alienation", in this case a form of alienation which language imposes upon itself through the medium of the artist. It is in the nature of language to work upon itself, and translation merely takes this work one step further (127).

Berman does not appear to register the consequence that the dialogical dimension of communication with the foreign is thereby reduced to an intermediary stage in this reflexive and cyclical dynamic whereby language carries out this work upon itself. He returns us unwittingly to the model of *Bildung* as a frame for interpreting the experience of the foreign. The guiding assumption of Ricœur's work, that translation must be rendered "impossible" if its dialogical dimension is to emerge as an end in itself, is in this sense justified.

It is the accentuating of the dimension of untranslatability, towards the end of enhancing the dialogical aspect of translation, which is most crucial in understanding Ricœur's contribution to our understanding of cultural error: this enhancing in itself does not take us much beyond Berman or his other interlocutors such as Venuti. Let us return to Ricœur on being "set in motion" by human plurality, as both the end and condition of possibility of translation: "Have we not been set in motion by the fact of human plurality and by the double enigma of incommunicability between idioms and of translation in spite of everything? And then, without the test of the foreign, would we be sensitive to the strangeness of our own language?" (*On Translation* 29)

Translation is "set in motion" not simply between the domestic and foreign, but also between the foreign which is external and the foreign which is internal to the domestic language. This exchange is an organic offshoot of Berman's model. In seeking to engage authentically with the foreignness of the source language, Berman exhorts us to harness "the speaking force" of the target language which "derives from its multi-dialectal roots". A translation which respects the dialogical exchange between domestic and foreign is one which pursues a "double movement:" it seeks also to unlock the often neglected or devalorized "meanings of the natural and native language" (160). In similar terms, Venuti advocates that we harness the foreignness within the target language to counteract the domesticating tendency of translation, drawing on

> the conventionalized language of popular culture ... to render a foreign text that might be regarded as elite literature in a seamlessly fluent translation. This strategy would address both popular and elite readerships by defamiliarizing the domestic mass media as well as the domestic canon for the foreign literature. (Venuti 12)

The translator can use popular idioms in the translation of putatively elite texts, breaking down frontiers between languages by breaking down boundaries within a linguistic community. We may likewise interpret Ricœur's reminder of "the other half of the problem of translation", that of "translation within the same linguistic community", as an example of this double movement (*On Translation* 24). "We rediscover, within our linguistic community", Ricœur tells us, "the same enigma of the identical meaning which cannot be found": we extend hospitality to the foreign by confronting the foreign which is within ourselves (*On Translation* 25).

It would appear that the meaning and purpose of Ricœur's idea of linguistic hospitality is ultimately quite orthodox. To the extent that we may remain within the framework established by Berman in seeking to address in "practical" terms the "theoretical" impossibility of translation, the theoretical abyss with which Ricœur confronts the translator does not ultimately seem that daunting. At first glance, the contribution of Ricœur, in practical terms, appears quite modest.

This is because it is in fact the unintended consequences of Ricœur's enhancing of the dialogical element, particularly of the attendant gesture of accentuating "impossibility", which are most significant in shaping our understanding of cultural error. We can bring out these consequences by engaging more closely with Venuti's extension of Berman's paradigm, specifically with regards to this appeal to the dimension of intra-linguistic translation as a means of negotiating the difficulties of inter linguistic translation. Venuti's appeal to the neglected and devalorized multiplicity of dialects within the target language is in response to the domestic drive of language, not to Ricœur's problematic of the impossibility of overcoming the heterogeneity which exists between languages; and it goes by the name of "scandal" rather than "hospitality."

The latter as a standard is to assume a heavier responsibility than the former: the potential for "scandal" is to assist merely in the production of a "good" as opposed to a "bad" translation; "hospitality", before distinguishing "good" from "bad", is to render translation possible in the face of its theoretical impossibility. It thereby also assumes a much more ambiguous status. We might turn Ricœur's formulation on its head: hospitality may rather be that which serves to conceal the impossibility of translation, an act of arch-"trumpery" to use the vocabulary of Berman. We may note Venuti's own grudging admiration for "the sheer achievement of boldly domesticating translations" orientated by the standard of correspondence as by a mirage (81).

We may further note the much deeper capacity for failure on the behalf a translation orientated by the standard of hospitality: the appeal to intra-linguistic translatability may descend into, or indeed may always represent, a spectacle whereby translation loses itself in its own internal abyss in the guise of extending hospitality to the foreign language. Once the horizon of the "impossibility" of translation imposes itself, a possibility for parody emerges as an unmistakable consequence of Ricœur's ethics of hospitality: a parody which "corrupts", to co-opt Ricœur's own vocabulary, the standard of hospitality from the inside.

In seeking to enhance the dialogical element of Berman's paradigm, it is this unintended consequence which stands out as Ricœur's singular contribution; and it is no minor one: through engagement with Ricœur we arrive at a new class of error. The title which I chose for this article is somewhat misleading. Certainly, Ricœur's theoretical framework allows for a conceptualization of cultural error in terms of the gesture of inhospitality exemplified by the domesticating translation. If not more dangerous then certainly more disconcerting, however, is the error of the parody of hospitality. At the risk of sliding into the abyss which Ricœur's work opens, we might argue that this possibility of parody did not suggest itself to him because a theory of correspondence continues to orientate his ethics of hospitality: to be precise, he presupposes that the foreign which opens within a linguistic community is of the same nature as the foreign which opens between linguistic communities. We might say that this presupposition raises the *spectre* of an original language, which has never fully departed the horizon, however much we turn towards the standard of hospitality.

Perhaps, then, the position at which we arrive by following Ricœur is one of multiple types of cultural error and, ultimately, a composite standard for judging them. Another *aporia*, beside that which opens between the theoretical impossibility and practical reality of translation, insinuates itself into the fabric of Ricœur's text: upon pursuing the dialogical dimension to its endpoint in hospitality, we are "thrown back" towards the standard of correspondence. There is a need to better conceptualize the relation of hospitality with correspondence, and to better interiorize this residual investment in the horizon of an original language. This is a need which is not formulated explicitly by Ricœur; however, it is one which forcefully suggests itself upon a more sustained cross-referencing of his short work on translation with the earlier work *Oneself as Another*.

3. From hospitality to correspondence

We are returned to the incompleteness of Ricœur's modelling of the ethics of translation and to the model of cultural error which emerges from it. There is notably an outstanding need to identify a way of negotiating between the standard of hospitality, projecting the error of inhospitality, and the standard of correspondence, projecting the error of incongruence. In this final section, I will suggest how we may proceed towards the negotiation with this *aporia* by returning to the theoretical framework of the earlier text.

The transition towards hospitality in Ricœur's work on translation echoes the transition towards solicitude in *Oneself as Another*. Solicitude as a normative standard is anchored by the face to face relation between two individuals, which is to say that it is "addressed to persons in their irreplaceable singularity" (*Oneself as Another* 263). Already in the encounter with another across speech, to recall, there is an implicitly ethical dimension, which is betrayed if we attempt to extract and express it in abstract terms. To seek to identify the other as a representative of a certain species endowed with a set of properties worthy of this gesture of solicitude is to lose sight of the immediacy of this interpellation by another. The idea of morality which emerges from the process of abstraction from this immediacy finds its exemplary in Kant who speaks not of solicitude but of respect which is bestowed upon all rational beings in compliance with a universal moral code.

We have here another of Ricœur's *aporia*: for Kant, the moral perspective can be considered universal only to the extent that it is purified of all attachment to the contingent circumstances of any empirically given situation, such as those of the face to face encounter, or from the extra-rational inclinations of the individual, such as the inclination towards solicitude. Ricœur's pitting of the situationally bound expression of solicitude to another individual across speech against the respect which the universal moral law incites us to accord to all individuals who possess certain identifiable properties is what, in his work on translation, takes on the form of the distinction between the standard of hospitality set against the standard of correspondence informed, either explicitly or implicitly, by the perspective of a universal language. The face to face relation of solicitude finds its corollary in the translator's focus on the discursive strategies which express hospitality or a lack thereof towards the translated text as to a partner in communication, set against a focus on the identification and reconstitution within the target language of its textual physiognomy.

The subsequent variations to which Ricœur subjects the relation between the ethics of solicitude and the morality of respect are thus of significance when considering the relation between hospitality and correspondence. We cannot rest content with the ethical standard of solicitude, Ricœur tells us: its implicit normative content must be rendered explicit and articulated abstractly from a universalizing perspective. This is because solicitude is inherently "corruptible" (*Oneself as Another* 221). To counteract the intrinsic normativity of the face to face relation enacted across speech is a violence which inheres to language. The face to face relation of solicitude is an expression of the way in which one individual is uniquely able to "affect" another individual, in essence to call them to themselves. This very same capacity for affecting the other is the source of language's violence to the extent that, in the situation of speech, there is always an active and a passive force: an "initial dissymmetry between the protagonists of the action – a dissymmetry that places one in the position of agent and the other in that of patient", and it is upon this dissymmetry that "all the maleficent offshoots of interaction, beginning with influence and culminating in murder, will be grafted" (*Oneself as Another* 219). By codifying in universal terms principally what is forbidden to interactions between individuals, the appeal to the universal perspective of moral law serves to right the trajectory of solicitude. While the call to respect under this universal law reduces the individuals in dialogue to interchangeable members of humanity, divesting them of their character as unique and irreplaceable, it also endows their relation with a reciprocity, which counters the inherent tendency of language towards violence. "The rule of universalization is a necessary condition for the passage from the ethical aim to the moral norm": the perspective of a universalizing moral law exceeds the horizon of the ethical perspective of solicitude; and yet, if recalled to its origins in the face to face relation of solicitude, it may serve the purpose of the latter (*Oneself as Another* 224).

It is this reconstructed appeal to the horizon of universality which does not make its way into the ethics of hospitality proposed by Ricœur within the field of translation; however, this transition is entirely organic. The "original sin" of language, the inherent violence of speech or "corruptibility" of solicitude, finds its reflection in the "domesticating tendency" of translation as identified by Berman and Venuti among others. We find here the same inherent violence of language diagnosed by Ricœur in *Oneself as Another*, one which puts the target language in the position of agent and the source language in the position of patient. In addition, we have just observed that Ricœur cannot himself avoid residual investment in the horizon of a perfect language as source of universality grouping together the plurality of historical languages. Referred more carefully back to the theoretical framework provided by *Oneself as Another*, we can perceive this residual investment in a new light. Rather than an epistemic crutch, the reference to this horizon now takes on the aspect of an ethical imperative. To be precise, a continued reference to the standard of correspondence from within the exercise of hospitality is required to counter the inherent violence of translation: the perspective of reciprocity which comes from being interchangeable refractions of the same perfect language is required to counter the inherent tendency of translation to fracture across the divide between agent and patient. We might also add that a recalling of correspondence from within the exercise of hospitality is what separates the latter from its parody against the background of the inherent corruptibility of this ideal.

We may thus appreciate the contribution which Ricœur makes to our understanding of cultural error only if we follow it step by step, as it leads us away from the rejection of correspondence and the horizon of a perfect language – and back again. We saw that Ricœur's rejection of this paradigm served as a vehicle for advancing the dialogical model of translation proposed by Berman. In pursuing this aim, however, Ricœur also exposes more forcefully the difficulties which accompany the dialogical turn. The further we pursue these difficulties the more we are returned, from an altered perspective, to our point of departure. What results from this circuitous path is a composite standard, poised between hospitality and correspondence, and correspondingly a notion of cultural error which must appeal to the latter standard in its negotiation between the danger of inhospitality and the danger of the parody of hospitality.

We might finally note that, with Ricœur, we thereby find ourselves torn between the competing trajectories of the abyssal reflection on the impossibility of translation and the utopian projection of the likes of Benjamin with which he otherwise seeks to dispense. Might we elaborate a perspective from which we may avoid this oscillation between extremes? This is a question which leads us beyond the confines of the present article.

Works cited

Benjamin, Walter. "The Task of the Translator". *Walter Benjamin: Selected Writings Volume 1*, edited by Marc Bullock and Michael Jennings. Harvard University Press, 1996, pp. 253-263.

Berman, Antoine. *The Experience of the Foreign: Culture and Translation in Romantic Germany*, translated by S. Heyoaert. Suny Press, 1992.

Drugan, Joanna; Tipton, Rebecca. "Translation, Ethics and Social Responsibility". *The Translator*, vol. 23, no. 2, 2017, pp. 119-125.

Eco, Umberto. *The Search for the Perfect Language*, translated by James Fentress. Blackwell, 1995.

Ricœur, Paul. *On Translation*, translated by Eileen Brennan. Routledge, 2006.

Ricœur, Paul. *Oneself as Another*, translated by Kathleen Blamey. The University of Chicago Press, 1992.

Venuti, Lawrence. *The Scandals of Translation: Towards an Ethics of Difference*. Routledge, 1998.

On the Websites of Others

Katja Grupp

Introduction

Newspapers distribute an infinite amount of information. If this information is brought to another culture in the language of that culture, the process necessarily involves linguistic translation. The information thus encounters a readership influenced by completely different ideological assumptions; this is true also with regard to the meaning of individual words. Moreover, a webpage that offers translated newspaper articles involves another form of transfer: from the printed word to translation on the internet. Since messages are often illustrated with images, the selection of images can lead to a shift of content statements and thus, to cultural errors.

In this article, I shall examine the translations of newspaper articles that are available on the Russian website *InoSMI.ru*. I will mainly look at articles dealing with Russia. This implies another form of transfer as the articles focus on the external view of Russia by comparison with an internal one. These seemingly neutral and objective translations are coloured by a kind of ideological subconscious, which gives errors the quality of Freudian slips (Freud 209-210). In the light of this observation, one cannot easily differentiate between intentional manipulation and the location of a discourse and/or its authors in an ideological field. My study analyses the effects of processes caused by these forces.

1. The Russian website *InoSMI.ru*

In today's globalized world, things can, it seems, be easily transferred from one continent to another. We might even forget how far China is from America or Europe as everything is available – if not today, then tomorrow at the latest. We as individuals are all connected via Facebook, Instagram, Whatsapp and other kinds of social media. However newspapers, which inform us on a less individual basis about domestic and foreign affairs, continue to exist. The remit of newspapers is to inform their readers in a trustworthy and in-depth fashion. In a seemingly ever-shrinking world, it is interesting to observe what foreign journalists publish.

Russia, the biggest country of the former Soviet Union, is still struggling to find a new identity after the fall of the Iron Curtain. My intention in this article is to analyse the cultural gaps between the self-image of Russia and the image of Russia as presented in translated articles. The question is, what image of Russia is transferred to Russian readers via their reading of foreign newspapers.

The presentation of content from other countries to Russian readers has a long tradition. For example the journal *Inostrannaya literatura* [Иностранная литература] published literature from abroad translated into Russian[1]. The transfer of this concept to the mass-media was a novelty that emerged after the end of the Soviet Union and the rise of the internet in the 1990s.

The website *InoSMI.ru* has existed since 2004. The name of the website, *InoSMI*, is the acronym of *Inostrannie Sredstva Massovoj Informacii* [Foreign Mass Media]. Its service is affiliated to the RIA Novosti news agency. Translations are published online on a daily basis. This website presents translated newspaper articles from all over the world. The range of topics varies, but most of the translated articles are analytical essays written by Western[2] journalists, dedicated to Russia. Factual information and news about cultural events in foreign countries, or about Russian foreign policy are rarely pub-

---

[1] One well-known example is the journal *Inostrannaya literatura* (Иностранная литература [Foreign Literature]), which was founded in 1955. In the Soviet Union, it was one of the most popular journals, which informed about other countries and their literature. Thanks to the journal, cultures from the other side of the Iron Curtain became known in the Soviet Union. In this way, readers became familiarized with foreign literature in translation (Menzel 143).

[2] The term "Western" here probably includes countries from the other side of the former Iron Curtain. *InoSMI.ru* differentiates between "foreign" and "Western" media.

lished in translation[3]. It is one of the most frequently cited websites by Russian journalists and thus, has a significant influence on public opinion in Russia (Fredheim 41). The translated articles inform readers in Russia about what is going on in other countries and also tell us about the image Russia and Russian politics have in foreign newspapers (41).

Translation is a key element in this process. It brings news from other countries and foreign languages into the Russian-speaking world. *InoSMI.ru* translates daily from more than 600 foreign newspapers. The translators and journalists from *InoSMI.ru* make use of more than 2800 newspapers and journals[4]. *InoSMI.ru* exists only in a web-format and therefore, it is interesting to think about the function of the internet as a source of information. This leads us to examine official or unofficial restrictions governing the content of websites[5].

In Russia, the attitude towards such information websites seems rather liberal (Rabitz 167), but not completely without control:

> The Internet filtering in Russia turned out to be unsophisticated; thousands of sites were blocked by mistake, and users could easily find ways to make an end-run around it. At the same time, very few people in Russia were actually sent to jail for posting criticism of the government online. (Soldatov 313)

As we can see from its website, *InoSMI.ru* is not only affiliated to the RIA Novosti news agency (Russia's international news agency) but is also sponsored by the Federal Agency on Press and Mass Communications of Russia (FAPMC). Therefore, the website can be seen as

---

[3] https://www.inosmi.ru.
[4] https://inosmi.ru/docs/about/us.html.
[5] https://themoscowtimes.com/news/internet-censorship-skyrockets-in-russian-in-2017-study-says-60389.

an influential instrument of official foreign policy and viewed as part of the state apparatus.

By analysing the topics chosen for translation, it becomes obvious, that mainly opinions and statements from foreign newspapers are translated. Thus, the function of *InoSMI.ru* does not seem to be that of informing Russian-speakers about what is going on in other parts of the world, but rather to indicate what other parts of the world think and write about Russia. The editor of the website *InoSMI.ru* is Marina Semenovna Pustil'nik, a specialist of international politics and economy[6]. Pustil'nik sees the reason for such a special interest in the way the country is seen and judged by foreign journalists as the result of the Russians' lack of self-confidence in the wake of the fall of the Soviet Union (Boy 2011).

The aim of foreign newspapers is to explain Russian politics, society, economy and so on to an interested but mostly ill-informed reader abroad. In contrast to that, the readers of the *InoSMI.ru*'s translations are mostly Russian speakers living in Russia, who read about their own country from another perspective. In this way, they see Russia through the eyes of others, on a website that represents the point of view of others. This imbalance concerning background knowledge seems to be important when analysing the translations. To underscore the reliability of the content, *InoSMI.ru* always provides a link to the original source of the article:

> The translations are brought to the reader without any kind of censorship. Moreover, most of the translations are presented as a result of a "foreignizing" translation strategy in order to preserve the original style and way of thinking found in the source text. (Van Puck 271)

---

[6] https://ria.ru/news_company/20090311/164475711.html.

2. "Everything that is worth translating"[7]

InoSMI.ru's slogan is "everything that is worth translating"[8] and the categories available on the website are: politics, economy, science, war and war-industrial complex, society, everything from today, long-reads, multimedia and news.

The transfer of newspaper articles into another language and another culture does not only concern words, but also includes the transfer of images into a different language (in this case into Russian). By images we mean metaphors or pictorial language. We shall also take into account the visual setting of each newspaper article. A newspaper article is most often combined with photographs, a photomontage, or some kind of illustration. Pictures in newspapers and magazines are salient as they catch the reader's eye and provide a visual opening on the topic. In the following, we shall also analyse pictures and photographs, considering them to be a part of the shift from one language and culture to another.

2.1 In medias res: dealing with the past

The (non-)celebration of the centenary of the Russian Revolution in 2017 was expected by the Western media for a long time. The new "rise of Stalin" under Putin[9] meant that the cruelty of the Stalinist era (notably the Great Purge, between 1936-1938) was less frequently mentioned in public, with the emphasis put on the historical importance of Stalin. The elimination of Stalin's cruelty in the 30s and 40s from official publications can be seen as a considerable change in the perception of Soviet history[10]. The title of the article in *The Guardian*

---

[7]   "ИноСМИ – Все, что достойно перевода" www.InoSMI.ru.
[8]   In summer 2018, it was changed into: "Как иностранные СМИ изображают Россию. Мы переводим. Вы делаете выбор" ["How foreign mass media imagines Russia. We translate. You choose"]. Hereafter, all the translations given in square brackets are my translations.
[9]   https://themoscowtimes.com/articles/stalin-rises-from-the-ashes-in-putins-russia-45743.
[10] www.cbc.ca/radio/thesundayedition/the-sunday-edition-november-12-2017-1.4396794/masha-gessen-on-how-totalitarianism-reclaimed-

on 3rd November 2017: "Putin's Russia can't celebrate its revolutionary past"[11] is translated as: "Путинской России приходится приукрашивать революционное прошлое"[12] [Putin's Russia has to embellish its revolutionary past]. We can observe a considerable shift in the meaning of the sentence, as the grammatical active "can't celebrate" is translated into "приходится приукрашивать" [has to embellish], with the translation implying that Russia is "required" to embellish its past.

When comparing the verbs "to celebrate" and "приукрашивать" [embellish], the modification undertaken by the translator becomes even more striking. The meaning of "приукрашивать" is "to gloss over", "to embellish", "to whitewash" or "to paint in bright colours", and in using this verb instead of stressing the inability to celebrate, the translator confers a different meaning on the headline of the article. The inability to celebrate (*Guardian*-version) becomes in the *InoSMI.ru*-version the requirement to put the revolutionary past into new, bright colours. The mental/psychological inability to celebrate the centenary takes on a new connotation in the Russian translation of *InoSMI.ru*: Putin's Russia is forced to whitewash the revolutionary past. The notion of inability ("can't") gets lost in the translation that is proposed by an unknown translator.

The gap between the original text and the translated version also shows, when looking at the translation of the subtitle. In the original version, it reads: "Putin's Russia can't celebrate its revolutionary past. It has to smother it". In the *InoSMI.ru*-version there is no subtitle. The verb "to smother" is not mentioned in the Russian version at all.

The next sentences in the *Guardian*-title are the following: "The Russian Revolution was a fight against the excesses of the rich. No wonder Vladimir Putin wants to ignore the centenary". It is,

---

russia-1.4396897 and 24.10.2017. www.nzz.ch/international/stalin-und-die-sehnsucht-nach-der-starken-hand-ld.1323741.

[11] https://www.theguardian.com/commentisfree/2017/nov/03/putin-russia-revolution-ignore-centenary.

[12] https://inosmi.ru/politic/20171104/240692086.html.

however, striking that these sentences are not translated into Russian on *InoSMI.ru*. The omission of the possible reason for the inability to celebrate the centenary gives an idea as to how the website alters the meaning of the original message. The subtitle in the *Guardian* suggests an explanation for the incapacity to celebrate the past and at the same time builds a connection between Russian history and the current (social) situation.

By removing the explanation in the Russian translation, the meaning of the original gets entirely lost. Therefore, the translation can be viewed as manipulative. The elimination of the explanation as to why Russia cannot celebrate its revolutionary past also gives the impression that the translated Russian version presents a plain and simple explanation of the present. The psychological background, explained in the subtitle, outlines the Russian struggle with the past only for the reader of the original *Guardian* article.

The article in the *Guardian* is illustrated by a dark picture, composed of a collage[13]. A shadow of Lenin, the dominant figure of the Russian Revolution in 1917, can be recognized covered by two very dominant and five smaller stylized flags of contemporary Russia. The colours (white/blue/red) of the flag are shining, whereas the background and the face of the person are dark, nearly black. The only detail corresponding to the bright flag is the iris within the dark face.

---

[13] https://www.theguardian.com/commentisfree/2017/nov/03/putin-russia-revolution-ignore-centenary.

https://www.theguardian.com/commentisfree/2017/nov/03/put in-russia-revolution-ignore-centenary

When one analyses the translation of newspapers, it is important to take account of the image in its impact on the message of the article. The pictures used in the original article are not identical to the translated *InoSMI.ru*-version, possibly for copyright reasons. The *InoSMI.ru*-version puts the picture first and arranges the texts after the picture.

https://inosmi.ru/politic/20171104/240692086.html

In contrast to the contemporary illustration by Nate Kitch, the Russian translation is embellished by a picture from an image bank[14]. The photograph shows a demonstration of soldiers bearing red revolutionary flags embossed with Lenin's face. The title of the picture: "Участники шествия в Омске, посвященного 99-й годовщине Великой Октябрьской революции» [Participants of the march in Omsk dedicated to the 99th anniversary of the Great October Revolution][15]. This pictorial reminder of the obviously

---

14 https://inosmi.ru/politic/20171104/240692086.html.
15 https://inosmi.ru/politic/ 20171104/ 240692086.html.

celebrated and uncritical link to the past (which does not correspond to the *Guardian* text) creates a completely different idea of the content. The translated text is embellished by a Russian image that can be seen as manipulative.

2.2 Putin and Brezhnev

Putin in his speeches and interviews often refers to the past – especially to the (re)popularized leaders of the Soviet Union. Brezhnev was the leader of the Soviet Union from 1964 to 1982, and the General Secretary of the Central Committee of the Communist Party of the Soviet Union. Due to this position in politics, he was one of the main figures during the Cold War. In contemporary Russia, Brezhnev represents the power of the USSR at that time[16]. On February 12th, Chris Miller wrote an article about Putin and how he refers to Brezhnev[17]:

ARGUMENT

Putin Isn't a Genius. He's Leonid Brezhnev.

Why Russia's strongman economy can't reform.

BY CHRIS MILLER | FEBRUARY 12, 2018, 4:17 PM

https://foreignpolicy.com/2018/02/12/putin-isnt-a-genius-hes-leonid-brezhnev/

---

16   https://www.dailymail.co.uk/news/article-2331709/Russias-favourite-leader-revealed-Leonid-Brezhnev-established-political-repression-awarded-military-honours-didnt-deserve.html.
17   https://foreignpolicy.com/2018/02/12/putin-isnt-a-genius-hes-leonid-brezhnev/.

The Russian translation in *InoSMI.ru*[18] reads as follows:

https://inosmi.ru./politic/20180217/241490358.html

The two sentences of the original title are combined in the translated version into one, which has the effect, that the connection between Putin and Brezhnev becomes even closer. The shift in the meaning has its origin in the small word "novyj" [new]. Whereas Chris Miller stresses that Putin is not a genius and equates him with Leonid Brezhnev, the *InoSMI.ru* translation says that Putin is a "new" Brezhnev. This phrase evokes the glory of the past combined with today's innovations. The subtitle "Why Russia's strongman economy can't reform" remains untranslated. The *InoSMI.ru* version starts directly with the author's text.

This shift in the translation has to do with the different image of Brezhnev in Russia and in the Western world. To Western eyes, Brezhnev represents the old, hard-line, conservative Soviet leader. Due to his political decisions at the time of the Prague Spring in Czechoslovakia, the invasion of Afghanistan and the crisis in Poland, Brezhnev's position underlined the non-agreement with democracy. Therefore, the image of Brezhnev in the Western world is quite negative. On the contrary, for Russians in 2018, Brezhnev is

---

[18]   https://InoSMI.ru./politic/20180217/241490358.html.

one of the most popular Soviet leaders[19]. Today, referring to Brezhnev for Westerners means being a Soviet hard-liner, whereas the Russian understanding of Brezhnev is a more positive one[20]. So being a "new Brezhnev"[21], as the translated version says, is positive. The manipulation in the translation is evoked by a different political understanding of Brezhnev and his role during the Cold War.

https://foreignpolicy.com/2018/02/12/putin-isnt-a-genius-hes-leonid-brezhnev/

---

[19] https://themoscowtimes.com/articles/brezhnev-most-popular-20th-century-leader-poll-says-24237.
[20] At the latest since the Warsaw Pact of Czechoslovakia in 1968 with increasing skepticism. This was exacerbated by the invasion of Afghanistan ten years later. Not to mention the increasing repression of dissidence and *refuseniks*. https://www.nytimes.com/1989/12/15/obituaries/andrei-sakharov-68-soviet-conscience-dies.html.
[21] https://inosmi.ru./politic/20180217/241490358.html.

The illustration of the article is very similar at first glance. In the article in *Foreign Policy*, the picture has the following caption: "A man looks at a caricature depicting Russian Premier Vladimir Putin as Leonid Brezhnev on his computer screen in Moscow on Oct. 5, 2011". Putin and Brezhnev are one person, wearing a uniform with medals.

The idea of depicting Putin and Brezhnev as a single person is also the idea of the illustration of the translated article in *InoSMI.ru*.

https://inosmi.ru./politic/20180217/241490358.html

However, the picture of this "new Putin-Brezhnev-person" is located not on a computer screen but in a street, where people are demonstrating. The Putin-Brezhnev-picture seems to represent the leader of the demonstrators. Policemen are between the poster of Putin-Brezhnev and the demonstrating people.

There is a small shift in the meaning of the translated article towards the still very popular Brezhnev. The untranslated subtitle, which announces why the economy cannot be reformed, does not correspond to the Brezhnev-Image of Putin. Brezhnev, like Lenin and Stalin, is still very popular among Russian people[22].

2.3 Turning to the present

In March 2018, presidential elections were held in Russia. It was predictable that Vladimir Putin, the incumbent president, would be re-elected. But Ksenia Sobchak announced in October 2017 that she would run for president. Sobchak, a TV anchor and journalist, is the first female presidential candidate in 14 years. She is the daughter of the first democratically elected mayor of Saint Petersburg, Anatoly Sobchak.

The translation of an article about the election period was produced in the run-up to the elections. Masha Gessen, a Russian/US independent journalist, wrote about Ksenia Sobchak and her pre-election tour in the US[23].

---

[22] https://derstandard.at/1363711778058/Lenin-Stalin-und-Breschnew-fuehren-Liste-der-beliebtesten-Kremlherrscher-an.

[23] https://www.newyorker.com/news/our-columnists/the-curious-case-of-the-television-star-running-against-vladimir-putin.

THE CURIOUS CASE OF THE TELEVISION STAR RUNNING AGAINST VLADIMIR PUTIN

By Masha Gessen February 12, 2018

https://www.newyorker.com/news/our-columnists/the-curious-case-of-the-television-star-running-against-vladimir-putin

The translation of the article from the *New Yorker* on the 12th of February, printed one month before the election, was published in *InoSMI.ru* on 14th of February[24].

---

[24] https://inosmi.ru./politic/20180214/241450522.html.

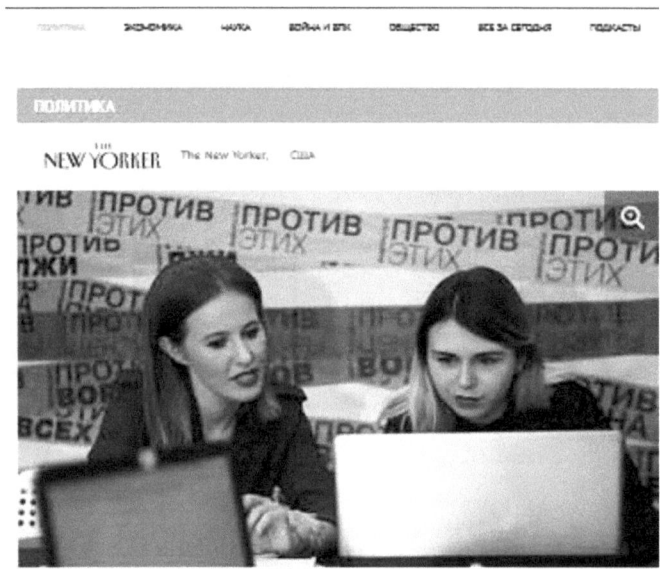

https://inosmi.ru./politic/20180214/241450522.html

When Masha Gessen writes about the "curious case" it demonstrates how unusual it is that an unnamed television star should attack Vladimir Putin in his renewed presidential bid. The translation sticks closely to the original and can be understood as follows: "[The] Curious Rivalry of a TV Star against Vladimir Putin"[25]. This is less spectacular and unique, but there is no shift in the general meaning. The translation of this article can be seen as an example of translations "brought to the reader without any kind of censorship" (van Puck: 271). The English original and the Russian version differ neither in message nor in meaning.

---

25   Hereafter, the translations in the body of the text are my translations.

Looking at the photograph accompanying the article, the Russian version of the TV Star Ksenia Sobchak is less glamourous than the original version in the *New Yorker*. On *InoSMI.ru*, Ksenia Sobchak is shown in discussion with another young woman, perhaps one of her campaign co-workers of her own age, whereas the photograph in the *New Yorker* shows a young woman in an TV studio, probably during an interview.

The New Yorker

Ksenia Sobchak has won praise from Russian activists and journalists. But no one gets on the Presidential ballot without Putin's permission.

https://www.newyorker.com/news/our-columnists/the-curious-case-of-the-television-star-running-against-vladimir-putin

InoSMI.ru

https://inosmi.ru/politic/20180214/241450522.html

Nevertheless, the translation of an article is more than words and images. Typically for online newspapers, interactivity with the reader is important. Comments on the articles appear immediately online, visible for all the other readers of the text. The reactions to the articles give an impression of how the (translated) texts and illustrations are perceived and understood. The readers of *InoSMI.ru* are fairly active in writing comments in response to the articles However, it is interesting to notice that the comments on the texts are quite negative. The commentators on the website *InoSMI.ru* write that a young inexperienced woman should stay away from politics: "Либеральный, слабый лидер не сможет управлять Россией" [A liberal, weak leader cannot govern Russia][26].

2.4 Whose comments?

«Путинейджеры» не хотят революции, западные СМИ этим разочарованы

https://inosmi.ru/overview/20180316/241726358.html

---

[26] https://inosmi.ru./politic/20180214/241450522.html

The title reads: "*Putinagers*[27] do not want a revolution, the Western mass media are disappointed". Readers of *InoSMI.ru*-articles are very active in expressing their views. In the following article, which is not a translation but a summary of opinions and texts from different newspapers, the comments made by Russian readers are very striking. They express their dismay and disgust about the expectation. Why should they have any reservations and resentments with regard to Putin?

> Judging by comments on *InoSMI*, Russian readers find the analysis of Western journalists selective and simplistic, portraying Russia as a one-man dictatorship where media is totally state-controlled, dissent is suppressed, elections rigged, and which meddles aggressively in other peoples' affairs and threatens its neighbors. (Weir 2018)

InoSMI.ru seems to work as a channel to communicate the disappointment not about Russian politics, the president or the social system, but about the view from outside Russia, in this case via the Western media. According to this assumption the comments seem to underline the legitimacy of the existing power and the politicians who are in power. The commentators seem to follow the statement of the Meeting of the Security Council. In November 2014, it was decided that there should be a national agreement without any conflict between national, religious ideas[28].

---

[27] The word *Putinagery* is a *portmanteau* word combining "Putin" and "Teenager", which refers to young people born and raised under Putin.

[28] „Необходимо знать и понимать, что разжигание конфликтов между людьми разных национальностей и верований, пропаганда националистической идеологии, массовые нарушения общественного порядка на этой почве, тем более призывы к насильственному свержению существующего строя, – это прямое проявление антинародного мышления, это прямые проявления экстремизма".

["It is necessary to know and understand that stirring up conflicts between people of different nationalities and beliefs, propaganda of

The following statement from a user called "Nika"[29] is representative of many of the comments made about this article.

> юные россияне, выросшие при Путине, не хотят революции
>
> [young Russians, raised under Putin, don't want a revolution]

> А почему они ее должны хотеть? Они имеют все что хотят, в пределах разумного, конечно, путешествуют со своими родителями, хорошо питаются, развлекаются, учатся, радуются жизни. Какая революция?
>
> [Why should they want one? They have everything they want, as far as possible, of course, they travel with their parents, have good food, fun, learn and enjoy life. Why revolt?]

https://inosmi.ru/overview/20180316/241726358.html

Another user, Donpedro, also stresses, that there is no need for revolution and war:

> Вам бы всё революции сеять. Были у нас и революции и войны. Стыдно, что мы, веря вам, подавались на такие

---

nationalistic ideology, mass disturbances of public order on this land, especially calls for the violent overthrow of the existing system, are direct manifestations of anti-people thinking, these are direct manifestations of extremism."] http://kremlin.ru/events/ president/ news-by-date/20.11.2014.

[29] https://inosmi.ru/overview/20180316/241726358.html.

провокации, уничтожая друг-друга почти весь 20 век. Нам революции и войны не нужны. И, дети наши не хотят такой жизни. И Путин не хочет, мы же видим, как он этого старательно избегает, хотя некоторые горячие головы его подталкивают долбануть кое-куда… Понимаю, что вам нужна Россия горящая, как Ближний Восток, но разочарую вас, господа: вот уж хрена вам!

[You would sow more revolutions. We had both revolutions and wars. It is a shame that we, believing you, voted for such provocation, and destroyed each other for almost the entire 20th century. We do not need revolution and war. And, our children do not want such a life. And Putin does not want it either, we see how he carefully avoids this, although some hot heads are pushing him to blow something up … I understand that you need an unstable Russia similar to the Middle East, but I will disappoint you, gentlemen: Fuck you!]

https://inosmi.ru/overview/20180316/241726358.html

The readers of *InoSMI.ru* are given the impression that the foreign press writes simplistically about Russia. In this text about the *Putinagers* who do not want a revolution, the Western media are taken in the title as one unit. When reading the comments on *Putinagers*, one gets the impression that all commentators are satisfied with contemporary Russian politics (in contrast to the politics of the past).

Conclusion

In analysing the translations of newspapers into Russian, I have highlighted differences between the original and the English version which display subtle but symptomatic deviations. These differences are not based on the linguistic quality of the translation, but rather on the tendentious manner in which *InoSMI.ru* presents the articles to the reader. As I have demonstrated, untranslated sub-headings, explanatory subheadings, and the selection of pictures also underline the clear differences between the source texts and articles in translated form, which very often are given an anti-Russian slant. As I mentioned, there is a knowledge gap between the readers of the original article and the Russian-speakers reading the translated article. This knowledge gap seems to be a deliberate aspect of the website *InoSMI.ru*. However, it is not only the translation, but also the selection of media and articles, which ensures that the Western media appear more critical than they actually are. The presentation of the articles and the pictures illustrate that the Russian version is more explicit and direct in contrast to the original newspaper article.

> In Russian translation, the Western media appear Russophobic and engaged in an information war against Russia, whilst small pockets of freedom, often on the Internet, present a counter-hegemonic narrative. Through this selection bias a view of the foreign press as high on opinion, low on evidence emerges. (Fredheim 82)

Viktoria Brunmeier considers the online strategies of the Kremlin to be quite subtle. The tendentious choice of the likely authentic statements on the website may be viewed as evidence of this. It is not about supporting Vladimir Putin openly, but rather about creating a platform for people to express their opinion (137).

One gets the impression that *InoSMI.ru* actively cultivates the stereotype of anti-Russian Western newspapers on the one hand, and the Russians, who are satisfied with Russian politics and the main politicians on the other hand. According to the Russian Security Council, "inciting national differences" and "propagating nationalist ideas" provokes extremism[30]. The aim of *InoSMI.ru* seems to directly

---

30   Необходимо знать и понимать, что разжигание конфликтов между людьми разных национальностей и верований, пропаганда нацио-

execute the programme of the Russian Security Council as thus expressed. We are dealing here with inaccurate translations based on cultural errors, but these errors are to a great degree determined by ruling ideologies or even by explicit administrative directives, giving them the quality of Freudian slips. The supposed foreignness of the sources translated in "Foreign Mass Media" is dissolved in the murky soup of Russian governmental and ideological interests.

налистической идеологии, массовые нарушения общественного порядка на этой почве, тем более призывы к насильственному свержению существующего строя, – это прямое проявление антинародного мышления, это прямые проявления экстремизма. www.Kremlin.ru.

Works cited

Brunmeier, Viktoria. *Das Internet in Russland: Eine Untersuchung zum spannungsreichen Verhältnis von Politik und Runet.* Reinhard Fischer, 2005.

Fredheim, Rolf. "What Kind of Control does Putin have over Russian Media". *Baltic Rim Economies*, vol. 2016, p. 37.

Fredheim, Rolf. "Filtering Foreign Media Content: How Russian News Agencies Repurpose Western News Reporting". *Journal of Soviet and Post-Soviet Politics and Society: 2015/1: The Russian Media and the War in Ukraine.* Columbia University Press, 2014, pp. 37-82.

Freud, Sigmund. *The Psychopathology of Everyday Life in Volume VI of The Complete Psychological Works of Sigmund Freud.* Vintage Classics, 2001 [1991].

Machala, Lubomír; Marta Vágnerová (eds.). *XIX. Olomoucké dny rusistů: Sborník příspěvků z mezinárodní konference, 30.08. – 01.09. 2007.* 1. vydání, Univerzita Palackého v Olomouci, 2008. Rossica Olomucensia XLVI-II.

Menzel, Birgit. "Die Zeitschrift *Innostrannaja Literatura* als Medium kultureller Übersetzung". *Kultur und/als Übersetzung: Russisch-deutsche Beziehungen im 20. und 21. Jahrhundert,* edited by Birgit Menzel; Christine Engel. Frank & Timme, 2011, pp. 143-75.

Menzel, Birgit; Engel, Christine (eds). *Kultur und/als Übersetzung: Russisch-deutsche Beziehungen im 20. und 21. Jahrhundert.* Frank & Timme, 2011.

Rabitz, Cornelia. "Ohne Zensur und doch nicht frei – Russlands Medienlandschaft". *Länderbericht Russland,* edited by Heiko Pleines and Hans-Henning Schröder. Bundeszentrale für Politische Bildung, 2010, pp. 153–71.

Soldatov, Andrej A., and Irina P. Borogan. *Ther Red Web: The Struggle Between Russia's Digital Dictators and the New Online Revolutionaries.* PublicAffairs, 2015.

van Puck, Piet. "Perevodčeskij web-sajt "inosmi" kak russkojasyčnoe zerkalo zapadnoj pressy". XIX. Olomoucké dny rusistů: Sborník příspěvků z mezinárodní konference, 30.08. - 01.09. 2007, edited by Lubomír Machala and Marta Vágnerová, 1. Vydání. Univerzita Palackého v Olomouci, 2008, pp. 271–74.

Webography

Boy, Ann-Dorit. "Russland schaut in den Pressespiegel". *Neue Züricher Zeitung,* 6 July 2011, www.nzz.ch/russland_schaut_in_den_pressespiegel-1.10835592. Accessed 19 19 December 2018.

"Brezhnev Most Popular 20th-Century Leader, Poll Says". *The Moscow Times.* 2013, themoscowtimes.com/articles/brezhnev-most-popular-20th-century-leader-poll-says 242 37. Accessed 3 December 2018.

Clines, Francis X. "Andrei Sakharov. 68, Soviet 'Conscience,' Dies". T*he New York Times.* 1989, Dec 15, www.nytimes.com/1989/12/15/obituaries/andrei-sakharov-68-soviet-conscience-dies.html. Accessed 19 December 2018.

Daily Mail Reporter. *Russia's favourite ever leader revealed.* 27 May 2013, www.dailymail.co.uk/news/article-2331709/Russias-favourite-leader-revealed-Leonid-Brezhnev-established-political-repression-awarded-military-honours-didnt-deserve.html. Accessed 3 December 2018.

Gessen, Masha on how totalitarianism reclaimed Russia. 2017, www.cbc.ca/radio/thesundayedition/the-sunday-edition-november-12-2017-1.4396794/masha-gessen-on-how-totalitarianism-reclaimed-russia-1.4396897. Accessed 3 December 2018.

Gessen, Masha. "The Curious Case of the Television Star Running Against Vladimir Putin". *The New Yorker*. 22 Dec. 2018, www. newyorker.com/news/our-columnists/the-curious-case-of-the-television-star-running-against-vladimir-putin. Accessed 3 December 2018.

Gessen, Masha creator. "Masha Gessen on How Totalitarianism Reclaimed Russia". CBC Radio, 16 Nov. 2017. www.cbc.ca/radio/thesundayedition/the-sunday-edition-november-12-2017-1.4396794/masha-gessen-on-how-totalitarianism-reclaimed-russia-1.4396897. Accessed 3 December 2018.

Gessen, Masha (Гессен,Маша). "Любопытное соперничество телезвезды с Владимиром Путиным". *InoSMI.ru*. 14 Feb. 2018, inosmi.ru./politic/20180214/241450522.html. Accessed 3 December 2018.

Hoffmann, David L. "Stalin Rises From the Ashes in Putin's Russia". 2015, themoscowtimes.com/articles/stalin-rises-from-the-ashes-in-putins-russia-45743. Accessed 3 Dec. 2018.

"Lenin, Stalin und Breschnew führen Liste der beliebtesten Kremlherrscher an: Michail Gorbatschow schneidet unter Befragten schlecht ab". *Der Standard*. 22 May 2013, der stan dard.at/1363711778058/Lenin-Stalin-und-Breschnewfueh ren-Lis te-der-beliebtesten-Kremlherrscher-an. Accessed 3 December 2018.

Merridale, Catherine. "Putin's Russia can't celebrate its revolutionary past. It has to smother it". *The Guardian*. 2017, www.the gu ardian.com/commentisfree/2017/nov/03/putin-russia-rev olution-ignore-centenary. Accessed 3 December 2018.

Merridale, Catherine (Мерридейл, Кэтрин). "Путинской России приходится приукрашивать революционное прошлое". *InoSMI.ru*, 2017, inosmi.ru/politic/20171104/240692086. html. Accessed 3 Dec. 2018.

Miller, Chris. "Putin Isn't a Genius. He's Leonid Brezhnev. Why Russia's strongman economy can't reform". *Foreign Policy*. 2018, foreignpolicy.com/2018/02/12/putin-isnt-a-genius-hes-leo nid-brezhnev. Accessed 3 December. 2018.

Miller, Chris (Миллер, Крис). "Путин – не гений, а новый Брежнев". *InoSMI.ru*. 2018, inosmi.ru./politic/20180217/ 241490358. html. Accessed 3 December. 2018.

Rüesch, Andreas. "Wieso es in Russland wieder salonfähig ist, Stalin zu verehren". *Neue Züricher Zeitung*. 2017. 24.10.2017. www.nzz.ch/international/stalin-und-die-sehnsucht-nach-der-starke n-hand-ld.1323741. Accessed 3 December 2018.

Weir, Fred. "Why the Kremlin publishes uncensored translations of Western news". *The Christian Science Monitor,* 2018, www.cs monitor.com/layout/set/print/World/Europe/2018/0228/ Why-the-Kremlin-publishes-uncensored-translations-of-Western-news. Accessed 3 December 2018.

Информация о проекте. n.d, inosmi.ru./docs/about/us.html. Accessed 3 December 2018.

"Главным редактором сайта ИноСМИ.ру назначена Марина Пустильник". *Новости агентства*. 2009, ria.ru/news_com pany/20090311/164475711.html. Accessed 3 December 2018.

"О внесении изменений в отдельные законодательные акты Российской Федерации в части регулирования деятельности некоммерческих организаций, выполняющих функции иностранного агента". *Gosudarstvennaja Duma*. 2012, asozd2.duma.gov.ru/main.nsf/%28SpravkaNew%29? Open Agent&RN=102766-6&02. Accessed 3 December 2018.

"Путинейджеры не хотят революции, западные СМИ этим разочарованы". *InoSMI.ru*. 17 Mar. 2018, inosmi.ru/over vie w/20180316/241726358.html. Accessed 3 December 2018.

Заседание Совета Безопасности: Владимир Путин провёл в Кремле расширенное заседание Совета Безопасности. Рассматривался проект Стратегии противодействия экстремизму в Российской Федерации до 2025 года. Kremlin.ru. 2014, kremlin.ru/events/president/news/470 45. Accessed 3 December 2018.

"The Echo We Hear is Not the Echo of Our Own Words and Even the Best Translation is Something Alien": On the Translation of German Exile Literature

Angela Vaupel

Introduction

Language works as a vessel for memories and experiences. Language carries education and culture; it is a key marker of cultural and/or national identity, and is central to social participation. However, what are the effects of being forced to leave your native language environment behind from one day to the next? For many exiled writers in particular, contact with their original audiences ceases to exist in exile and their literary work is published in translation only. Because of the forced nature of exile, members of one language community more often than not become cut-off from the living flow of their native language; this was definitely the case before the age of the internet and global communication. The richness of associations, meta-levels in meaning, different language styles, and the topicality of any spoken language have to be ascertained anew when learning a non-native language.

Thus, for professional writers, actors, artists in exile, the switch to another language environment is a life-changing experience which may have positive or negative consequences for their productivity. This study aims to investigate the complexity of exile literature written by German-language exiles between 1933 and 1945. It will examine specific case studies with reference to the post-1945 history of reception in Germany and beyond. It will seek to measure the impact of translation on the work of German-speaking exiles and their artistic production, addressing the problems that arose during the translation process. It will consider the positive or negative implications of translations, including the issue of (possibly deliberate) cultural errors.

Many historians, like Horst Möller (1984), have emphasized the irreparable blow dealt to Germany's intellectual legacy as a result of the massive emigration of its scientists, politicians, artists, academics and intellectuals between the years 1933-1945. Although several exiles returned to their homeland after the war, and some were reinstated in their former positions, many critics have argued that both the exiles and Germany itself suffered unthinkable damage. As Azade Seyhan says:

> both the German intellectuals in exile and the culture they left behind endured multiple losses. Many major thinkers and writers, such as Stefan Zweig, Walter Benjamin, and Kurt Tucholsky took their own lives in exile; others could not establish themselves in a foreign culture nor continue their scholarly or artistic work. (qtd. in Bermann and Wood 277)

Furthermore, German-Jewish academics and authors were faced with additional harassment when their work was forcibly expelled from their German mother tongue by a perverse and absurd Nazi law, which, as early as in 1933, categorized all publications by Jewish professors as "translations from the Hebrew" – a language which, of course, most Jewish Germans knew only via their religious tradition (286). Hence, what survived of German intellectual culture during the twelve years of the "Thousand-Year Empire" was preserved and reproduced in various sites of exile and, in some cases, within the invisible spaces of inner emigration.

Many *émigrés* who left Germany and the German-speaking regions in the wake of Hitler's rise to power held on to their native language and their reflections on the "language problem" became a *leitmotif* in their literary works, personal notes and letters. Theodor Adorno and Hannah Arendt, for instance, saw a strong connection between their philosophical ideas and their German mother tongue, both craving intellectual exchanges in their native language in order to work productively. Philosopher Ernst Bloch, who returned from exile to the East-German city of Leipzig in 1948, stated in his 1939 lecture *Zerstörte Sprache – zerstörte Kultur* [A Destroyed Language – A Destroyed Culture][1] that one cannot demolish a language without demolishing one's culture internally. The opposite is also true, one cannot preserve and develop a culture without speaking the language in which this culture originates and lives. To be banned into a "no-man's-land in between languages" is Michael Hamburger's apt description of the state of writing in exile (qtd. in Röser 1). Likewise, Günther Anders, speaking about his exile experience in his diaries, declares "we became stammerers", "stammerers even in two languages. While we couldn't speak French, English or Spanish properly yet, our German had already started to crumble" (90)[2].

Unlike today, when many educated people are capable of speaking (non-native) English as a *lingua franca*, German-language exile writers of the period 1933-1945 were faced with a linguistic exile in addition to their displacement, which caused specific challenges and marginalization. Moreover, their professional existence and creativity was threatened by traumatic experiences or economic hardship. Some authors were forced into silence by the loss of their working language due to their amputation from the community of German speakers. On the other hand, however, it is exile literature in particular that goes beyond the monolingualism of most national literatures through its embrace of codeswitching, multi- or plurilingualism. For these writers translation became a topic and means of literary production through their working "between the languages".

Metaphors of space and botany are often used by exiled authors in an attempt to describe their insular existence between lan-

---

[1] Hereafter, the transaltions in the body of the text are my translations.
[2] "Stammler sogar in beiden Sprachen: Denn während wir unser Französisch, Englisch oder Spanisch noch nicht gelernt hatten, begann unser Deutsch bereits Stück für Stück abzubröckeln" (Anders 90).

guages. This is the case, for instance, in Peter Weiss's autobiographical novel *Vanishing Point* (1965), in Klaus Mann's autobiography *The Turning Point* (1942), which was originally written in English, or in his father Thomas Mann's famous perception of the German exiles as the representatives of "the other" Germany. Along with Klaus Mann, Hans Sahl, and Hilde Domin, other exile authors like Lion Feuchtwanger and Carl Zuckmayer explored the "language problem" in detail in their literary work as well as within lectures, articles, diaries or letters by pointing out the additional challenges they faced. Not only were they isolated from what Feuchtwanger called the "lively stream of the mother tongue" (535) but their native language had become "polluted" by Nazi jargon and propaganda.

Nonetheless, both authors stress the positives of their "inbetweeness" as exiled writers, for the writer's sensitivity towards using native language increases, and the exposure to the non-native language serves as a corrective *aqua fortis* to literary expression, like a "trunk-knife"[3] that cuts away any stylistic blunder. Taking these thoughts further and considering critical reflections by Hans Sahl or Hilde Domin, for instance, on the impossibility of adequately translating the meta-meanings of the German words for "home" and "homelessness" into English, it becomes obvious that for these exile writers their first language is no longer attached to a homeland or to German culture.

Because of their homelessness and their existence within a no-man's-land, and with a native culture severely marked by Nazi barbarism, literary exiles' writing in German could no longer refer to their home culture. In this context, Sahl speaks of German as an "exterritorial language" (145) and German-language exile literature thus exceeds the realm and concept of a national literature (Rösler 3). This may also be true for the topics and subjects of exile narratives, as Feuchtwanger states in his reflections on writing in exile:

---

[3] "Wurzelmesser"

Gradually, whether we want it or not, we ourselves are changed by the new environment, and with us everything we create. There is no way to the inner vision but through the outer one. The new country in which we live influences the choice of our topics, influences the form. The poet's outer landscape changes his inner landscape. (550)[4]

1. The translation of German-language exile literature

Walter A. Berendsohn, who is widely considered to be the first researcher on the subject of German-language exile literature, confirmed the dominant role and scope of German exile literature, especially regarding its translation. He refers to the *Index Translationum*, a database of translated books worldwide, initiated by the League of Nations (today it is continued by UNESCO) in 1932: the index demonstrates impressively that even prior to 1939 German exile literature was widely translated into various languages. Berendsohn argues that German exile literature actually represented German literature within contemporary world literature, rather than the German literature produced in the Third Reich that toed the ideological line (Benteler 1).

According to Berendsohn, translations are the prerequisite for an international literary exchange beyond national and linguistic borders and, therefore, a central indicator of a work that has attained world literature status. Many of the exiled authors held on to their native German as their literary language, while others switched codes or even wrote in more than one language not native to them. The decision to keep writing in German or to adopt another language

---

[4] "Allmählich, ob wir es wollen oder nicht, werden wir selber verändert von der neuen Umwelt, und mit uns verändert sich alles, was wir schaffen. Es gibt keinen Weg zur inneren Vision als den über die äußere. Das neue Land, in dem wir leben, beeinflußt die Wahl unserer Stoffe, beinflußt die Form. Die äußere Landschaft des Dichters verändert seine innere."

may have been made for programmatic or pragmatic reasons, however, in any case translations became inevitable and a permanent challenge for the production of literary texts in linguistic exile.

The Leo Baeck Institut, which is devoted to the history of German Jews and comprises large archival databases, lists the important publishing houses of German-language exile literature, such as the S. Fischer Verlag in Vienna and Stockholm, El Libro Libre in Mexico, Pantheon Books, the L.B. Fischer Publishing Corp., the Pacific Press in Los Angeles, the Malik Verlag in Prague (later in London), and the Aurora Verlag in New York. Querido and the German unit of well-established publisher Allert de Lange, both based in Amsterdam, need to be added to this list since, as early as in 1933, the two Dutch publishers issued dozens of titles by German authors who were not prepared to compromise with the Nazis or could no longer publish in their homeland(s) because they were Jewish.

They worked on a relatively large scale until 1940, the year Holland was occupied by the Nazis. Although they were blacklisted in the Third Reich, and hence unable to reach German-speaking audiences, many exile literature texts were published in translation first, and only after 1945 in their original German if at all. For example, Arnold Zweig's novel *The Axe of Wandsbek* was directly translated from the German manuscript into Hebrew to be first published in Israel in 1943 (1959 in German by Aufbau). Anna Seghers' exile novel *Transit* was first published in its English translation by James Galston in Mai 1944[5], then in Spanish (translated by Angela Selke and published under the title *Visado de Tránsito* by Nuevo Mundo in 1944) and in French (translated by Jeanne Stern, published in 1947 by La Bibliothèque Française).

The original German typescript got lost during Seghers' years in exile and the German publication of *Transit* is a re-translation into German from the translations in other languages. Furthermore, many of the exiled writers operated as translators as soon as

---

5 Published by Little and Brown in Boston and taken over in 1945 by the London publisher Eyre and Spottiswoode with the title *Transit Visa*.

they had sufficient foreign language skills and frequently out of material need. This was for instance the case for Rudolf Frank, one of the most active translators in exile, as well as for Stefan Zweig who, even before his exile, regarded himself not only as a writer but also as a translator and cultural mediator.

2. Lost in translation? The issue of cultural errors

Translation covers a wide variety of activities which are usually aimed at making texts accessible to people who are not familiar with the language in which the text is produced. For the translation of poetic, literary or philosophical texts, the "transmission of meaning cannot be separated from the way that meaning is articulated or signified" (Weber 65). In other words, meaning is not carried by language alone but is negotiated between readers from within their own contexts of culture. As a result, translation becomes necessarily a form of interpretation, mediation or manipulation between two different "linguacultures" (Katan 75). Literary translators' efforts to render one language system into another thus require a profound awareness of broad cultural, as well as specific linguistic values. As Bermann says, "how much of the 'otherness' of the 'foreign' should the translator highlight? How much of the foreign should he mute or erase in order to make texts easier for the 'home' (target) audience to assimilate?"

The problems posed demand judgment calls as ethical as they are practical or cognitive (Bermann 5). As a result of this dilemma, cultural errors can often be observed in the translation of literary texts. In some cases, they are due to a lack of knowledge of cultural concepts outside the source culture. In other cases, they may be generated by failed cultural transfers. This means that the translator may have been well aware of the connotations of a certain concept, but has not been able to transpose them appropriately into the target culture.

The latter is particularly the case for the translation of regional varieties of the source language. The aforementioned exile writer Anna Seghers' thoughts about the "improvement" of grammatically incorrect passages, or the eradication of regionalisms in her work, was later problematized by her in letters to attentive readers:

> "It is not enough, even if the word is wrongly chosen, to use the terminologically and grammatically correct expression in its place; the new expression must at the same time be correct and also fulfil the same purpose rhythmically and tonally ... by using other vowels or more or less syllables the feeling which the sentence is to bring about" could be destroyed, and thus the effect impaired. (Schlenstedt 7)[6]

And elsewhere she explains why her particular regional idiom is important to her:

> For example, I myself ruthlessly bring out of my own dialect (I am from the Rhine) even expressions and idioms which do not correspond to the grammatical rule, because I find them more beautiful, clearer, etc., and that is what many writers do, probably all of them. (Schlenstedt 7)[7]

The fact, though, that partial or even complete equivalents exist in the target language does not in itself mean that assimilation is the

---

[6] „Es genügt nicht, selbst wenn das Wort falsch gewählt ist, an seiner Stelle den begrifflich und grammatisch richtigen Ausdruck zu setzen, der neue Ausdruck muß zugleich richtig sein und auch rhythmisch und klanglich denselben Zweck erfüllen ..., durch andere Vokale oder durch mehr oder weniger Silben könnte das Gefühl zerstört" werden, „das der Satz bewirken soll", und damit die Wirkung beeinträchtigt."

[7] "Zum Beispiel bringe ich selbst aus meinem eigenen Dialekt (ich bin vom Rhein) rücksichtslos sogar Ausdrücke und Redewendungen, die der grammatischen Regel nicht entsprechen, weil ich sie schöner, deutlicher usw. finde, und das machen sehr viele Schriftsteller, wahrscheinlich alle."

best translation strategy. One possible solution to this kind of problem would be a careful proofreading by someone who is both native speaker of the source text and who possesses adequate knowledge of the culture of the region with which the original text is impregnated. In other words, translators must be fully aware of the importance of the "culture filter" (Katan 75) in translation and of their own cultural limitations.

Sociologists and Cultural Studies scholars focus especially on the influence of and relationship between culture and power relations in society. Culture, according to Jenks, is considered the result of the "pressures that social structures apply to social action" (qtd. in Katan 87). Arguably, in Seghers' case the point could be made that her translators' preference of grammatically correct standard German over the author's original use of regionalisms displays the uneven power relationship between "high", i.e. standard, and "low", i.e. vernacular language (although perhaps not intentionally). However, with regards to instances that refer to an inability of appropriate transposition despite the translator's cultural sensitivity, it may be that conflicting contemporary conditions (e.g. censorship) or ideological precepts impinge on the translation by moulding or manipulating it.

Hence, the system in or from which the translator works is itself under question and the translator intervenes between competing power systems, as the translator sometimes no longer facilitates but take sides, and as readers we must be aware that texts (and the translator) are carriers of ideologies. This has to an extent been the case for German-Jewish *émigré* author Lion Feuchtwanger's historical novels *Waffen für Amerika* [Arms for America] and *Die Jüdin von Toledo* [The Jewess of Toledo], both written in Feuchtwanger's native German during his exile in the USA (1940-1958) and published as translations into English and other languages.

3. Cultural Errors? Lion Feuchtwanger's historical novels *Waffen für Amerika* and *Die Jüdin von Toledo*

Lion Feuchtwanger (1884-1958) fled Europe during World War II and found refuge in Los Angeles from 1941 until his death in 1958. He began his literary career as a theatre critic and playwright during the 1910s and 1920s in Munich but became internationally known for his historical fiction./During his 17 years in Southern California, he wrote primarily historical novels including the two volumes of *Waffen für Amerika* [Arms for America], also named *Die Füchse im Weinberg* [The Foxes in the Vineyard] and published in America under the title *Proud Destiny*. *Die Jüdin von Toledo* [The Jewess of Toledo], also known under the title *Spanische Ballade* [A Spanish Ballad], was published in 1956 under the English title *Raquel, The Jewess of Toledo*.//

/ During his long career as a writer, Feuchtwanger wrote 19 plays, 19 novels, and numerous short stories and essays. His works have been, and continue to be, published in many countries and have been translated into more than 30 languages. Unlike many of his fellow emigrants and escapees, Feuchtwanger already had a large overseas audience for his novels in translation before he was forced into exile. With the income from his writings, he was able to assist many other German-Jewish and anti-fascist writers in exile.

The reasons for the change in titles are twofold – some of Feuchtwanger's original German book titles were changed for translated editions in order to reach new and broader audiences, e.g. his novel *Paris Gazette* (from the original German title *Exil, 1940*). It was thought that the original title would limit the readership to a politically aware contemporary (European) audience, already critical of the political climate of its time. This is also true for another two novels, however, for reasons more complex than just to meet the taste of new audiences: *Proud Destiny* is the title of the English language translation of Feuchtwanger's first novel in two volumes *Waffen für Amerika*, written after his dramatic rescue to the USA from an enemy alien prison camp in occupied France.

The novel's plot features social progress springing from the American and French Revolutions. More precisely, the narrative focuses on the effort of supporters of the American Revolution, such as playwright Pierre de Beaumarchais and American envoy Benjamin Franklin, to gain French aid for the revolutionaries of the new United States of America. Feuchtwanger's novel, published during the Cold War in 1947, evoked a notable response in the Soviet Union, based on a misunderstanding of the original German title as an alleged promotion "of Anglo-American global hegemony". Representing the USA as a progressive force, "even in a 170-year-old setting, was undesirable in the context of the political hostilities of the late 1940s" (O'Dochartaigh 32).

Thus, while the change of the original title *Waffen für America* to *Füchse im Weinberg* for the East German edition of 1952, or *Proud Destiny* respectively, does not constitute a cultural error in terms of being a linguistically accurate translation, it demonstrates the second, cultural aspect of conflicting contemporary conditions which Feuchtwanger's editors responded to in order to avoid clashes with his Soviet and East German publishers in particular, and as so not to endanger the further appearance of his books in the East.

Though Feuchtwanger never accepted the criticism of the novel's original title as justified, he agreed to change any references to "imperialist" America and to the supply of weapons. Once they were removed, his work was published in the East. The American title of the novel can, however, be read as a tribute to his country of refuge and as a reminder of America's moral responsibility to protect human rights and liberties for which it fought in the American War of Independence and in World War II. Moreover, the title *Proud Destiny* delivered a culturally sensitive meta-message that took on a timely relevance with the rise of McCarthyism in the States, but which was largely lost on the American readership. American critics praised the author of *Proud Destiny* for his progressive "Americanization" as stated by *The New York Post* on 18 September 1947:

Whether it is the French or American influence ... The writing is far from Teutonic, and the whole effect tough, firm, and solid, as light, charming and tragi-comic as the period it presents (qtd. in Koepke 100-101)

or by *The Buffalo News* on 13 September 1947: "Since 1940, Feuchtwanger has lived in the United States, and perhaps as some indication of his powers of absorption, ... is remarkably free from the author's former heaviness of style" (qtd. in Koepke 100-101). These references to the author's cultural assimilation can be found neither before nor later in the book reviews. The subject matter has obviously played a decisive role for American critics.

Yet, Feuchtwanger was also keenly aware of the shortcomings in his translator William Rose's rendering of the novel. For instance, on March 21st 1947, Feuchtwanger wrote to him:

Sometimes my diction seemed visibly over-coloured to you, and you then took away colour, you gave only two or only one, or none at all, of about three attributes that I give to a person or a thing. This must sometimes be to the advantage of the sentence; on the other hand, I check my pages very rigidly to find out whether I can delete an adjective or a phrase, and what remains is only what seems indispensable to me. Of course it happens that I repeat adjectives, but then it happens deliberately, because I want to give them to the person or the situation as a *leitmotif*. (Adrian Feuchtwanger 261)[8]

---

[8] "Manchmal schien Ihnen meine Diktion sichtlich überfärbt, und Sie nahmen dann Farbe weg, Sie gaben etwa von drei Attributen, die ich einem Menschen oder einer Sache mitgebe, nur zwei oder nur eines, oder auch gar keines. Das muß manchmal zum Vorteil des Satzes sein; andernteils prüfe ich meine Seiten sehr scharf nach, um ausfindig zu machen, ob ich ein Adjektiv oder eine Wendung streichen kann, und was

Another problem identified by Feuchtwanger was overall wordiness. The standard expansion rate when translating from German to English is about ten per cent due to German's compound nouns. In the case of *Proud Destiny*, the German manuscript of over 300,000 words turned into 360,000 words in the English galley proofs and had to be cut down accordingly: "The cuts included, for example, the removal of a touching scene in which Franklin admits self-doubt to his grandson William" (262). As he bemoaned in his letters, Feuchtwanger had already struggled to capture the statesman's human side, and as a result, cuts such as this were obviously irritating (262). Feuchtwanger's criticisms evidently took their toll on the translator, who eventually severed their professional relationship.

While the polarisation of Cold War, and its opposing ideologies, were the reason for the changes to the German titles of Feuchtwanger's America novel, it was somewhat different reasons that led to the changed title of his novel *Die Jüdin von Toledo* (1955). This novel deals with intercultural mediation and the plea for mutual understanding between different ethnic groups. Disappointed by the hysterical, anti-liberal policies of the USA and disillusioned by the political developments in the Soviet Union, East and West Germany, Feuchtwanger turned to the cultural wealth of Judaism in his penultimate novel *Raquel, The Jewess of Toledo*, which is based on a Spanish medieval legend. In terms of material history, he draws on a number of famous models, including Lope de Vega's and Franz Grillparzer's literary adaptations of the subject of the "beautiful Jewess".

The novel was first published in English with its literally translated original title *The Jewess of Toledo* by Pacific Press in Los Angeles, but a German-language edition entitled *Spanische Ballade* for the West German Europäischer Buchklub [European Book Club] had been published one year earlier in 1954. Market-economy reasons were supposedly the deciding factor for the title change. The

---

stehen bleibt, ist nur das, was mir unentbehrlich scheint. Natürlich kommt es vor, daß ich Adjektiva wiederhole, dann aber geschieht es mit Absicht, weil ich sie dem Menschen oder der Situation als Leitmotiv mitgeben möchte".

question is, why was the original title not considered to be marketable? It seems reasonable to assume that the change of title into the inoffensive "Spanish Ballad" was intended to evade too sensitive "Jewish themes", such as the brutal expulsion of Iberian Jews during the Spanish Reconquista, as implied by the original title. In other words, the publisher aimed to avoid a possible anti-Semitic rejection by the German audience. Once more it is the dimension of cultural sensitivity that caused Feuchtwanger's advisers to change the original German title of the book, in order to avoid a cultural error less than ten years after the end of World War II and the Holocaust (still a taboo subject at the time). This may have affected the success of the novel in Adenauer's Republic (Vaupel 153). The title selection of "A Spanish Ballad", however, makes the discrimination and historical expulsion of the Jewish minority a Spanish problem entirely. That is, any indirect allusions to German guilt and responsibility for the more recent, 20th-century genocide of European Jewry, do not come up in the first place – which, of course, is antithetical to the overall lesson of Feuchtwanger's novel.

4. Reception and Conclusion

Although the various title changes for both novels are not so much about real translation errors, they nevertheless show how contemporary political ideologies, and perhaps exaggerated concessions to contemporary sensitivities, required these changes. Thus, they provide cultural testimony to the atmosphere of the time. The return to the original titles in subsequent years (both *Waffen für Amerika* and *Die Jüdin von Toledo* were again used as titles in later German editions) reflects the transformations within the post-war political climate and a form of cultural advancement. It can be argued that literary policy and the development of German post-war literature became a symptom of the temporal-political conditions in both parts of Germany: Feuchtwanger was appropriated by his East German critics as an exclusively anti-fascist and purely politically motivated writer, as it corresponded to East Germany's political self-image.

While the author's bourgeois origins and left-liberal attitude were critically conceded, his belief in socialism as a progressive social order was regarded as the main element and motivation of his valuable work for the "socialist reader". The significance of Judaism and Feuchtwanger's own Jewish cultural roots as equally strong and motivating elements in his *oeuvre* was, however, largely ignored by the East German literary criticism, at least until the 1980s, and seen as a mere biographical side note.

Exile literature as such was particularly important in the founding phase and the early years of the German Democratic Republic (GDR) in order to promote a common consensus among the various political forces in the emerging "socialist society". The anti-fascist stance became the common denominator for supporters and critics of socialist unity policy in the GDR, and exile literature generally stood for this anti-fascist tradition and had the special task of acting as a form of positive German heritage, i.e. as a starting point for the development of an independent "national" GDR literature. In this context, bourgeois authors such as Feuchtwanger and others were acknowledged, albeit while playing a subordinate role in direct comparison with the promotion of socialist authors of exile literature such as Anna Seghers, Willi Bredel or Johannes R. Becher.

In West Germany, standardized criteria of reception, such as the imperative of unconditional text immanence valid until the 1970s, had to be overcome in favour of socially critical literary analyses. As a result, the reception of exile literature was much delayed. Within West German literary reception history there are attempts throughout to depoliticize authors of exile literature and, especially in the case of Feuchtwanger, to distinguish them from serious "poets" as high-circulation trivial "writers" and thus discredit them. The heterogeneity and political disunity of the exiled writers and their literary production in exile, often regarded as qualitatively inferior, served as "proof" of the alleged infertility and ineffectiveness of exile as such.

While the ignorance of exile literature, and the long-standing exclusion of its authors in West Germany, was primarily caused by the suppression of the National Socialist past and the ostrich mentality of a post-war restorative society, the initial enthusiastic adaptation of exile literature in East Germany was to a certain extent also part of a displacement mechanism, namely the rejection of an admission of complicity by the "anti-fascist" East German state in the all-German catastrophe (255–258).

The reception history of German-language exile literature in general, and Feuchtwanger's works in particular, thus illustrate the extent to which literature is a reaction to the social environment alongside aesthetic language art – and vice versa, and to how much literature can lead to extreme polarization. Naturally, this also refers to the role of translations as acutely prominent in the literary output of exiled authors. In addition to the described problems, which may include (self-)censorship in order to become published at all or winning new/foreign audiences, it has become clear that the literature of exile from Nazi Germany has produced innovative forms of multilingualism in different ways, some of which can be described as *translational* writing methods (Benteler 82).

In this context, translation can then be regarded within the text as an aesthetic tool that represents and reflects the need for translation, and the confrontation with foreign languages in exile. Although motives of loss of speech and speechlessness may play a central role in exile literature, through multilingual writing methods and internal translations (e.g. a common procedure in the work of exiled authors Hilde Domin or Mascha Kaléko) the texts possess a fundamental cross-national and cross-linguistic quality. In turn, this reveals an innovative and alternative "self-design in exile" (82), which in relation to language is in clear opposition to more traditional ideas of exile, such as that of the *émigrés* (or the diaspora) as "preservers" of the mother tongue.

It is difficult – if not impossible – to assess if the classification of cultural errors still apply to these cross-national and cross-linguistic type of texts which go beyond national culture categories. The corpus of exile literature translations thus demonstrates, more often than not, that the long-prevailing notion of unity of culture, territory and language is hardly relevant. Instead of a "dialogue between the cultures", the texts display cultural interconnectedness and entanglement. In this context, translation increasingly becomes the leading perspective for any form of cultural contact (Bachmann-Medick 246). It no longer serves merely as a vehicle for faithful mediation between polar defined, original cultures, but as a reciprocal process between cultures. This suggests that a territorial understanding of culture is overcome – or at least subversively infiltrated.

Works cited

Albrecht, Richard. "'Zerstörte Sprache – zerstörte Kultur'. Ernst Blochs Exil-Vortrag vor siebzig Jahren: Geschichtliches und Aktuelles". *Träume gegen Mauer – Dreams against Walls. Bloch-Jahrbuch 13*, edited by Francesca Vidal. Talheimer, 2009, pp. 223-240.

Anders, Günther. *Die Schrift an der Wand. Tagebücher 1941-1966*. Beck, 1967.

Bachmann-Medick, Doris. *Cultural Turns. Neuorientierung in den Kulturwissenschaften*. Rowohlt, 2009.

Benteler, Anne. "Übersetzung als literarisches Schreibverfahren im Exil am Beispiel von Mascha Kaléko und Werner Lansburgh". *Cadernos de Tradução*, vol. 38, no.1, 2018, pp. 65-85, DOI: 10.5007/2175-7968.2018v38n1p65.

Benteler, Anne. "Überleben in der Übersetzung – oder Lost in Translation? Übersetzung im Exil – Exil als Übersetzung". *Exilograph. Newsletter der Walter A. Berendsohn Forschungsstelle für deutsche Exilliteratur*, no. 22, 2014, pp. 1-5.

Bermann, Sandra; Wood, Michael (eds.). *Nation, Language, and the Ethics of Translation*. Princeton UP, 2005.

Bermann, Sandra (ed.). "Introduction". *Nation, Language, and the Ethics of Translation*, edited by Sandra Bermann and Michael Wood. Princeton UP, 2005, pp. 1-11.

Domin, Hilde. *Rückkehr der Schiffe*. S. Fischer, 1962.

Feuchtwanger, Adrian. "The Proud Fabric? A Translator's Perspective on 'Waffen für Amerika' in English Translation." *Feuchtwanger und Berlin*, edited by Geoffrey V. Davis. Feuchtwanger Studies, vol. 4. Peter Lang, 2014, pp. 259-267.

Feuchtwanger, Lion. "Der Schriftsteller im Exil (1943)". *Ein Buch nur für meine Freunde*. S. Fischer, 1984, pp. 533-538.

Hamburger, Michael. "Niemandsland-Variationen." *Zwischen den Sprachen. Essays und Gedichte*. S. Fischer, 1966, pp. 26-34.

Heimannsberg, Joachim, et al. *Klaus Mann: Tagebücher 1940-1943*. Edition Spangenberg, 1991.

Jenks, Chris. *Culture*. Routledge, 1993.

Katan, David. "Translation as Intercultural Communication". *The Routledge Companion to Translation Studies*, edited by Jeremy Munday. Routledge, 2009, pp. 74-93.

Koepke, Wulf. "Die Exilschriftsteller und der amerikanische Buchmarkt". *Deutsche Exilliteratur seit 1933*, edited by John M. Spalek; Joseph Strelka, vol. 1. Franke, 1976, pp. 89-117.

Möller, Horst. *Exodus der Kultur: Schriftsteller, Wissenschaftler und Künstler in der Emigration nach 1933*. Beck, 1984.

O'Dochartaigh, Pól. "The Present Sense of an Historical Novel: Feuchtwanger's Waffen für America". *Refuge and Reality. Feuchtwanger and the European Émigrés in California*, edited by Pól O'Dochartaigh; Alexander Stephan. Rodopi, 2016, pp. 31-41.

Röser, Claudia. "Im Niemandsland zwischen den Sprachen? Sprachwechsel und Mehrsprachigkeit in der Exilliteratur". *Exilograph. Newsletter der Walter A. Berendsohn Forschungsstelle für deutsche Exilliteratur*, no. 18, 2012, pp. 1-4.

Sahl, Hans. "Gast in fremden Kulturen". *Ich lebe nicht in der Bundesrepublik*, edited by Hermann Kesten. List, 1964.

Seyhan, Azade. *German Academic Exiles in Istanbul: Translation as the "Bildung" of the Other*, edited by Sandra Bermann and Michale Wood. Princeton UP, 2005, pp. pp. 274-289.

Vaupel, Angela. *Zur Rezeption von Exilliteratur und Lion Feuchtwangers Werk in Deutschland: 1945 bis heute*. Peter Lang, 2007.

Weber, Samuel. "A Touch of Translation: on Walter Benjamin's 'Task of the Translator'", edited by Sandra Bermann and Michael Wood. Princeton UP, 2005, pp. 65-79.

Zuckmayer, Carl. "Kleine Sprüche aus der Sprachverbannung". *Gedichte 1916-1948*. Suhrkamp, 1948.

Webography

Feuchtwanger Memorial Library. USC lib., 2017, www.libguides.usc.edu/feuchtwanger. Accessed 12 June 2018.

Kirkus Book Reviews, 2018, www.kirkusreviews.com. Accessed 9 September 2018.

Leo Baeck Institute, 2016, www.lbi.org/collections/library/highlights-of-lbi-library-collection/german-exile-literature collection. Accessed 9 September 2018.

Universität Mainz. Silvia Schlenstedt, Kommentar zu Anna Seghers' *Transit*, www.seghers-werke.germanistik.uni-mainz.de/leseproben/transit_leseprobe.shtlm. Accessed 30 December 2018.

On the Translation of Bulgakov's *A Young Doctor's Notebook* into the Language of the Cinema

Marina Tsvetkova

Introduction: cinema adaptation as a "double translation"

This chapter examines cultural errors in a case of a "double translation", when a literary text is transferred not only into a different cultural setting with its own traditions but also into a different medium. The focus of my study is the miniseries *A Young Doctor's Notebook* directed by Alex Hardcastle and Robert McKillop. The TV series is based on a collection of short stories of the same name by the celebrated 20th century Russian writer and playwright, Mikhail Bulgakov, known in the West mainly for his novel *The Master and Margarita*, first published in 1960.

Even though the series is labeled a "period" drama and its characters and places have Russian names, the script written by Mark Chappell, Alan Connor, and Shaun Pye completely rearranges the original and adapts it to make it quite contemporary and "British". When I say "British", what is most striking in the adaptation is the prevalence of the British sense of humour, considered by the British themselves to be one of the major virtues of their nation. Most authors who try to define British (or English) humour (Fox, Jarski, Mikes, and others) are unanimous in their opinion that it is based on irony, understatement and "underreaction", self-mockery, is "silly, sardonic, nasty, naughty, wry, surreal and nutty" (Jarski XV), "soaked with cynicism and marinated in bile" (XVIII).

I.Q. Hunter and Laraine Porter point to the "'eccentric' British strain of whimsy, surreal nonsense and downright silliness that leads from Lewis Carroll and Edward Lear to the anarchic "madcap comedy" of the Crazy Gang, The Goons, who made two films, *Down among the Z. Men*, (1952) and *The Case of the Mukkinese Battlehorn* (1956). Richard Lester's *The Bed Sitting Room* (1969), *Monty Python* and Viv Stanshall's *Sir Henry at Rawlinson End* (1980)" (Hunter, Porter 2). All of these characteristics make British humour as well as British comedy "untranslatable" to other cultures. What distinguishes British humour from its foreign counterparts is its dominance and pervasiveness.

As Rosemarie Jarski wittily puts it, "humour is not something we add on to our lives; it is our take on life" (XVIII). This peculiar British attitude towards life can be seen as responsible for most of the transformations of Bulgakov's stories as reimagined by the filmmakers. This kind of "misreading" of the original via the British mode of interacting with the world can be viewed an example of a cultural error, which, ironically, resulted in the huge success of the miniseries in Britain. However, what I wish to explore here is to what extent those choices can be ascribed to a form of "cultural error", or whether they are part of a deliberate strategy followed by the film makers. This is the central question in my discussion.

In the case of a film adaptation, the source text cannot remain unchanged as it has to be translated from one medium to another. As one of the most prominent experts in film adaptation studies, George Bluestone claims:

> changes are *inevitable* the moment one abandons the linguistic for the visual medium... The film becomes a *different thing* in the same sense that a historical painting becomes a different thing from the historical event which it illustrates. It is fruitless to say that film A is better or worse than novel B as it is to pronounce Wright's Johnson's *Wax Building* better or worse than Tchaikowsky's *Swan Lake*. (5-6)

This makes the very question of fidelity to the adapted text pointless. The transformation of a prose text into a film is a field of studies, which has been recently investigated from different angles. It started, like Translation Studies, via contrastive analysis aimed at the investigation of the degree of fidelity of the film adaptation to its source (the latest example of such an approach, proving that the fidelity debate is not over, is a book of essays edited by David Kranz and Nancy Mellerski 2008) and has continued with the studies of the motives behind adaptations. As Linda Hutcheon argues, in *A Theory of Adaptation* (XV), "the idea of 'fidelity' to that prior text is often what drives any directly comparative method of study. Instead, I argue here, there are many and varied motives behind adaptation and few involve faithfulness".

One of the major motives, especially in contemporary society, is to make the adaptation "fit for consumption" by its viewers. In a case such as ours, when an adaptation works not only at the crossroads of different media, but of two different cultures, an example from the intercultural communication process suggested by the Russian scholars Valerii Zusman, Victor Zinchenko and Zoya Kirnoze (55) might be usefully applied to it. The authors use the word "meta-artifact" in the case of the target culture to stress the distinction between the original and its copy. When applied to literary text translation, the theory stresses the inevitable adaptation of the text to a new target culture.

To convert a text from one language into another, one has to become its reader (i.e. to understand and interpret it) first. Every understanding and interpretation is unique, it cannot be identical to what was meant by the author, and this is exactly the point in the process when all sorts of cultural errors may occur. The translator is simultaneously both a reader and a new author, working on the border of two cultures: that of the original and that of the culture in which the translation is introduced. This view is supported by George Bluestone, "in the fullest sense of the word, the filmist becomes not a translator for an established author, but a new author in his own right" (62).

The two cultures exist in two different realities and two different national traditions (synchronically as well as diachronically). Even if the translator is determined to stick as closely to the original as possible, he or she cannot avoid following cultural types and stereotypes attributive to their native tradition. Thus, the translated text is influenced by the individuality of the translator, by the tradition and reality of the culture which the translator belongs to, as well as by cultural errors made by the translator as a result of not being culturally sensitive as the case may be.

Consequently, any translation is bound to differ from the original. If the changes made to the original (even though they are the result of cultural errors) in order to adapt a work of art to the "horizon of expectations" of the reader in the target culture (formed by their own traditions and reality), the translation is usually a success, provided that the exotic foreign flavour of the original is partly preserved. Zusman *et al.*'s theory is also helpful in the case of a "double" translation, the main difference being that instead of a reader in the target culture, we will have a viewer and the film adaptation will stand in the place of the "meta-artifact" (to highlight its inevitable infidelity to the original).

1. Bulgakov's cycle and its film versions

The short stories on which the series is based were written by Bulgakov in the 1920s and inspired by his own experiences as a young doctor, practising from 1916-1918 in a small village hospital in the Smolensk region. Bulgakov published the stories from 1925-1926 separately in journals and did not see them as one single entity. As a result, one can find unnecessary repetitions here and there, and in some stories the setting where the action takes place is called Murievo, in the others it is referred to as Nikolskoye. Scholars (Yanovskaya, Sokolov) later discovered that Bulgakov had intended to bring the publications together in one volume. This was accomplished after his death. The debate still continues in Russia as to which stories should be included.

In the Russian tradition, the cycle usually comprises "The Embroidered Towel", "The Steel Windpipe", "Baptism by Rotation", "The Blizzard", "Black as Egypt's Night", "The Vanishing Eye", and

"The Speckled Rash". "Morphine" (which is thematically close to the stories mentioned above) was published 1927 and scholars did not find any evidence that the author meant it to be a part of the cycle. The "Notes" are written in the first person and we do not know the name of the narrator. In "Morphine", the narrator has a name – Vladimir Bomgard; however, the protagonist of the story is one Doctor Polyakov, whose diary Bomgard publishes.

Alan Connor, in an article for *The Guardian*, refers to different collections in English and French which the co-writers used when working on the script: Michael Glenny's version, published in 1975, Paul Lequesne's in 1994, and Hugh Aplin's in 2011. All of them include the core hospital stories as well as different extra stories, which makes the cycle read differently. In the eyes of Connor, this justifies the rearrangements they made to the script to create a coherent story out of a disjointed diary form: "Like many editors before us, we have reordered Bulgakov's stories and decided which to emphasize. Unlike them, we've written new scenes to make sure our two doctors had a coherent adventure" (Connor).

The first season of the series *A Young Doctor's Notebook* (released in 2012)[1] is based on Bulgakov's stories mentioned above, while the second one *A Young Doctor's Notebook and Other Stories* (shot in 2013)[2] borrows only the main character and the characters of the hospital staff from the stories of the cycle as well as the story "Extraordinary Adventures of a Doctor", included in Paul Lequesne's French edition.

Bulgakov's narrator illustrates the autobiographical strain in his writing. The author also worked as a doctor in a remote hospital in the settlement called Nikolskoye from September 1916 to September 1917 and then for a year in a hospital in the small town of Vyazma. By that time, however, Bulgakov already had some experience as an army doctor, while the narrator is two years younger than the author, and fresh graduated from university. Apparently, these changes were made to sharpen the key theme of the cycle – the

---

[1] Hereafter, referred to as *Notebook*.
[2] Hereafter, referred to as *Notebook and Other*.

initiation of a young man into a profession, where his patent lack of experience might cost people their lives.

In the film, the biographical nature of the short stories is emphasized – the young doctor (played by the prominent British actor Daniel Radcliffe) resembles the young Bulgakov, while the mature doctor (played by a well-known American actor Jon Hamm) is the very picture of Bulgakov in his 40s. Thus, all the strange things which happen in the film could be taken by the viewers as real facts drawn from the life of the Russian writer, thus making the action more thrilling by adding a frisson of realism.

The first season starts with a framing episode from the doctor's later life (made up by the script writers) in which officials from the GPU (the acronym for the equivalent of the KGB in Stalin's time) are searching the doctor's study in Moscow. Contrary to expectations, they are not searching for the proof of his counter-revolutionary subversion but rather for the evidence of his morphine addiction. This hint at Stalin's repression is a plot device designed to make the series more attractive to Western viewers, for whom repression forms an important part of the stereotype of Soviet Russia. The frost and the dreary vastness of the landscape help to create the exotic flavour of the country as well. They further contribute to the USSR's image as a barbaric place.

The film recounts the story of a newly qualified doctor posted to a remote rural hospital in the village of Muryevo, who gradually becomes a morphine addict. Thus, the plot of Bulgakov's "Morphine" is foregrounded making it the pivotal story in the series. The main character takes the name of the narrator of the story, Vladimir Bomgard, as opposed to Polyakov. The scriptwriters probably found the sound of the name Bomgard stranger, funnier, and more suitable for the comic miniseries they were making.

As for the plot twists, they come directly from the diary kept by Polyakov. Like Doctor Polyakov, the central character in the film keeps a diary. The miniseries is arranged as flashbacks the elder Vladimir Bomgard experiences while reading the notebook he kept during his stay in Muryevo. Therefore, the script places the theme of a young man developing a morphine addiction front and centre (and it is true that Bulgakov himself developed a morphine addiction while working as a doctor). The subplots, borrowed from the stories which make up Bulgakov's "Young Doctor's Notebook", are centred around this theme.

The focus on the issue of drug addiction makes Bulgakov feel contemporary and attractive to young viewers. It is interesting to note that in 2008 a film entitled *Morphine* was shot by Andrey Balabanov. In this film, Bulgakov's short story of the same name was used as the central premise, as it was in the TV series, the first season of which appeared four years later. Balabanov also changed the central character's name (Sergey Vasilyevich) to Mikhail to emphasize the parallels with the writer's biography. The plots from other stories of *The Young Doctor's Notebook* are incorporated into the overarching plot as episodes from Doctor Polyakov's medical practice.

The young medic helps deliver children, performs amputations, fights the horrifying ignorance of his rural patients, all the while gradually becoming more and more dependent on morphine. In his film, the Russian director, however, concentrated exclusively on that tragic, final facet of the story. In full compliance with the original, the main character commits suicide when he realizes his own inability to break the vicious cycle of morphine addiction. Given the similarities with *The Young Doctor's Notebook,* it is difficult to imagine that neither the writers nor the producers of the TV series saw Balabanov's screen version. However, the connection goes unreferenced in the final credits.

2. The cultural error of the filmmakers and its consequences

The scriptwriters read the tragic story of the degradation of a bright graduate of the Moscow Medical University from "Morphine" through the lens of British humour, and they blended it with the ambivalent attitude that is characteristic of *The Young Doctor's Note-*

book stories, where the dramatic and the ironic coexist. This results in a very special production where horrific yet humorous scenes abound; their mood betrays the spirit of Bulgakov's work, which is characterized by a mixture of laughter, melancholy and bitterness.

In all the details of the production, the exaggerative choices made by the filmmakers are obvious. Bulgakov described the stages of addiction in great detail in "Morphine", and the scriptwriters comically elaborate on these details. For instance, the GPU man enumerates the side effects of morphine abuse (neither this character, nor the symptoms are present in the original story): anxiety, depression, nausea, insomnia, muscle spasms, high blood pressure, rapid weight loss, frequent and uncontrollable bowel movements, involuntary ejaculation.

It is interesting to note, that the last two signs are not mentioned in medical books and seem to be invented especially for the series to help to develop an atmosphere of grotesque and dark humour. The sense of macabre grotesque is enhanced by the use of a reverse faux Cyrillic writing in the title cards and credits, as well as the elder doctor's physical interjections into his own flashbacks to his first year out of college. This move might be prompted by the inner voice verbalizing the most horrible fears of the young doctor in "The Embroidered Towel". In the story, the dialogues of the main character and the voice are full of self-irony and even sarcasm:

> "Let's see now ... they tell me admissions are almost nil at the moment. They're breaking flax in the villages, the roads are impassable..."
> "That's just when they will bring you a hernia," thundered a harsh voice in my mind, "because a man with a cold won't make the effort over impassable roads but rest assured they'll bring you a hernia, my dear doctor".
> There was something in what the voice said. I shuddered.
> "Be quiet," I said to it. "It won't necessarily be a hernia. Stop being so neurotic. You can't back out once you've begun".
> "You said it!" the voice answered spitefully.

> "All right then... I won't take a step without my reference book ... If I have to prescribe something I can think it over while I wash my hands and the reference book will be lying open on top of the patients' register. I shall make out wholesome but simple prescriptions, say, sodium salicylate, 0.5 grammes in powder form three times a day".
> "You might as well prescribe baking soda! Why don't you just prescribe soda?" the voice was blatantly making fun of me.
> (Bulgakov 192)

The internal voice "thunders" like the voice of God, it speaks "spitefully", it "bluntly makes fun" of the young doctor. In the story, this creates a weird effect of a split personality. In the series, however, this technique is brought closer to the grotesque, which makes the viewers suspect a personality disorder. For example, the older Bomgard teases his younger self and eats the page from the medical book with the description of a difficult case of child birth, while the former is trying to snatch the page from his mouth; the older and the younger Bomgards share a bath sitting face to face, sleep in one bed etc.

The turning of Bulgakov's cycle into a dark comedy, with elements of obscene humour, farce, and sarcasm so characteristic of British culture is the crucial change made to the original texts in order to conform to audiences in the target culture. To a certain extent, it is suggested by the style of Bulgakov's short stories – which are at times ironic, and at times dramatic. However, Bulgakov never goes as far as to present the narrator or the other characters as slapstick comedy caricatures, in contrast to the scriptwriters who labeled their film as "comedy-drama".

Though most critics argue that there is more comedy than drama in it: "the stories have been made more comic and less grimly stark than the originals" (Sutcliffe) "emphasizing the grotesque and comic at the expense of the melancholy and satirical" (Hale). In this case, we can speak of a clear-cut example of a cultural error: the filmmakers misread Bulgakov's text by "reading into" it a cultural mode characteristic of British culture in which comedy is "the most popular genre of the... cinema" (Hunter, Porter 2). This cultural error becomes a pivot on which the cinematographic version of Bulgakov's cycle is based.

3. Features of dark comedy in the TV series

Dark comedy (or black comedy) is a sub-genre of comedy which makes light of subject matter that is generally considered taboo, particularly subjects that are normally viewed as serious or painful, namely such issues as violence, disease and death. According to *The Encyclopedia Britannica*, this type of comedy is based on the juxtaposition of "morbid or ghastly elements with comical ones," deriving humour from the shocking and unexpected (*Britannica.com*). Though black comedy often incorporates irony, farce, low comedy and straightforward obscenity, it usually goes beyond merely telling jokes and tends to alternate between comedy and tragedy.

The miniseries corresponds exactly to the description of black comedy as a genre. Reviewers compare the *A Young Doctor's Notebook* with such TV comedies as *The Evil Dead* (Aveling), *Mighty Boosh* (Waywell) and others of the same kind. The central character pulls out a patient's tooth with a piece of bone to the accompaniment of the widely known Russian folk song *Kalinka*. The overemotional relatives of the patients are neutralized by formaldehyde and then dragged away by their legs. At the funeral of one of the midwives, Pelageya, the paramedic who died of typhus, appears in a buffoon wig, made from the tail of a horse, which died in the previous episode. The older Bomgard, when travelling in a boxcar in the company of an indigent, one morning discovers that the diary (which he was rereading) is missing pages, and the following dialogue ensues between the travelling companions:

> Bomgard: "There are pages missing".
> Man: "I ate a lot of borshch".

Bomgard: "October, November..."
Man: "Bad borshch".
Bomgard: "You wiped your ass with Christmas?"
(*Notebook and Other*, episode 2, 00:32-00:33)

Furthermore, the episodes of the series are full of horrific, yet funny, gags characteristic of dark comedy, inconceivable in Bulgakov's stories most of which were published in medical journals: the doctor takes so long to saw off a patient's leg with a blunt saw, that the midwives and the paramedic assisting him fall asleep. Later on, he clumsily slips on and nearly falls down into the pool of blood where the sawn-off piece of leg is floating. Pus spurts right into the face of the young doctor when he punctures an abscess and the staff barely avoids dropping Pelageya's corpse in the narrow corridor when taking it out of the hospital.

The plot based on medical matters helps to saturate the TV series with dialogue filled with dark jokes. Bomgard's eulogy, given at Pelageya's funeral, comes off in the best tradition of farce: "It is incomprehensible even to me, a doctor, that Pelageya, built as she was, like an ox, could be felled down by something so small as a typhoid louse" (*Notebook and Other*, episode 4, 01:44-02:01). The jokes about syphilis run throughout all the episodes of both seasons; the entire neighborhood is infected, and the young Bomgard has a debilitating fear of being infected himself. In Bulgakov's cycle, the theme of syphilis appears only in one short story "The Speckled Rash".

In general, all kinds of sexual or scatological jokes, can be found throughout the miniseries. For instance, the paramedic, when he appears in the corridor after the first delivery Bomgard has to attend, asks with a straight face, "Is it me... or does she have the most unusually shaped vagina?" Bomgard answers in the same British manner, "Well... I have had... a long... and arduous journey" (*Notebook*, episode 1, 19:10-19:25). Needless to say, this joke was introduced by the filmmakers and not borrowed from Bulgakov's stories.

4. British humour in the TV series

Sexual or scatological jokes, so called "dirty jokes", are a regular feature of contemporary British comedy. According to Chiara Bucaris and Luca Barra, since the late 90s – early 2000, humour containing

> unconventional, often-humorous, and explicit treatment of subjects such as sex, death, homosexuality, and illness have become more pervasive in Anglo-American television programming. From *Inside Amy Schumer* and *The League of Gentlemen* to Super Bowl commercials, stand-up comedy specials, and new generation, single-camera sitcoms, forms of edgy, transgressive, dark, and even taboo humour have in the last few years increasingly become part and parcel of both television programming and the viewing experience (1-2).

By inserting jokes of that kind, the filmmakers seriously deviate from Bulgakov's original and destroy the predominantly grimly stark spirit of his sketches of young doctor's life with only the occasional glimpse of irony and satire.

There are many scenes containing classical elements of physical comedy and knockabout in the series: the short Bomgard arrives to the remote rural hospital where he is posted dragging a suitcase larger than himself; the midwives dress him in a huge labcoat which belonged to Leopold Leopoldovich (his predecessor), who was much taller and broader than him.

The jokes in the film have a recognizable British character: they are based on making puns and playing on words (Tebbe 2-3). Natasha (a character from the second season, the plot of which is fabricated completely by the scriptwriters), trying to explain how much she enjoys the warmth she and her brother found in the hospital says: "Once again, thank you for your kindness. I haven't felt such warmth since I sat and watched the Bolsheviks burn down my childhood home" (*Notebook and Other*, episode 2, 09:03-09:10).

When she visits the young Bomgard, who shot himself in the leg during the party the day before, they have the following conversation:

> Natasha: "I feel guilty. If I hadn't suggested you join the White Guard this would never happen."
> Bomgard: "I had no regrets. I wanted to aid your cause."
> Natasha: "Then, perhaps, you should join the Bolsheviks."
> Bomgard: "How would that help? ... Oh... Right."
> (*Notebook and Other*, episode 2, 16:04-16:18)

Another good example is the dialogue between the younger and the older versions of Bomgard. Younger Bomgard exclaims: "I am a doctor. It is my duty to help these people". His exalted monologue is interrupted by the desperate cries of a father, bringing his dying daughter to the hospital. Older Bomgard retorts: "I believe, duty calls" (*Notebook*, episode 2, 08:53-09:01).

There is also the type of British jokes that is frequent when something humorous is said or done by a person, while s/he does not exhibit a change in emotion or facial expression. This is the so-called "dry humour" or "dry wit" (Rishel 166). When Bomgard hears that some soldiers have appeared on the horizon, he assumes that these are the Bolsheviks and rushes to install the red banner at the entrance to the hospital.

The paramedic watches what he is doing and quietly speculates aloud about the symbolism of the red banner. After a long and pompous speech he remarks: "[it] captures everything the Bolsheviks stand for. I must say, doctor, it shows a tremendous courage to display this symbol with the White Guard moments from the door". Whereupon, the horrified Bomgard hastily disappears with the banner, and the paramedic philosophically quips: "Courage, but tempered with cunning" (*Notebook and Other*, episode 2, 03:37-04:30). Natasha, when she notices an amateurish self-portrait painted by Bomgard, whispers: "Extraordinary". Bomgard, proud of himself confesses: "Oh, it's actually self-portrait." Natasha: "Oh, I see. Of whom?" "Bomgard: "Me." Natasha: "Well, this is almost beyond fauvism. So deceptively childlike" (*Notebook and Other*, episode 2, 10:50-11:18).

5. The image of the protagonist in the series

In the miniseries, in accordance with the demands of the genre of black comedy, the interpretation of the protagonist differs completely from that of the narrator in Bulgakov's stories. Bulgakov's narrator is a young man, a bright graduate of the Medical University in Moscow – new to his job as a country doctor. He is full of doubts and phobias, but he copes with all the difficulties he faces with poise (successfully helping a difficult birth, saving a little girl dying of diphtheria by inserting an iron pipe into her trachea, decisively performing his first amputation, and saving the life of a girl who suffered from an injury caused by a robber). The paramedic and the midwives constantly note the narrator's professionalism despite his youth. Anna Nikolaevna and Pelageya Ivanovna (the midwives) keep repeating that he has not done any worse than Leopold Leopoldovich, whom they both admire and praise.

Bomgard, in the miniseries, is shown in a comic light from the very first scene on. He looks like a teenager and is extremely short, which makes it difficult to believe that he is a doctor. Both midwives treat him as if he were a child. Anna Nikolaevna wishes him good night, reminds to brush his teeth, instructs him not to lose the keys of the drugstore, and makes all sorts of humiliating remarks about his lack of experience. The young doctor feels their condescension keenly and tries to acquire a more imposing look; he starts to wear a beard like Leopold Leopoldovich and incessantly enumerates his academic achievements everywhere: "top of the class... fifteen fives. Unprecedented! ... I have read every book in the Imperial Moscow University library" (*Notebook*, episode 1, 03:50-03:54).

Despite all his efforts, the midwives and the paramedic continue to treat the young doctor ironically. After the first amputation, instead of the words of encouragement said by Pelageya Ivanovna in the short story, the characters in the film have the following conversation:

> Anna Nikolaevna: "You performed many amputations, doctor?"
> Bomgard (lies): "No, not really... three."
> Anna Nikolaevna: "It looked like your first."
> Bomgard: "Of course, my first... leg, definitely."
> Anna Nikolaevna: "Well, you've come to the right place. You'll have plenty of opportunities to improve."
> (*Notebook*, episode 2, 18:19-18:43)

This episode comes from the story "The Embroidered Towel" where the situation is portrayed as follows:

> "I suppose you've done a lot of amputations, doctor?" Anna Nikolaevna asked suddenly. "That was very good, no worse than Leopold"... I glanced suspiciously at their faces and saw respect and astonishment in all of them. (Bulgakov 10)

The comic nature of the character of young Bomgard is accentuated by the insertion of episodes of an explicitly farcical student performance "Moscow Quacks" into the series, in which Bomgard plays the part of the crazy Doctor Bunkers, as well as two scenes done in *Commedia dell' arte* style, in which Bomgard is shown as either the miserable Piero or the sinister Doctor. The fact that Daniel Radcliffe is best known for his part as Harry Potter no doubt prevents the viewers from taking him seriously and contributes to the comic interpretation of Doctor Bomgard's character which contradicts Bulgakov's presentation of the main character.

6. Minor characters and the setting in the series

Like the main character, the whole system of side characters in Bulgakov's cycle is redefined. The hospital staff is depicted with a touch of caricature. The individuals are eccentrics and are more like the characters from Dickens or Smollett than the characters of Bulgakov's cycle. Anna Nikolaevna – the elder midwife and the epitome of righteousness – worships Leopold Leopoldovich as if he were a pagan god. In contrast to Bulgakov's plot, the young doctor has an affair with masculine Pelageya, despite finding her ugly and repelling. This storyline was borrowed from "Morphine," in which Doctor Polyakov has an affair with a nurse, Anna Kirillovna by name, who serves in his hospital. The scriptwriters changed the name to Pelageya Ivanovna, which sounds funnier to an Anglophone audience. It is not the only place in the film where the filmmakers poke fun at "strange" Russian names with their awkward patronymics.

Bomgard throughout both seasons calls the paramedic "feldsher" (a word used in Russia for people of this profession), which resembles a surname. At the end of the second season, it appears that the feldsher's name is Demyan Lukitch. After a couple of comic, fruitless attempts to repeat it, Bomgard asks: "May I call you feldsher?" (*Notebook and Other*, episode 4, 15:16-15:20). When the feldsher and Pelageya die, their first names and patronymics are inscribed on their grave markers without surnames.

The paramedic is transformed into a gay man (in the first season he flirts with Bomgard and in the second season has an affair with a White Guard officer). He tells everyone the same story: a joke about Palchikov, who bought the most dazzling pair of trousers to persuade a girl he loved to marry him, but the bride died on the day of their wedding. Leopold Leopoldovich, who is present in the hospital in spirit due to the presence of his portraits and self-portraits everywhere, the unprecedented assortment of medical instruments, and the library of Turkish erotic books he collected (the last detail was imagined by the script writers). Patients, who are described by Bulgakov ironically, though not without compassion, are depicted exclusively in a comic way in the film. Even the beautiful

Natasha is wounded, not by a bullet but by a chandelier which falls on her.

The exotic atmosphere of Russia, thoroughly crafted by the filmmakers, serves as a supplementary decoy for the British viewers. The image of Russia in the TV series corresponds with the usual stereotypes connected with the country in the British mind: it is the domain of eternal frost (though Bomgard spends two years in Muryevo no other season except winter is depicted; the wooden house where the rural hospital is situated is always shown covered with snow); local people are barbaric (the looks and the behaviour of Bomgard's patients are represented in a demeaning way); there is no civilization in the country (the only shop in the neighbourhood is half a day away and is open only in August).

Conclusion

The contrastive analysis of Bulgakov's short stories and its TV adaptation has revealed how the original was transformed. The key transformation can be viewed as a clear-cut example of a cultural error: the filmmakers misinterpreted Bulgakov's ambivalent attitude with its unique combination of irony and melancholy and they re-envisaged his work in terms of British culture, converting the cycle into a dark comedy. The rest of the transformations were carried out to help adapt the original to the "horizon of expectations" of contemporary British viewers. First of all, the plot of the series revolves around a story of a bright graduate of a prestigious university who becomes a drug addict and, therefore, focuses on one of the urgent issues in our contemporary world. Additionally, the exotic Russian setting, which is perfectly consistent with the age-old perception of the country (frost, snow, lack of civility, barbaric, ill-mannered people, vast space etc.) increased the attractiveness of the TV production. Supplementary attractions consisted in exploiting stereotypes of Russia: the Bolsheviks, raids, GPU/KGB, repression.

At the same time, this exoticism is combined with black comedy, one of the most popular genres in the British film tradition.

The filmmakers (even in the case of the first season when it was based on Bulgakov's writing) present the plot, the characters, and the dialogues in the best tradition of black comedy with its eccentricity, low farce, knockabouts, at once funny and disturbing, as well as grotesque, bitter sarcasm, macabre medical jokes, deadpan humour, witty wordplay, and the use of understatement and irony, so that many jokes go unnoticed by those not familiar with it.

In spite of the changes introduced by the filmmakers, or rather because of them, the series was well received by both viewers and critics, and nominated for two awards. *The Guardian* stated that the first season gave the Sky Arts channel "the best viewing figures in its seven-year history" (Sweney). In this respect, we can ask if cultural errors of that type should be regarded as a mere trifle. In the TV production under analysis, they have a rather sinister function connected to enabling and fulfilling British stereotypes of the foreigner in a political climate of xenophobia (Beauchamp *et al.*).

It is interesting to note, that the first season was shot during the period of Mark Duggan's death, when the riots across London and other British cities in 2011 became a serious trigger for the escalation of xenophobic feelings in Britain. The TV series is an illustration of how "innocent" cultural errors betray the original and enhance the xenophobic attitude of the British viewers towards Russia and the Russians (Sakwa), while cultural transfer should foster and encourage harmony between cultures, rather than misunderstanding and hatred.

Works cited

Bluestone, George. *Novels into Film.* University of California Press, 1961.

Bucaris Chiara, and Barra Luca. "Mapping Taboo Comedy on Television". *Taboo Comedy: Television and Controversial Humour.* Palgrave, Macmillan. 2016.

Bulgakov, Mikhail. *A Country Doctor's Notebook*, translated by Michael Glenny. Neville House Publishing, 2013.

Fox, Kate. *Watching the English. The Hidden Rules of English Behaviour.* Hodder, 2004.

Hutcheon, Linda, O'Flynn . *A Theory of Adaptation.* 2nd ed. Routledge, 2013.

Hunter, I.Q.; Porter, Laraine. *British Comedy Cinema.* Routledge, 2012.

Jarski, Rosemarie. *Great British Wit. The Greatest Assembly of British Wit and Humour Ever.* Eubury Press, 2005.

Kranz, David L. and Mellerski, Nancy (eds.). *In/Fidelity: Essays on Film Adaptation.* Cambridge Scholars Publishing, 2008.

Mikes, George. *English Humour for Beginners.* Penguin, 1980.

Rishel, Mary Ann. *Writing Humor: Creativity and the Comic Mind.* Wayne State University Press, 2002.

Sokolov, Boris. *Bulgakovskaya Entziklopedia.* Mif, 2000.

Tebbe, Teo. *The Funny Side of the United Kingdom. British humour with special regards to John Cleese and his works.* Grin Verlag, 2007.

Yanovskaya, Lidia M. "Kommentarii k *Zapiskam Yunogo Vracha*". *Izbrannye Proizvedeniya v dvukh tomakh*, vol. 1. Dnipro, 1989, pp. 745-765.

Zinchenko, Victor *et al. Mezhkulturnaya Kommunikatziya. Sistemny Podkhod.* Vector TiS, 2003.

Webography

Aveling, Nick "A Young Doctor's Notebook and Other Stories". *Time Out,* 13th December 2012. https://www.comedy.co.uk/tv/a_young_doctors_notebook/press/2/. Accessed 17 November 2018.

Britannica. com. www.britannica.com/topic/black-humor. Accessed 25 November 2018.

Beauchamp, Zack. "Brexit was fueled by irrational xenophobia, not real economic grievances". *VOX,* updated 27 June 2016, https://www.vox.com/2016/6/25/12029786/brexit-uk-eu-immigration-xenophobia. Accessed 25 November 2018.

Goodfellow, Maya "Britain's raging racism calls for more than symbolic safety pins". *The Guardian,* Fri 1 June 2016, https://www.theguardian.com/commentisfree/2016/jul/01/britain-racism-safety-pins-brexit-migrants-xenophobic. Accessed 25 November 2018.

Connor, Alan A. "Young Doctor's Notebook: From the Operating Table to the Screen." Review of *A Young Doctor's Notebook*, by Alex Hardcastle and Robert McKillop. *The Guardian,* Tuesday 4 December 2012, www.theguardian.com/tv-andradio/ 2012/dec/04/young-doctors-notebook-hamm-radcliffe. Accessed 21 January 2017.

Hale, Mike. "Into the Heart (and Other Assorted Body Parts) of Old Russia. Daniel Radcliffe and Jon Hamm in *A Young Doctor's Notebook*". *The New York Times,* October 1 2013, www.nytimes.com/2013/10/02/arts/television/daniel-radcliffe-and-jon-hamm-in-a-young-doctors-notebook.html. Accessed 2 May 2018.

Kelly, Jon. "In numbers: Has Britain really become more racist?" *BBC News Magazine*. 10 August 2016, https://www.bbc.com /ne ws/magazine-36964916. Accessed 25 November 2018.

Sakwa, Richard. "Russo-British Relations in the Age of Brexit", *Russie.Nei.Reports*, No.22, Ifri, February 2018. https://ww w.ifri.org/sites/default/files/atoms/files/sakwa_russo_brist ish_relations_2018.pdf. Accessed 25 November 2018.

Sutcliffe, Tom. "A Young Doctor's Notebook – Daniel Radcliffe is innocent and Jon Hamm is knowing in this ham-fisted show". Review of *A Young Doctor's Notebook*" by Alex Hardcastle and Robert McKillop. *The Independent*, Friday 7 December 2012,www.independent.co.uk/artsentertainment/tv/review s/television-review-a-young-doctors-notebook-daniel-rad cliffe-is-innocent-and-jon-hamm-is-knowing-in-8390497.ht ml. Accessed 2 May 2018.

Sweney, Mark. "A Young Doctor's Notebook delivers Sky Arts' best ever figures". *The Guardian*, 7 Dec 2012, www.theguardian. com/media/2012/dec/07/sky-arts-john-hamm-daniel-radcliffe. Accessed 2 May 2018.

Waywell, Chris "A Young Doctor's Notebook and Other Stories". *Time Out*. Thursday 21 November 2013. https://www.timeout. com/london/tv-reviews/a-young-doctors-notebook-and-other-stories. Accessed 17 November 2018.

Filmography

A Young Doctor's Notebook. Season 1, written by Mark Chappell, Alan Connor, and Shaun Pye, directed by Alex Hardcastle and Robert McKillop, Sky Arts 1, 2012.

A Young Doctor's Notebook and Other Stories. Season 2, written by Mark Chappell, Alan Connor, and Shaun Pye, directed by Alex Hardcastle and Robert McKillop, Sky Arts 1, 2013.

Tom Paulin's Destabilising Translations: Misunderstandings, Errors, Manipulations

Stephanie Schwerter

1. Introduction: Tom Paulin's approach to politics, poetry and translation

This chapter concentrates on the notion of cultural errors in the context of Tom Paulin's translations of Russian poetry. As a poet, Paulin came of age as a part of a new generation of Northern Irish writers, including Seamus Heaney, Paul Muldoon, Derek Mahon, Ciaran Carson and Medbh McGuckian. He is one of the major Northern Irish poets attempting to express his political views on contemporary Northern Ireland through the lens of Russian poetry. Choosing translation as a mode of discourse, he seizes upon the differences and similarities of Northern Ireland and pre- and post-revolutionary Russia to shed a new light on the Northern Irish conflict, widely referred to as "the Troubles".

In the following, I shall explore the boundaries between error, rewriting and manipulation, focussing on Paulin's translation of three Russian poems: "Voronezh" by Anna Akhmatova, "It's After One" by Vladimir Mayakovsky, and "To Chaadaev" by Alexander Pushkin. The translations of the three works appear in Paulin's poetry collection *The Road to Inver* with the subtitle *Translations, Versions, Imitations 1975-2003* (2004). The way in which the poet approaches his sources varies considerably. Whereas in some cases, he engages with the foreign original intensively before moving away from it, in others, he digresses significantly from the source text after a short involvement with the original. In Paulin's work, the concepts of "translation", "version" and "imitation" cannot be precisely distinguished from each other, as often the limits between translation and transformation are not clear-cut. In my analysis, I shall refer to Lawrence Venuti's concept of domestication and foreignisation (19-

20), as well as to the writings of André Lefevere and Clive Scott, who consider translation as "rewriting" (Scott, *Translating Rimbaud's "Illuminations"* 6) or acts of "experimental writing" (Lefevere, *Translation, Rewriting* vii).

Cultural errors may take different shapes and forms. Frequently, they occur when translators ignore or misunderstand the underlying cultural references of a term or a concept in the source text. In this context, the cultural error is due to an insufficient knowledge of the source culture and might generate an entirely different reading of the given text in its translation. Another kind of cultural error may happen when a translator understands the implicit cultural connotations of a term or concept but is unable to transfer it in an adequate way into the target culture. This type of error may be the source of ambiguous translations, which are prone to lead the audience in the wrong direction or leave them confused about the source culture.

A translator might also commit a cultural error by consciously or subconsciously eliminating the cultural connotations of a given term. A further kind of cultural error can be a "creative error" in the sense of a modification, which has been intentionally introduced into the target text by the translator in order to confer on the source text a different meaning. In some cases, the elimination of certain shades of meaning can be judged as inadequate as important pieces of information become omitted. This "error" may even amount to a kind of manipulation of the readers as they might be unaware of the alterations made by the translator, believing that they are confronted with a faithful translation of the original. Unable to decode the different meaning of a term or concept conferred by a translator on a term or concept, they may not know that they are actually being manipulated. In the following, we shall explore the different types of cultural errors occurring in Tom Paulin's translations of Russian poetry. In the context of Paulin's translations, the question arises as to which types of errors have been committed unintentionally and which modifications have been introduced consciously to convince reader of a certain political discourse. In order to understand Paulin's way of translating, it is necessary to comprehend his political ideals and his personal approach to translation.

It is difficult to classify Paulin on political and ideological lines. As the son of a Scottish father and an Irish mother, he was born in Leeds and spent his childhood and youth in Belfast (Hufstader 190). His viewpoints are generated by his own ethno-religious background and his rejection of it. Although he was a member of Belfast's Protestant community, the poet turned his back on Ulster Unionism as a young man, when he became aware of the social inequality created by the British establishment (Haffenden 158). Paulin came to support the Civil Rights movement and to sympathise with the Catholic community, initially believing that "greater social justice in Northern Ireland could be achieved within the context of the United Kingdom" (*Ireland* 16). Despite his sympathy for the Catholic community, he has refused to recognise the Catholic and Protestant Churches as instances of power and control. Pleading for a "secular republic", he cherishes the idea of a United Ireland in form of a "non-sectarian, republican state, which comprises the whole island of Ireland" (16).

Paulin considers it the duty of his poetry to "give a sense of history and society" the better to promote an understanding of the Northern Irish situation (Haffenden 16). His political engagement may have had some bearing on his interest in Russian literature. Paulin argues that due to its implicit and coded nature, poetry composed during the Soviet area is the "most advanced form of political verse" ("Introduction" 52). The subtexts of political writing from the east seem to have encouraged him to reflect on the society in which he grew up. According to Paulin, a poet has to move out of his/her own culture in order to be able to understand it (Haffenden 157). In this sense, it could be argued that through Russian poetry, Paulin attempts to move away from Northern Ireland in order to achieve the required distance to reconsider his own cultural environment from a fresh angle

In his poetry collection *The Road to Inver*, Paulin translates works by 34 European poets. He ends his collection with a poem entitled "Une Rue Solitaire" – written in French and English – in which he engages with the general difficulty of translating poetry. The title suggests that translators have to go down a "lonely road" in order to achieve their work. This means that they are often left alone in order to find the right tone or meaning of a word or a phrase with nobody preventing him/her from committing errors. "Une Rue Solitaire" could be perceived as an explanation of Paulin's method of translation followed in *The Road to Inver*. The lines: "You find the poem's title/ But not the poem" (100) hint at the fact that the reader of a certain poem might be able to track down the original by its title, but might not always find in the translation the exact content of the source text.

Thus, Paulin suggests that in his collection of poetry, the boundaries between translation and creation might become blurred. A further line in his poem reads as an encouragement addressed to translators to detach themselves from the original text: "try write it out in your own form/ of this language" (100). In the context of Paulin's poem, taking liberties in a translation would mean inserting a personal voice into the target text. Referring to the act of translation itself, the speaker of the poem states:

> [...] it's not – nay never – not at all
> what you want to say
> [...] you squeak down the wrong way
> (100)

In these lines, Paulin subversively hints at the impossibility of translation, suggesting that transferring a poem from one cultural context into another while at the same time maintaining its political subtexts, tone and rhyme structure is rather unfeasible. In this sense, Paulin implies that a poet is bound to commit errors in his search for the right word or phrase.

Concerning his translations of Russian poetry into English, it is striking that Paulin employs free verse instead of imitating the rhyming patterns of the originals. This decision may have been motivated by linguistic as well as artistic considerations. In the case of Russian-English translations, rhyme is particularly difficult to transfer as phonetically, morphologically and syntactically the two languages show considerable dissimilarities. In "Problems of Translation", Nabokov points to the fact that in contrast to English words, Russian terms never carry more than one accent. Apart from that, polysyllabic terms in Russian are more frequent than in English (118). The poet Joseph Brodsky even goes so far as to claim that translations from Russian into English are "one of the most horrendous mindbenders" (Volkov, 86).

He further argues that even "a good, talented, brilliant poet" would be "incapable of restoring a Russian poem in English" (86). Therefore, it is possible that Paulin opted for free verse in order to avoid the aforementioned linguistic difficulties. However, it is also likely that the poet chose free verse to inscribe his translations with his own voice. According to Scott, free verse "activates the page as an expressive arena" (*Translating Rimbaud's* 16), which enables the translation to "perform itself" (28). The expressive freedom provided by the use of free verse might have encouraged Paulin in his choice of poetic form.

In my subsequent analysis, I shall argue that Paulin follows a "domesticating" approach in his translations. According to Venuti, a domesticating translation is marked by a transparent and fluent style, which minimises the foreignness of the target text. A foreignizing translation strategy, on the contrary, aims at non-fluent or "estranging" translations, which are designed to underline the foreign identity of the source text (15). In a personal email exchange, Paulin admitted that he is not fluent in Russian and therefore had to rely on pre-existing translations. However, he refused to reveal the word-to-word translations from which he established his own poetic translations. Paulin merely mentions that in the case of Akhmatova's poem, Anne Pasternak Slater, Boris Pasternak's niece, did a literal translation for him[1].

---

[1] Personal email from Tom Paulin: 13th of February 2008.

As Paulin bases his translations on literal translation made by others, he may ignore the modifications the Russian originals may have undergone in their first translation. In this way, the poet is possibly not aware of potential cultural errors committed by the first translator. Nevertheless, it is not the aim of this chapter to analyse the linguistic differences between the Russian originals and their first English translations and Paulin's subsequent translations. The main focus is on Paulin's poetic choices. In the following, I shall accompany the Russian poems with my own word-to-word translations, which intend to convey the content of the poems to a non-Russian-speaking audience without aiming at rendering the rhyme structure.

2. Domesticating Anna Akhmatova's "Voronezh"

Paulin's "Voronezh" is a translation of an eponymous poem by Anna Akhmatova. While the Russian original was written in 1936 during the Stalin era, Paulin's translation was published in 1986 during the Northern Irish conflict. Akhmatova dedicated "Voronezh" to her fellow poet Osip Mandelstam, who at the time was living in exile in the city of Voronezh because of a satirical poem he had written on Stalin. Akhmatova visited her banished friend twice and wrote two cycles of poems, in which she expresses her rejection of the totalitarian state. "Voronezh" alludes to Mandelstam's situation during his exile. The reader is able to decode the reference to the poet's banishment in Voronezh due to the fact that the poem is dedicated to Mandelstam.

However, Paulin, in his translation, deletes the dedication to the Russian poet and thus erases a whole subtext, which refers to a famous case of deportation having taken place during the Stalin era. On a more general level, Mandelstam's exile has come to stand for the cruelty of the Stalinist regime. Therefore, it could be said that the fact that the poem is dedicated to Mandelstam amounts to a cultural error as the whole subtext referring to the terror under Stalin entirely disappears. For a Russian speaking reader, the name of the city of Voronezh, combined with Mandelstam's name, clearly refer to the Stalinist era. It is possible that Paulin decided to delete the reference to the Russian poet as he might have presumed that the dedication to Mandelstam would not have the same meaning for an English speaking audience as it does for a Russian readership. Nevertheless, even if Paulin had been aware of the allusion to exile and banishment, his decision to obliterate the references to Russian history could be regarded as inadequate, as a whole dimension of the poem becomes erased.

In the first stanza of her poem, Akhmatova describes the city as frozen and covered with snow, evoking dispossessed peasants begging in the streets. Thus, she renders the cold atmosphere as well as the poverty reigning during the Stalin area. Paulin's translation of the beginning of the poem remains faithful to the Russian original. However, as the translation continues, he introduces considerable alterations into the target text. Akhmatova's poem runs on with a reminiscence of past Russian glory:

И куликовской битвой веют склоны могучей, победительной земли.	And the slopes of the mighty victorious earth are blowing with the memories of the Kulikovo Battle.	The earth's stout as a bell – it hums like that battle on the Field of Snipes.
(Akhmatova, 267)	(my translation)	(Paulin, *The Road* 44)

It is striking that Paulin entirely eliminates the reference to the Battle of Kulikovo, which has played an important role in Russian history up to the present day. The historic combat took place on the Kulikovo field next to Voronezh in 1388. It marked the beginning of the expulsion of the Mongols from territories, which later became part of the Russian empire. The battle was more about protecting culture and traditions than a mere fight for territory. Historians frequently regard the historic battle as the birth of the Russian nation as it provided Russia with the foundation for cultural unification (Timofeychev, 2017). In her poem, Akhmatova refers to the Battle of Kulikovo in a subversive way in order to attract attention to the hopelessness of the situation during the Stalin area. The poet implies that in the context of the frozen city of Voronezh, the glorious past seems far away and has become overshadowed by suffering in persecution.

It is rather unlikely that the reference to the historical Russian battle ignored by Pasternak's niece, who provided Paulin with her word-to-word translation. Therefore, we could argue that Paulin intentionally chose to delete the allusion to Russian history. Concerning historical references occurring in poetry and prose, Lefevere explains that authors use historical and literary allusions to "give a sharper edge to the point they make" (*Translating Literature* 22). These allusions, however, may present an obstacle for translators, especially for translators of poetry, who operate in a different cultural environment. Lefevere suggests that the translator first needs to find out the importance of the historical event in the source culture before "cast[ing] around for relevant analogies" in the target culture (*Translation Rewriting* 92).

If the translator feels that a hint at a certain historical event from the source culture does not enhance the meaning of the translation, he or she might prefer to delete it. In his translation of "Voronezh", Paulin might have decided to obscure the allusion to the Battle of Kulikovo, supposing that Anglophone readers might not be knowledgeable about this particular detail of Russian history and would perhaps become confused by the reference to an unfamiliar event. Similar to the omission of the dedication to Mandelstam, it could be asked whether Paulin's choice amounts to a cultural error as a whole historical dimension of the poem becomes lost.

However, a close examination of the term "Fields of Snipes" shows that the poet managed to maintain an underlying link to the historic combat. At first sight, it seems that Paulin merely replaces the factually excising "Field of Kulikovo" with "Fields of Snipes", which appears to be an imaginary battlefield. Nevertheless, a linguistic analysis of the term "Field of Snipes" uncovers a witty wordplay, which is most likely inaccessible to the common reader. "Field of Snipes" reads as a loose etymological translation of "Поле Куликово" ("Pole Kulikovo"), the Field of Kulikovo, where the historical battle took place. "Поле Куликово" literally translates as "The Field of Stints", from "поле" ("pole"), meaning "field" and "кулик" ("kulik"), referring to a "stint", a short-legged shorebird to be found in northern Eurasia. In his translation, Paulin replaces "stint" with "snipe", a slightly different kind more family in Europe. Both birds, "stint" and "snipe", belong to the family of sandpipers, which includes a huge variety of wading bird living in the marshes. Employing "snipe" instead of "stint", Paulin choses a polysemous word, which allows him to play with its different connotations. With the term "snipe", Paulin at the same time refers to a species of birds and to a gunshot. In this way, the poet links images of nature with urban violence.

In the context of Paulin's poem, "Fields of Snipes" alludes to the gunshots fired by British soldiers and Northern Irish paramilitaries during the Troubles. Phonetically hinting at "sniper", the term "snipe" evokes the hidden gunmen on Northern Irish streets and thus reinforces Paulin's reference to Northern Ireland. In so doing, Paulin establishes a coded link between the historical battlefield of Kulikovo and the Troubles. Furthermore, the poet replaces the line "slopes of the mighty victorious earth" by "the earth's stout as a bell" and thus confers to the battlefield a less glorious note. Through the adjective "stout" and the noun "bell", he implies heaviness and rigidity and suggests an uncompromising dispute. In addition, the dark onomatopoetic verb "hum" attributes an alarming atmosphere to the battle.

Hence, he suggests that the Troubles have turned into a threatening conflict, marked by intolerant attitudes. Through his allusions to urban war and violence, Paulin generates a gloomy atmosphere in his poem and points to the austere mood reigning in Northern Ireland during the Troubles. By obscuring the reference to the battle of Kulikovo, the poet intentionally choses not to integrate a foreignizing element into his translation. The allusion to Russian history is substituted with a coded hint at Northern Ireland, which underscores Paulin's use of a domesticating approach to translation. In this way, he attempts to imbue his poem with references drawn from his own cultural environment in order to attract attention to the situation in the region.

3. Manipulation and rewriting in the translation of Vladimir Mayakovsky's "It's After One"

In his translation of Vladimir Mayakovsky's poem "It's After One", Paulin goes even further in his domesticating approach than in "Voronezh". His departure from the original shows already in the choice of title. Instead of translating the poem's title, Paulin renames Akhmatova's work "Last Statement". In this way, he not only obscures the connection to the source text but also implies that his translation has to be read as "a creative act" (Scott, *Translating Rimbaud's* 13) or a form of "experimental writing" (6). At the beginning of his translation, Paulin remains relatively close to the Russian poem while diverging increasingly from the original as the poem goes on. It could be argued that he enters a relationship with Mayakovsky, which amounts to "co-authorship" (Scott, *Translating Baudelaire* 9) as he confers on the target text a new political dimension, literally transferring the poem from Russia to Northern Ireland.

Mayakovsky composed his poem shortly before committing suicide in 1930. Putting his writing in the service of the Soviet regime, he intended to support the creation of a new proletarian state. Mayakovsky was convinced that the Russian Revolution would be a "cleansing force", and that through his poetry he could contribute to revitalizing life in the Soviet Union (Hosking 434). Notwithstanding his devotion to the state, his writing was dismissed by Lenin as "literary hooliganism" and recognised by Stalin only after his death (Brown 201). Disappointed by love and betrayed by the "splendid-sounding ideas of communism", Mayakovsky at the age of 37, considered his life to be over (Blake 29). The poet had become aware of the conflict between the ideals and the reality of communism and felt increasingly oppressed by Soviet bureaucracy. His disaffection with the actual application of communist ideas under Stalin finds its parallel with Paulin's disappointment over Northern Irish Unionism, which he considered as the causes for social inequality in the region (16).

His translation was entitled "Last Statement". Thus, Paulin refers directly to Mayakovsky's death. The fact that the Russian original partially appears in the letter Mayakovsky left on his desk before committing suicide explains Paulin's choice of title. At first glance, the Russian poem reads as a love poem in which the speaker announces the end of a relationship. It most likely alludes to Mayakovsky's separation from Tatyana Yakovleva, whose refusal to marry him left the poet devastated. However, in the light of the poet's last letter, it becomes clear that more than grieving his failed love affair, he expresses his disappointment with life.

In the following lines, Mayakovsky subtly hints at the failure of communism and his lost love by using a pun, which is extremely difficult to transfer into another cultural environment:

Как говорят, инцидент исперчен.	As one says, the incident is over-peppered/ closed.	We bit green chilies and we're through.
(Mayakovsky 286)	(my translation)	(Paulin *The Road* 37)

In the above-mentioned lines, Mayakovsky plays with the sounds of the words "исперчен" ("isperchen"/ "overpeppered) and "исчерпан" ("ischerpan"). The latter is a term, which in official bureaucratic Russian is commonly used in the phrase "инцидент исчеран" ("intsident ischerpan"), meaning "the incident is closed". Instead of using the word "исчерпан" ("ischerpan"/ "closed"), which a Russian speaker would naturally expect after "инцидент" ("intsident"), Mayakovsky employs the entirely unexpected term "исперчен" ("isperchen"/ "overpeppered), which seems wholly out of context (Blake 313). Suggesting administrative vocabulary without actually using it, the poet introduces a political dimension into his lines. On the first narrative level, the poet seems to express with dark humour that his relationship is over, declaring his love affair as terminated in an administrative way. On the second narrative plane, however, he refers to Soviet bureaucracy and, in a larger sense, to the Soviet state, which both became a burden to him. Implying that the incident is closed, Mayakovsky communicates that he is as much "done with" the Soviet establishment, as he is with his former girlfriend.

The collocation инцидент исперчен ("the incident is overpeppered") conjures up the idea of something spoiled. Using the image of pepper, he implies that things became too "hot" and therefore had to be finished. With his ironic word play, Mayakovsky expresses sarcasm about the collapse of his political ideals and his failed love affair. At the same time, the poet articulates the idea of "closure" in both readings of the pun.

As my linguistic analysis of the poem has revealed, Mayakovsky's lines carry references to Soviet Russia as well as to the poet's private life, which only a reader familiar the reality of post-revolutionary Russia is able to decode. Mayakovsky himself considers the translation of his poems as a "difficult business". He argues that western translators know very little about Soviet poetry and therefore are unable to carry across most of the hidden cultural allusions. In this context, Mayakovsky claims that "verses can only be wholly understood if you have a feeling for the whole underlying system of a language because some things, like word-play and puns, are almost untranslatable" (Triolet 63).

In *Last Statement*, Paulin does not make an attempt to translate Mayakovsky's pun. The question arises whether Paulin was unaware of the underlying cultural context or whether he felt constrained by the semantic dissimilarity of the two languages and therefore went for an alternative image. In *Translating Literature*,

Lefevere explains the difficulty of transferring wordplays from one language into the other (52). In a pun, the author plays with the evident and the less obvious, unusual meaning of a word. The clash between the "norm" and the "deviation from the norm" gives the message of the pun a specific weight. If the target language, however, does not have a similar term with equally dual connotations, the pun might be irretrievably lost (52). Mayakovsky in his poem does not use an unusual meaning of "исчерпан" ("ischerpan") but replaces the term with an entirely different word, which makes the translation of the pun even more complicated.

In his translation, Paulin had to find an alternative to render Mayakovsky's image of "over-spiciness", as the English language does not contain two words that only slightly differ phonetically from each other and express the same idea as the Russian term. Opting for the line "we bit green peppers", he eliminates the semantic ambiguity of the Russian word play. Consequently, he deletes the hint at Russian bureaucracy and in this way obliterates Mayakovsky's criticism of Soviet Russia. With the line "we are through", Paulin maintains the idea of the end of a relationship.

Through the adjective "green", Paulin introduces a subtle reference to Ireland. As a result, Ireland's national colour "green" in combination with "chilies" evokes the "spiciness" of the Northern Irish situation. In this sense, Paulin subversively articulates his disagreement with British rule over Northern Ireland. Having created social inequality, the British government led the region into political unrest and thus "spoilt" its atmosphere. Through the introduction of a new image, as Paulin moves further away from the original and blurs the historical and cultural distance between the source and the target texts. According to Lefevere, all rewritings of an original text reflect a certain ideology and function in a manipulative way in order to operate in a given society (*Translation, Rewriting* 132). In the translation of Mayakovsky's poem, a certain "manipulation" becomes evident. Paulin moves away from his source after a short engagement with it attributing to his translation a new political dimension. While Mayakovsky in his poem voices his rupture with Russian communism, Paulin in his translation announces his break with Ulster Unionism. Thus, it could be argued that Paulin tries to communicate his own political view in his poem through the lens of the Russian original.

4. Rewriting Alexander Pushkin's "To Chaadaev"

Paulin's translation of Alexander Pushkin's poem "To Chaadaev" is entitled "A Nation, Yet Again". Among Paulin's translations of Russian poetry, "A Nation, Yet Again" departs more considerably from the original than any other poem. For that reason, we could say that Paulin pushes his "domesticating approach" to its extremes. The poet remains faithful to the original for only a few lines before digressing from the Russian poem almost entirely, only keeping a few loose links to the content of Pushkin's work. This method shows Paulin's desire to recreate the Russian original in a new form and to transpose it into a new environment. "A Nation, Yet Again" follows the source text in a general way, maintaining the central theme, the quest for political and social equality.

Whereas Pushkin explicitly criticizes the Tsarist regime, Paulin follows a more indirect approach in order to engage with the situation in Northern Ireland as he does in "Voronezh" and "It's After One". Pushkin's poem is dedicated to Pytor Yakovlevich Chaadaev, a Western oriented Russian philosopher of the 19th century, who was critical of the Orthodox Church. Due to his progressive political convictions, Chaadaev was declared insane by the Russian state and placed under medical supervision[2]. Pushkin admired Chaadaev for his courage and his revolutionary ideas. Alluding to a political dissident in the title of his poem, the Russian poet highlights the subversive nature of his lines.

Paulin establishes a link between Tsarist Russia and his own cultural environment by modifying of the Russian original to "A Nation, Yet Again". With the title of his poem, the poet hints at the Irish

---

[2] Cf. https://www.britannica.com/biography/Pyotr-Yakovlevich-Chaadayev

rebel song "A Nation Once Again", written by Thomas Osborne Davis in 1840. The song promotes the ideal of a United Ireland, free from English rule. Paulin's choice of title can be read on different narrative levels. With the underlying allusion to the Republican song, the poet subversively expresses his own political ideal of a "non-sectarian, republican state, which comprises the whole island of Ireland" (*Ireland* 17).

It is, however, striking that Paulin in his title does not adopt the exact wording of the song title but slightly alters it. Changing "A Nation Once Again" to "A Nation, Yet Again", and adding a comma after "nation", the poet attributes to the title an ironic dimension. Kennedy-Andrews claims that by inserting a comma, Paulin "disrupts" the "Republican mantra 'A Nation Once Again'" and thus expresses his "hesitation about traditional concepts of 'nation'" (189). Through his subversive play with the subtleties of the English language, Paulin mocks the fact that despite many promises, the desired nation state has not yet been created. In so doing, he attributes the failure to both the Northern Unionist and the Southern Republican establishments, finding them guilty of having been unable to find a peaceful solution to the Northern Irish conflict via a country which exists outside a religious framework.

By changing the title of Pushkin's poem, the implied link to Russian history becomes entirely deleted. In this sense, it could be asked whether Paulin's decision to erase a whole dimension of the poem could be regarded as a cultural error. Even if his translation departs considerably from the source text, the central idea, the quest for political and social equality is maintained. Thus, we might argue that through his translation, Paulin intents to recreate Pushkin's poem in a different historical and political environment. The poet attempts to reconfigure "To Chaadaev" in his own terms and tries the employ the source text as an arena within which his own political ideals can be aired.

Analyzing Pushkin's poem, we have to consider the Russian poet's political convictions as they run through the lines in form of a politicized subtext. Pushkin was critical of the tsarist regime and identified with the Decembrists, a group of young liberal officers, who fought against tyranny and tried to overthrow the tsar (Kopilov 78). Throughout his poem, Pushkin implicitly expresses his stand against the Tsarist regime. In the following lines, he openly calls for the overthrow of the Tsar:

но в нас горит ещё желанье, под гнётом власти роковой нетерпеливою душой отчизны внемлем призыванье.	But the desire is still burning inside us under the yoke of fatal power with our impatient soul we listen to our fatherland's appeal.	I'm tense now: talk of sharing power, prophecies of civil war new reasons for a secular mode of voicing the word *nation*.
(Pushkin in: Arendt 170)	(my translation)	(Paulin, *The Road* 65)

With "yoke of fatal power" Pushkin clearly hints at Tsarist oppression, while the "desire" which is "burning" inside the Russian population reads as striving for freedom. The "fatherland's appeal" is to be read as Russia's longing for a non-authoritarian state.

In contrast to Pushkin, who chooses patriotic language, Paulin employs contemporary vocabulary to communicate his own political ideas. Classic terms such as "yoke" and "fatherland" become replaced by modern concepts such as "power sharing" and "civil war", which in the context of Paulin's poetry clearly hints at the Troubles. Whereas Pushkin supports the victims of the Tsarist Empire, Paulin takes the side of the disadvantaged Catholics in Northern Ireland. However, even if the poet empathizes with the Catholic community, he does not identify with the values cherished by the Catholic Church and appeals for a "secular republic" (*Ireland* 18), which in his poem becomes expresses through the wish for a "secular mode of voicing the word *nation*". Thus, Paulin suggests that political and social equality can merely be reached on the basis of a value system free from religious bigotry. In this sense, he appeals for pluralism and the acceptation of otherness in order to achieve what he calls "a wide and cultivates cosmopolitan outlook" on the national question (18). Whereas Pushkin in his poem calls for the overthrow of the Tsar, Paulin uses his translation in order to articulate his support for the Northern Irish Civil Rights movement.

5. Conclusion

In the context of Paulin's translations of the three poems explored above, it is impossible to determine to which extent certain translational choices made by the poet are due to an insufficient knowledge of specific aspects of the source culture and thus could be judged as cultural errors. Regarding Paulin's approach to translation as a form of rewriting, it is, however, very likely that most of his digressions from the different source texts have been introduced intentionally in order to give voice to his own political views. In this sense, it could be debated whether his choice to recreate the Russian poems in a different spatial and temporal context is justifiable and whether this particular process could be regarded as a cultural error.

If we consider the facts that the Russian Empire was an autocratic monarchy in which the majority of people lived as serfs, the Russian Revolution and the Civil war that followed brought death and starvation to millions of people and that Russia under Stalin was a police state covered with prison camps in which prisoners were deliberately worked to death or killed, it can be argued that Paulin is taking considerable liberty to imbue the Russian originals with Northern Irish connotations and thus to establish a link between the Tsarist empire or Stalinist Russia with the Troubles. Whilst not wishing to downplay the gravity of the Northern Irish conflict, the relationship created between the two situations could be seen as an overstatement. However, Paulin's exaggeration might be seen as a response to the attempts of the British government and the media to play down the import of the Northern Irish conflict. Paulin deletes certain dimensions of the originals while at the same time adding new elements to them. Delocalising and dehistoricising the originals, the poet transfers the Russian poems into a different cultural environment and inserts further voices into his translations. On the one hand, this approach could be interpreted as an attempt made by Paulin to manipulate his readership in order to win it over to his own political ideas. On the other, the poet's digression from his sources allows him to achieve a detachment from his own cultural environment in order to communicate new perspectives on the Northern Irish Troubles.

It could be argued that in his translations, Paulin does not aim at a one to one comparison between Russia and Northern Ireland. Establishing a link between a contemporary conflict and historical periods of political tensions, he tries to achieve a detached view on the Troubles through amplification. Whether Paulin's translation can be regarded as cultural errors or not relies on the interpretation of the poet's translational approach. In a purist sense, the omission of certain cultural dimensions of a given source text can be seen as unforgivable cultural errors. In a larger sense, however, Paulin's translation can be seen as creative acts of rewriting which, in the manner of Walter Benjamin, contributes to the revival and survival of the originals (75-82).

Works cited

Akhmatova, Anna. *Stikhotvoreniya*. Slovo, 1995.

Arndt, Walter. *Pushkin Threefold*. George Allen, 1972.

Benjamin, Walter. "The Task of the Translator". *The Translation Studies Reader*, edited by Lawrence Venuti *Second Edition*. Routledge, 2008, pp. 75-83.

Blake, Patricia (ed.). *The Bedbug and Selected Poetry by Vladimir Mayakovsky*. Indiana University Press, 1975.

Haffenden, John. *Viewpoints. Poets in Conversation*. Faber, 1981.

Hosking, Geoffrey. *Russia and the Russians. From Earliest Times to 2001*. Penguin, 2002.

Hufstader, Jonathan. *Tongue of Water, Teeth of Stones. Northern Irish Poetry and Social Violence*. The University of Kentucky Press, 1999.

Kopilov, I. L. *Vsya russkaya literatura*. Sovremenny literator, 2003.

Kennedy-Andrews, Elmer. *Writing Home. Poetry and Place in Northern Ireland. 1968-2008*. Brewer, 2008.

Lefevere, André. *Translation, Rewriting and the Manipulation of Literary Fame*. Routledge, 1992.

Lefevere, André. *Translating Literature. Practice and Theory in a Comparative Literature Context*. The Modern Language Association of America, 1992.

Mayakovsky, Vladimir. *Polnoe sobranie sochineniy*. Vol. 10. Gosudarstvennoe Izdatelstvo khudozhestvennoy literatury, 1958.

Nabokov, Vladimir. "Problems of Translation: *Onegin* in English". *The Translation Studies Reader*, edited by Lawrence Venuti, *Second Edition*. Routledge, 2008, p. 115-127.

Paulin, Tom. *The Road to Inver. Translations, Versions, Imitations*. Faber, 2004.

Paulin, Tom. *Writing to the Moment. Selected Critical Essays.* Faber, 1999.

Paulin, Tom. "Introduction". *The Faber Book of Political Verse*, edited by Tom Paulin. Faber, 1986, p. 15-52.

Paulin, Tom. *Ireland and the English Crisis.* Bloodaxe Books, 1984.

Scott, Clive. *Translating Rimbaud's 'Illuminations'.* University of Exeter Press, 2006.

Scott, Clive. *Translating Baudelaire.* University of Exeter Press, 2000.

Triolet, Elsa. *Mayakovsky, Russian Poet*, translated by Susan Muth. Hearing Eye, 2002.

Venuti, Lawrence. *The Translator's Invisibility. A History of Translation.* Second Edition. Routledge, 2008.

Volkov, Solomon. *Conversations with Joseph Brodsky*, translated by Martin Schwartz. The Free Press, 1988.

Webography

"Pyotr-Yakovlevich-Chaadayev". https://www.britannica.com/biography/Pyotr-Yakovlevich-Chaadayev. Accessed 14 May 2018.

Timofeychev, Alexey: "The Battle of Kulikov When the Russian Nation was Born", 19.06.2017, hwww.rbth.com/ arts/his tory /2017/07/19/the-battle-of-kulikovo-when-the-russian-nati on-was-born_806685. Accessed 08 May 2018.

(Mis-)reading Cultural References

How Khayyám Got Lost in Translation: Cultural Errors and the Translators of the *Rubáiyát*

Bentolhoda Nakhaei

Introduction

The present chapter aims to offer a meticulous analysis of the way the cultural lexemes and their connotative significations are rendered in selected translations of the *Rubáiyát*. Language can be viewed as "a social phenomenon, which is naturally and inextricably intertwined with culture" (House 32), as a result the meaning of each linguistic element is defined within its own linguistic culture. The collection of Khayyám's poems could also be regarded as a collection of linguistic elements, which are embedded in Persian culture and literature. That is to say, the meaning of each linguistic element in the *Rubáiyát* could be understood with reference to the cultural and literary context enveloping it. Thus, the way cultural metaphors and their connotations are translated plays an essential role in the reception of this literary work in the West.

This article evaluates the change of meaning, the levels of comprehension, and the reception of the *Rubáiyát* by examining the four English and French translations of Khayyám's masterpiece. Within a morpho-semantic framework, I intend to assess the cultural errors made by the 19th and 20th-century translators as a result of their faulty understanding of the *Rubáiyát*'s figurative use of lexis. I will examine the translation of cultural metaphors in the Persian quatrains, responding to the following questions: despite the constraints in discourse and ethics, to what extent did Edward Fitz-Gerald, Arthur John Arberry, Jean-Baptiste Nicolas, and Gilbert Lazard succeed in transferring the cultural implications of the metaphorical language in their translations? Did they commit errors while translating the connotative significance of the cultural lexemes of the

Persian quatrains? If so, how did the inexact translations of the *Rubáiyát* affect its comprehension and reception in the West? Did these errors lead to the destruction of the expressions and idioms of the source text? The focus of the present study is on the ten quatrains, which are common to the four English and French translations, which were published in 1859, 1863, 1949, and 1997.

In 1859, Edward FitzGerald translated Khayyám's collection of quatrains into English. John Arthur Arberry translated the *Rubáiyát* into English in 1949. In 1867, Jean-Baptiste Nicolas translated 464 quatrains into French. More than a hundred years later, in 1997, Gilbert Lazard also translated the Persian quatrains into French.

Edward FitzGerald[1] was the first translator who introduced Khayyám's collection of quatrains to the West via his first edition of 1859 (including 75 quatrains). His translation was based mainly on the Ouseley manuscript. This text, discovered by Cowell among a mass of uncatalogued material in the Bodleian Library, Oxford, in 1856, contains 158 quatrains. FitzGerald, himself explains in a letter to his professor of Persian the approach he adopted in his translation: "my translation will interest you from its form, and also in many respects in its detail, very unliteral as it is. Many quatrains are mashed together, and something lost, I doubt, of Omar's simplicity, which is a virtue in him. But there it is, such as it is" (FitzGerald 346-347).

The first edition of FitzGerald's translation went unsold. However, as Gordon S. Haight explains, in 1860, a bundle of the anonymous pamphlets was discovered by chance on the penny shelf of Quaritch's second-hand bookstall by two young men, Dante Gabriel Rossetti and Algernon Charles Swinburne (8). Following the appearance of the second edition of the translation eight years later, enthusiasm for the *Rubáiyát* spread so quickly in England that in 1929 the price of a single copy of the pamphlet went for £8000. Haight highlights the fact that FitzGerald himself regarded his version as "not strictly a 'translation' at all, and, as if conscious of

---

[1] The English poet, writer, and translator.

this, on the title-page of the subsequent editions changed *Translated* to the vaguer word *Rendered"* (8).

During the 19th century, FitzGerald's translation received special attention when Swinburne and Rossetti found FitzGerald's translated pamphlet, referring to his quatrains in their literary works. From that moment on, Khayyám's quatrains and his point of view created a revolutionary vogue against Victorian norms in the West. The publisher Macmillan outlines the way in which FitzGerald's translation was received by the different layers of 19th century society:

> In his fiftieth year, FitzGerald printed a little paper-bound pamphlet of translations which he called THE RUBÁIYÁT OF OMAR KHAYYÁM ... Suddenly the poem became a favorite. The mocking quatrains of the eleventh-century Persian were used as a challenge by the nineteenth-century undergraduates, repeated by rebellious lovers, and flung out as a credo by restless men and women. There had already been an undercurrent of protest against the rigidity and moral earnestness of the period. The RUBÁIYÁT served as a small but concentrated expression of the revolt against Victorian conventions ... the younger men and women made FitzGerald-Omar a vogue. (FitzGerald 394)

Among the English translations of the 20th century, Arthur John Arberry's translation is regarded as the closest in terms of content to Khayyám's quatrains. However, since Arberry paid careful attention to the exact translation of the sense of the text, the poetic form of the *Rubáiyát* is transformed into prose. Jean-Baptist Nicolas was among the pioneers who translated the *Rubáiyát* into French during the 19th century. Nonetheless, Nicolas' translation is regarded as the most complete. In 1867, he rendered 464 quatrains into French.

Among the French translations of the 20th century, Gilbert Lazard's translation is considered the closest in content, and, to some extent, in form to the *Rubáiyát*. It could be argued that he kept the poetic form. However, he did not recreate the same metrical pattern of the Persian quatrains in his translation.

1. Cultural errors in the context of Bassnett's, Lefevere's, and Schleiermacher's theories

Susan Bassnett likens language to "the heart within the body of culture", pointing out that "the surgeon, operating on the heart, cannot neglect the body that surrounds it, so the translator treats the text in isolation from the culture at his peril" (17). A translator must thus take into consideration the cultural context in which the text has been written. Lotman also believes that "no language can exist unless it is steeped in the context of culture; and no culture can exist which does not have at its center, the structure of natural language" (22). According to Ros Schwartz and Nicholas de Lange, the translator is mostly considered as a mediator.

As a matter of fact, he/she tries to convey "something that is language-and culture-bound into another culture, to achieve an equivalent effect" (Bassnett and Bush 215). It is therefore crucial that the translator should possess a sufficient understanding of both the target and the source culture and language. Moreover, the translator enriches "the life of the culture into which the transplant is made" (215). In other terms, translation is conferring a benefit on the culture from which the work is taken. In this way, the translator brings home foreign goods. Therefore, according to Bassnett and Bush, he could also be regarded as an importer who "spot[s] and take advantage of gaps in the range of cultural products available on the home market" (215).

Thus, it is important that the translator understands and transfers the meanings of the sub-text of the work correctly. The translator must also bear in mind the fact that he/she should not insert his/her own point of view in the underlying networks of the significations of the original work. That is to say, he/she plays the role of a mediator, who should remain neutral between the author and the reader of the target language. As Schwartz and de Lange have said "the translator is in some ways an intermediary between the original author and the new public" (17).

Omar Khayyám conveyed his thoughts and feelings mostly via a symbolic use of words. Since the language of the *Rubáiyát* is figurative, he employs images, metaphors, similes, personifications, and idioms with specific 11th-century linguistic and cultural references to Persian literature and mysticism. In his quatrains, Khayyám expressed his philosophical ideas about the riddles of life and the perplexities of human beings in this world via multifaceted and extended metaphors. Specifically, his figurative expressions of mysticism are mostly depicted via earthly images, amorous affairs, or religious and cultural references. In other terms, he referred to one ordinary notion in terms of another – mostly to describe his mystical experiences via worldly concepts and/or to express his opposition to the religious repression and hypocrisy of his era. These metaphorical images could only be understood in reference to Persian culture. The differences between cultures and languages may create misunderstandings between nations. If a translator misses the cultural connotation hidden in the image of each lexical item applied by the Persian poet, his/her translation leads to cultural misunderstandings, or errors.

From the 19th century, a vogue started among translators from colonizing nations – such as FitzGerald – to select canonical texts from the so-called uncivilized or less civilized nations in order to transform them and make them more presentable to the "home culture". In such cases, Clive Scott believes that the translator turns the text into a canvas, a space to operate his/her own imagination, a place to manipulate the original author's message (111). In the same vein, Bassnett believes:

> Translators into English served for centuries as agents of the empire, ransacking colonized or dependent territories for their literary treasures, to be taken home for display like shrunken heads in a museum for the edification of their compatriots. The absence of respect for the source culture

that they often demonstrated is epitomized in the words of Edward Fitzgerald, the nineteenth-century translator of Rubáiyát of Omar Khayyám: "it is an amusement for me to take what liberties I like with these Persians who (as I think) are not poets enough to frighten one from such excursions, and who really do want a little Art to shape them". (217)

From the statements above, it is possible to view FitzGerald's treatment of Khayyám's poem as the metaphorical domestication of a wild animal, which is tamed and ennobled in his English language text.

Friedrich Schleiermacher believes that translation from a different language into another one should reflect its source language. In his lecture "On the Different Ways of Translating", he explains the process as follows: "the reader should be able to guess the Spanish behind a translation from Spanish, and the Greek behind a translation from Greek. If all translations read and sound alike (as they were soon to do in Victorian translations of the classics), the identity of the source text has been lost, leveled in the target text" (Bassnett, Lefevere 7-8). Among the selected translators of the *Rubáiyát*, Arberry and Lazard attempted to stay faithful to the culture of the source text. That is to say, they did not allow their own subjectivity to intrude while translating culture-bound metaphors of Khayyám's work. They tried their best to replace the Persian images with close images in terms of meaning and culture in English and French. Nicolas also tried to transfer the same metaphorical images, however, most of the time he failed to understand the underlying meaning of metaphors in Persian. That is why he translated in a word for word fashion rendering every image, without paying attention to the transfer of the correct meaning.

2. Translation of Khayyámian metaphors

The study of metaphors in a literary text is the study of how the author has created the "reality" of the world in his text. And the study of translation could be regarded as the analysis of the interaction of cultural elements. In other terms, translational practice is one of the ways that a culture comes up with dealing with the other language and culture (Bassnett, Lefevere 13).

One of the problematic issues in literary translation is the translation of metaphorical and cultural expressions. The translation of metaphors could be one of the most challenging issues for translators, as Michael Hanne states, "it requires us to draw on a great range of our imaginative, cultural and linguistic resources" (208). The translation of metaphors often implies resorting to stylistic procedures. Since the stylistic features of each language is different from any other, this complicates the task of the translator. Due to the existence of fossilized structures and linguistic and cultural imagination, the transfer of meaning in the passage from one language and culture (i.e. Persian) to others (i.e. English and French) may certainly be questioned. In other terms, metaphors can be said to be impossible to translate; however, the task of finding an equivalent image between the semantic domains of two different languages, which may have little in common, can be a challenging undertaking.

This makes the task of the translator significantly more difficult since when he/she wants to translate a metaphor, he/she is faced with a vast range of differences between two language systems. In addition, each language has its own particular metaphors, whose connotative meanings are not only linguistic but also culture-specific. In order to ease this struggle, Michael Hanne suggests the translator should choose one of the following procedures: "as a literary translator, one often feels the need ... to find some way of transmitting elements of cultural context along with the text itself, perhaps in the form of a translator's introduction, endnotes, or some other device" (213). To avoid cultural errors in the translation of the *Rubáiyát,* Nicolas has clarified the cultural images by giving explanations between parentheses. Lazard has also given explanations about the differences between two language systems and cultures in the introduction of his translation.

However, through a close study of the four translations, it becomes clear that FitzGerald deleted lots of Persian metaphors and changed the meaning of the Persian quatrains. This can be seen, for instance, in the translation of the fourth common quatrain:

Persian quatrain	FitzGerald's translation	Literal translation
هر /سبزه/که/بر /کنار / جوئی/رسته/است Hœr sœbzə kə bœr kənʌr-ə dʒʊɪ rœstœst²	And this delightful Herb whose tender Green	Each grass that has been grown up near a stream
گوئی/ز لب/فرشته خوئی رسته/است Goʊɪ zə/lœb-ə fərə-ʃtə khoʊɪ rœstœst	Fledges the **River's lip** on which we lean	As if it has been grown up from the **lips** of a **faery temper**
پا/بر /سر /سبزه/تا/به/ خواری/ننهی Pʌ bœr sœr-ə sœbzə tʌ bə khʌrɪ nœnəhɪ	Ah, lean upon it lightly! For who knows	Don't put your foot contemptuously on the grass
کان/سبزه/ز خاک/لاله /روئی رسته/ است. Kʌn sœbzə zə khʌk-ə lʌlə roʊɪ rœstœst. (Forughi and Ghani 77)	From what once lovely **lip** it springs unseen. (FitzGerald, 25)	Since that grass has been grown up from the soil of a **tulip-faced**. (My translation)/

Table I. FitzGerald's translation of metaphors in the Fourth Common Quatrain

---

² The phonetic transcription presented in the table above and the following tables rely on the *Aryanpur Progressive English-Persian Dictionary*.

In the quatrain in question, there are three metaphors. The first one is /lœb/ لب = "lip", which is a metonymy standing for the "lover". FitzGerald kept the same image but used it in the second stanza. In the fourth stanza, he repeated the same Persian image, however, such an image does not exist in the fourth stanza of the original quatrain. In the original text, more precisely, in the second stanza, there is another metaphor, i.e. /fəraʃtə khouɪ/خوئی فرشته = "faery" temper. In this metaphor, Khayyám has likened the lover to someone who has angelic traits. FitzGerald deleted this metaphor. Instead, he replaced the image with the image of a "river."

Thus, the Western reader of FitzGerald's translation misunderstands the concept, employed by the Persian poet. The last metaphor is /lʌlə rouɪ/لاله روئی = "tulip-faced". This metaphor is also deleted in FitzGerald's translation. This type of deletion is repeated over and over, not only throughout the ten common quatrains but also throughout his translation of the Persian quatrains. As a result, FitzGerald's voice and vision stand between the Western reader and the original Persian text. Above all, the British translator has given a harmonizing beauty and an epicurean taste of his own to Khayyám's *Rubáiyát* in order to make it more acceptable to the tendencies of the Victorian era. Apparently, FitzGerald did not want to trouble the reader with the strangeness of the Persian text and therefore brought the author as close as possible to the reader, illustrating what Schleiermacher described as a domesticating translation.

In what follows, the translations of the culture-bound images of five Khayyámian metaphors in the seventh common quatrain have been selected for analysis on a micro-level. Table II, below, first presents the original text alongside the four translations. At the end, a literal translation is also given.

Persian quatrain	FitzGerald's translation	Arberry's translation
افسوس/که/نامه ی جوانی/طی/شد æfsʊs kə nʌmə-yə jævʌnı təy ʃʊd	Alas, that **Spring** should vanish with the **Rose**!	Alas, that the **scroll of (my) youth** has been rolled up,
وان/تازه/بهار زندگانی دی/شد vʌn tʌzə bæhʌr-ə zəndəgʌnı dəy ʃʊd	That/**Youth's sweet-scented Manuscript** should close!	And that the fresh **spring of life** has **turned to winter**:
آن مرغ طرب/که/نام/او/ بود/شباب ʌn mʊrgh-ə tæræb kə nʌm-ə oʊ bʊd ʃæbʌb	The **Nightingale** that in the Branches sang,	That **joyous bird** whose name was youth-alas,
فریاد/ندانم/که/کی/آمد/ کی شد. færyʌd nædʌnæm kə kəy ʌmæd kəy ʃʊd. (Foroughi and Ghani 80)	Ah, whence, and whither flown again, who knows! (FitzGerald 44)	I know not when it came, (or) when it departed. (Arberry 109)

Persian quatrain	Nicolas' translation	Lazard's translation
افسوس/که/نامه ی جوانی/طی/شد /æfsʊs kə nʌmə-yə jævʌnı təy ʃʊd/	Hélas! **Le décret de notre adolescence** touche à son terme!	Hélas, j'ai tourné les pages **du livre de la jeunesse**,
وان/تازه/بهار زندگانی دی/شد /vʌn tʌzə bæhʌr-ə	Le frais **printemps de nos plaisirs** s'est écoulé	Le vert **printemps de mon âge** au sombre **hiver** a fait

zəndəgʌnı dəy ʃʊd/		place ;
آن مرغ طرب/که/نام/او / بو د/شباب /ʌn mʊrgh-ə tæræb kə nʌm-ə oʊ boʊd ʃæbʌb/	Cet **oiseau de la gaieté** qui s'appelle la jeunesse,	Et **ce bel oiseau de joie**, Je ne sais quand il s'en vint
فر ياد/ندانم/که/کی/آمد/ کی شد. /færyʌd nædʌnæm kə kəy ʌmæd kəy ʃʊd/. (Forughi and Ghani 80)	Hélas! Je ne sais ni quand il est venu, ni quand il s'est envolé ! (Nicolas 109)	Ni je n'ai vu quand soudain il s'est envolé de moi ! (Lazard 39)

Table II. The Translation of Four Metaphors in the Seventh Common Quatrain among the Four Selected Translations

In the quatrain under study there are five culture-specific metaphors: 1) *Nameye javani* /nʌmə-yə jævʌnı/, 2) *Bahare zendegani* /bæhʌr-ə zəndəgʌnı/, 3) *Dey* /dəy/, 4) *Morghe tarab* /mʊrgh-ə tæræb/, and /*Shabab* /ʃæbʌb/.

In the following lines, an analysis of the way the translators rendered each metaphor will be presented in further detail. Starting the analysis with the first Khayyámian metaphor, in Persian the meaning of the word *nameh* /nʌmə/ is "a/ page on which a text is written", i.e. "letter". The word *javani* /jævʌnı/ also means "youth". In this metaphor, Khayyám likened "the period of juvenescence to a certain amount of pages on which this period will be inscribed and will eventually pass" (Nakhaei 141). From Khayyám's time until the present day, this metaphor is part of the myth-kitty of Persian literature; today it is still used by Persian poets, authors, and even by ordinary people. With regard to the way the translators handled this culture-specific metaphor, in FitzGerald's translation, the metaphor appeared in the second stanza as "youth's sweet-scented manuscript".

In his rendition, FitzGerald first juxtaposed the metaphor in the second line and then modulated the Persian image via addition of an olfactive dimension to the image of "page or letter". As a consequence, the image that Khayyám wanted to transfer is changed in FitzGerald's translation. The image is ennobled. Therefore, the reader of FitzGerald's text is intrigued by a more beautiful image. However, Arberry kept the Persian image and translated it as the "scroll of youth". Arberry's translation is closer in terms of meaning and form to the original text. With regard to the French translations, Nicolas chose the word *le décret* as the equivalent for the Persian word of *letter*. This selection of equivalence shifted image of the metaphor and changed its meaning.

The image is wrong, thus the meaning that Nicolas transfers via his translation is also erroneous. For the word "youth", he selected *adolescence* and added the possessive adjective of *notre*. Nicolas changed the point of view of the first stanza via a metaphorical modulation on the level of *sense*. This changes the understanding of the readers. On the other hand, Lazard chose an exact French equivalent for the Persian word of *nameh*, i.e. *les pages*. He also retained the image of "youth" in his translation, i.e. *jeunesse*. But, he modulated the middle of the metaphor by adding the image of *livre*. This addition changed the meaning of the metaphor and the quatrain as a whole. When we compare FitzGerald's translation with his English counterpart's, i.e. Arberry's and then Nicolas' translation with Lazard's, we can see that Arberry's and Lazard's translations are closer to the source text in terms of meaning, and, to some extent, of form.

Thus, we can say that Arberry and Lazard successfully transferred the underlying cultural meaning of the image. However, FitzGerald and Nicolas both misunderstood the image of the metaphor and also created linguistic and cultural misunderstandings for their readers. As a result, the errors in translation of this metaphor made by these two translators influenced the reading and the reception of the *Rubáiyát*. FitzGerald's translation presents Khayyám as a noble atheist and Nicolas' rendition introduces him as a rigid orthodox.

As already stated, the second metaphor is *bahare zendegani* /bæhʌr-ə zəndəgʌnı/. In Persian, the word *bahar* means "spring", and the word *zendegani* means "life". In this metaphor, Khayyám has likened "the period of youth to the spring of life". Among the English translations, FitzGerald translated the metaphor as "spring". In his translation, he changed the place of stanza one with stanza two. As a result, the metaphor is displaced and found in FitzGerald's first stanza. Moreover, in his translation, the English poet deleted the object (using Newmark's expression), i.e. "life". Therefore, the Persian metaphor is highly modulated and the point of view of the second stanza of the original text is presented differently. The cultural baggage of the metaphor is deformed as a result.

However, in Arberry's translation, the exact metaphoric images exist. With regard to French translations, it must be said that in Nicolas' translation the Persian metaphor is expanded to include several new images, i.e. *le frais printemps de nos plaisirs.* As a result, the original object of "life" is deleted and the images of *frais* and *plaisir* are added. Moreover, the selected object is personalized via the possessive adjective of *my*. The point of view and meaning of the metaphor is changed through this modulation. In Lazard's translation, it is clear that his translation of the metaphor is closer to the original text, i.e. *le vert printemps de mon âge.* However, like Nicolas, Lazard also deleted the image of *life* and has added images of *vert* and *âge*.

This sort of modulation also affected the form and the underlying layers of meaning of the Persian metaphor. It is clear that in the French translations, none of the versions render the exact cultural connotative meaning that the Persian poet intended to offer to his readers. These changes create cultural and linguistic errors for readers of Nicolas' and FitzGerald's translations. As a result, this affects the comprehension of the underlying signification of the quatrain in general and creates a global misunderstanding of Khayyám's work.

The third metaphor is *Dey* /dəy/. This word is the name of one of the months in the Persian calendar, which corresponds to *January* in the Western calendar. In this quatrain, Khayyám has used the metaphor of *Dey* to refer to the end of *the period of old age*. FitzGerald replaced the metaphor with the image of the *rose*. In this way, the original image, with its cultural and literary implications, is completely changed and the point of view of the Persian poet was also modified. Like FitzGerald, Arberry also chose a different image, i.e. "winter". He slightly modulated the Persian image and, as the consequence, the point of view and the underlying meaning of the metaphor are also slightly changed.

With regard to the French translations, Nicolas changed the grammatical category of the original metaphor from noun to verb, i.e. *s'écouler*. In this change, not only the image and its underlying meaning are deformed but it also modifies the point of view of the Persian poet. On the other hand, Lazard chose an equivalent to Arberry's by using *le sombre hiver*. However, he added the image of *darkness* to the "winter", which could be seen as an amplification of the original metaphor. On the whole, all the four translators modified the Persian image and its meaning.

The last metaphor is *Morghe tarab* /mʊrgh-ə tæræb/ which is likened to *Shabab* /ʃæbʌb/. In Persian, the word *morgh* /mʊrgh/ signifies "bird", and the word *tarab* means "joy". *Shabab* /ʃæbʌb/ also designates youth. Like the metaphor of *bahare zendegani* /bæ hʌr-ə zəndəgʌnɪ/, this metaphor is also inscribed in the literary and cultural myth-kitty of Persian literature. The metaphor is still used by Persian poets, authors, and it is also employed in people's every day speech. In his translation, FitzGerald deleted the whole Khayyámian metaphor and replaced it with the word "nightingale". He changed the image, the meaning, the form and, above all, the point of view of the author, likening it to tropes found in English poetry.

As a result, the readers of FitzGerald's translation gain a different point of view of Khayyám's quatrains. FitzGerald's readers are led to see connections with the English tradition which were added by the translator. This choice was a key element in aiding the adulation of Khayyám in Britain. Yet, we can view it today as a cultural error. Arberry did his best to keep the Persian image by rendering it as *joyous bird*. Thus, the reader of Arberry's translation has the same understanding of the underlying signification of the metaphor as an Iranian reader might have. In the French translations, Nicolas rendered this metaphor as *oiseau de la gaieté*, which also corresponds to the Persian metaphor. The reader's point of view, gained as a result of Nicolas' translation, is the same as that of the Iranian reader's. However, Lazard added the image of *beauty* to the original image by saying: *ce bel oiseau de joie*. Therefore, a slight modulation can be observed on the level of both form, and meaning in Lazard's rendition. As the result, the reader's understanding of Lazard's translation is slightly changed.

Finally, the last metaphor – a personification – is شباب /ʃæbʌb/ which means "youth" in English. In his English version, FitzGerald deleted this anthropomorphic metaphor. It is clear that the content and the sub-text of the Persian quatrain underwent more transformations in FitzGerald's version. On the other hand, Arberry represented the same metaphorical image. Likewise, in French, Nicolas literally reproduced the same personification. On the contrary, like FitzGerald, Lazard deleted the metaphor in question. As a result, in his translation, Khayyám's point of view and the underlying meaning of the quatrain, to some extent, were changed. Furthermore, in the final analysis, after a quick comparison of FitzGerald's translation with Arberry's, Nicolas', and Lazard's versions – which are mostly literal renditions – a great variation between linguistic and more importantly, cultural meanings can be observed. The following table summarizes the translational analysis discussed above on the basis of Newmark's (88-91) and Larson's (254) theories about the translation of metaphor.

Metaphorical expressions of the Persian quatrain	Type of metaphor	FitzGerald's translation	Arberry's translation
نامه ی جوانی /nʌmə-yə jævʌnɪ/	Simile	Replacing the image in the SL with a standard TL image	Replacing the image in the SL with a standard TL image
بهار زندگانی /bæhʌr-ə zəndəgʌnɪ/	Complex metaphor	Deletion of the original metaphor	Reproducing the same image in the TL
دی /dəy/	One-word metaphor, i.e. metonymy	Conversion of metaphor to sense	Conversion of metaphor to sense
مرغ طرب /mʊrgh-ə tæræb/	Replacing the image in the SL with a standard TL image	Reproducing the same image in the TL	Reproducing the same image in the TL
شباب /ʃæbʌb/	Anthropomorphic metaphor, i.e. personification	Deletion of the original metaphor	Reproducing the same image in the TL

Metaphorical expressions of the Persian quatrain	Type of metaphor	Nicolas' translation	Lazard's translation
نامه ی جوانی /nʌmə-yə jævʌnɪ/	Simile	Replacing the image in the SL with a standard TL image	Replacing the image in the SL with a standard TL

			image
بهار زندگانى /bæhʌr-ə zəndəgʌnı/	Complex metaphor	Replacing the image in the SL with a standard TL image	Replacing the image in the SL with a standard TL image
دى /dəy/	One-word metaphor, i.e. metonymy	Conversion of metaphor to sense	Conversion of metaphor to sense
مرغ طرب /mʊrgh-ə tæræb/	Replacing the image in the SL with a standard TL image	Reproducing the same image in the TL	Reproducing the same image in the TL
شباب /ʃæbʌb/	Anthropomorphic metaphor, i.e. personification	Reproducing the same image in the TL	Deletion of the original metaphor

Table III. Translational analysis of metaphors of the Seventh Common Quatrain

Apart from misunderstanding the level of underlying metaphorical significations, certain translators failed to translate simple words: this is the case for FitzGerald. In his letters to his professor of Persian, FitzGerald wrote: "Persian is certainly a very beautiful language so far words go, but its grammar is sadly defective" (Graves and Ali-Shah 32). Moreover, Omar Ali-Shah, in his historical preface to his translation mentions that FitzGerald always picked the nearest meaning of the words based on his own intuitive guess. He also gives two examples of FitzGerald's expression of bewilderment in understanding the meaning of Persian words in the *Rubáiyát* in his correspondence with Professor Cowell:

1. In a letter dated June 1857, he says "نوح/nouh/" must be the mystical shout of Dervish. However, the actual Persian

word in the source text is "نره/nœrə/" which means "cry" in English. 2. In another letter dated August 1857, FitzGerald states that the term "او داند/ʊ dʌnœd/" in stanza fifty of his translation might be some technical call in polo. Notwithstanding, it is the third person singular present indicative of the verb "دانستن/dʌnəstœn/" meaning "to know" in English and in general the term means "he knows". (32)

Last but not least, Ali-Shah points out that FitzGerald had a very difficult time learning the complex grammar of Persian alone but for "the poor help of Johnson's Persian English dictionary" (32).

Conclusion

Ideally, the translator should possess an extensive knowledge of the culture of the source and target languages, i.e. they should be bilingual and/or bicultural. In this regard, Robert Wechsler believes that "the process of translation is a trial from beginning to end: discovering and building the evidence (knowledge of the author's works, of the cultural and artistic context of his works, and often of his life)" (Bassnett, Bush 217-218). However, this is often not the case, and even if the translator has a high degree of practical knowledge of both languages, he/she may constantly suffer from the gaps in his/her knowledge concerning certain cultural aspects of the source language. Competence in this regard could presuppose adequate knowledge of the "cultural relevance of expressions" and "of their historical background and traditional usage" (242).

With regard to FitzGerald's competence in comprehending Persian, A.J. Arberry says: "to try to understand is one thing, to seek to reproduce is another. FitzGerald's actual errors of understanding can now be detected readily enough; they are not few, but they are not unduly numerous, considering the material at his disposal and the limited extent of his experience of the Persian language and literature" (*The Romance of the Rubaiyat* 21).

However, there are cultures, which are regarded as dominant, such as British and French. As a result, they are likely to deal with the Other (i.e. in this case the Persian Other), in a way that corresponds to their acquisitive, domesticating impulses. Usually, dominant cultures do not care much for the subtleties of other cultures. These homogeneous cultures consider their own way of seeing and reflecting as the natural way, which is the best way of dealing with other cultures. Thus, when another foreign element enters their world, they immediately shape, mould, and then naturalize it.

This study illustrates the multiple deletions and misunderstandings of Khayyamián's images in FitzGerald's translation, which caused the destruction of underlying networks of significance of the *Rubáiyát*. The deformation of Persian images in the key metaphors in his translation resulted in the qualitative impoverishment of the source text. In addition, with his free choice of images and lexis, and his attempt to make Khayyám's work conform to the Victorian conventions of his era, FitzGerald deformed the metaphorical web of the Persian work, which amounts to the destruction of expressions and idioms as per Berman. This could also be considered as an act of ethnocentrism and ennoblement as Khayyám's style is also deformed. However, the analysis of the translation of metaphors in Nicolas' translation showed that these two translators tended to clarify and expand metaphors by adding certain glosses between parentheses for their audience. Arberry and Lazard's translations demonstrated that they succeeded not only in comprehending the connotative and culture-bound meanings of the metaphors but also in rendering them with slight nuances in French.

Thus, it could be said that the traces of the unwillingness to adapt to the Other is observed most of all in FitzGerald's translation. In this regard, Bassnett asserts:

> Edward Fitzgerald (1809-63), who is best known for his version of *The Rubaiyat* of Omar Khayyam (1858), declared that a text must live at all costs with a transfusion of one's own worst life if one can't retain the Original's better ... In

other words, far from attempting to lead the TL reader to the SL original, Fitzgerald's work seeks to bring a version of the SL text into the TL culture as a *living entity*, though his somewhat extreme views on the lowliness of the SL text, ... indicate a patronizing attitude that demonstrates another form of elitism. (73)

One comes to the inescapable conclusion that neither FitzGerald – due to his patronizing attitude – nor, to some extent, Nicolas – due to his tendency for clarification and expansion– succeeded completely in conveying culture-bound images and Khayyám's subjectivity. However, Arberry and Lazard tried their best to transfer the underlying meanings of the cultural terms. Language, culture, and translation are three interconnected elements. There are many concepts and traits which are not defined in another culture. This varies from culture to culture. Persian culture is very different from Western cultures such as English or French culture. Therefore, it is difficult to comprehend the cultural subtleties of each notion in Persian and to transfer them via a different linguistic system into the English or the French culture.

On the whole, recurrent cultural errors – either due to colonial attitudes or lack of knowledge – in the translation of the *Rubáiyát* led to a global misinterpretation of Khayyám's work for decades in the West. To conclude, one may wonder how should the unique cultural features of Persian quatrains be transmitted in English and French? What steps can be taken to avoid the major cultural errors that FitzGerald and Nicolas made in their translations? Maybe those Western translators, such as Lazard, and scholars, such as Edward Said, who lived and were steeped in both cultures might help bridge the gap for Western readers via their translations and intellectual works, i.e. *Orientalism*.

Works cited

Arberry, Arthur John. *The Rubā'īyāt of Omar Khayyam: Edited from a Newly Discovered Manuscript Dated 658 (1259-60) in the Possession of a Chester Beatty BSQ with Comparative English Versions by Edward FitzGerald, E.H. Whinfield and the Editor.* Emery Walker Limited, 1949.

Arberry, Arthur John. *The Rubā'īyāt of Omar Khayyām.* Emery Walker limited, 1974.

Arberry, Arthur John. *The Romance of the Rubaiyat: Edward FitzGerald's First Edition Reprinted with Introduction and Notes.* Ruskin House, 1959.

Arberry, Arthur John. *Omar Khayyám: a New Version Based upon Recent Discoveries.* John Murray, 1952.

Aryanpur Kashani, Manuchehr. *The Aryanpur Progressive English-Persian Dictionary.* Jahan-e Râyâneh, 1377/1998.

Bassnett, Susan. *Translation Studies.* Routledge, 1980.

Bassnett, Susan, and Peter Bush. *The Translator as Writer.* Continuum, 2006.

Bassnett, Susan; Lefevere, André. *Constructing Cultures: Essays on Literary Translation.* Cromwell, 1998.

Dole, Nathan Haskell; Walker, Belle M. *The Persian Poets.* Wentworth Press, 2016.

FitzGerald, Edward. *Letters of Edward FitzGerald.* Macmillan and Co, 1894.

FitzGerald, Edward. *The Rubáiyát of Omar Khayyám: Rendered into English Quatrains, The Five Authorized Versions.* Walter J. Black, Inc. Roslyn, 1942.

Forughi, Mohammad Ali; Ghani, Ghasem. *Rʊbʌbɪyʌtə Umærə Khæyʌm, (Eng. Tr: Rubáiyát of Omar Khayyám).* Asatir Publishing House, 1371 [1390]/ [1992] 2011.

Graves, Robert; Ali-Shah, Omar. *The Rubaiyat of Omar Khayyam: a New Translation with Critical Commentaires*. Cassel, 1967.

Hanne, Michael. "The Translation of Metaphors". *The Translator as Writer*, edited by Susan Bassnett and Peter Bush. Contimuum, 2006.

House, Juliane. *Translation as Communication Across Languages and Cultures*. Routledge, 2016.

Larson, Mildred L. *Meaning-Based Translation: A Guide to Cross-Language Equivalence*. University Press of America Inc., 1984.

Lazard, Gilbert. *Omar Khayyâm : Cent un Quatrains*. Orphée/La différence, 1997.

Maine, F. George. *Rubáiyát of Omar Khayyám: Rendered into English Verse by Edward FitzGerald*. Collins, 1953.

Nakhaei, Bentolhoda. *Critical Analysis of the Stylistic Transformations in the 19th and 20th-century English and French Translations of Omar Khayyám's Rubáiyát: Exploring the Common Quatrains in FitzGerald, Arberry, Nicolas, and Lazard*. Doctoral Dissertation. Sorbonne Nouvelle-Paris 3, 2016.

Newmark, Peter. *A Textbook of Translation*. Prentice Hall International, 1988.

Nicolas, Jean Baptiste. *Les Quatrains de Khèyam*. L'imprimerie Impériale, 1867.

Too Graphic a Novel?
Charlie Hebdo, Cultural Connotations, and Change of Register in the German Translation of Luz' *Catharsis*

Marie Schröer

> What is most often called "relevant"? Well, whatever feels right, whatever seems pertinent, apropos, welcome, appropriate, opportune, justified, well-suited or adjusted, coming right at the moment when you expect it – or corresponding as is necessary to the object to which the so-called relevant action relates: the relevant propositions, the relevant decision, the relevant translation ... This word "relevant", this present participle that functions as a predicate, is here entrusted with an exorbitant task. Not the task of the translator, but the task of defining – nothing less – the essence of translation. This word, whose relation to French and English is not very certain or decidable ... also retains an obscure Germanic filiation, thus comes to occupy a position that is *doubly* eminent and exposed.
> Jacques Derrida, "What is a 'relevant' translation?" (368)

Introduction

On January 7, 2015, twelve people were murdered in a terror attack on the French satirical newspaper *Charlie Hebdo*. Having arrived too late for the editorial meeting, cartoonists Luz and Catherine Meurisse survived. In the aftermath of the attack, *Charlie Hebdo* became the topic of controversial debates on the freedom of expression and the necessity of overstepping the borders of the so-called good taste, for instance by mocking religions. In the US and in Germany, several left-wing voices condemned the journal's blasphemy and intolerance. Scholars more familiar with the tradition of the magazine, its past as the equally controversial *Hara-Kiri: Journal bête et méchant*[1], and the taboo-breaking spirit of "French humour" in general tried to explain *Charlie Hebdo* to a non-French audience, stating that the out-of-context translations of disparate covers did not correctly reflect the magazine's spirit. The truncated translation of magazine extracts, especially the magazine's covers, can be described as the result of cultural errors.

In May 2015, four months after the attack, Luz published *Catharsis*, an autobiographical comic dealing with the traumatic event. Four months later, the German translation, *Katharsis*, was published by S. Fischer – a renowned literary publishing house, which however rarely publishes comics or – as they are often called in the quest for reputation – graphic novels. The speed of the release of the German edition, combined with the fact that it was released by one of the most well-established German publishers, shows that the subject seemed both important and urgent[2].

The general relevance of the topic of the comic cannot be denied. In this context, this chapter discusses the "relevance" of the

---

[1] *Hara-Kiri. Journal bête et méchant* [Stupid, Evil Journal] appeared from 1960 to 1989 (at irregular intervals). Its black-humoured, ostentatiously vulgar approach did not spare the de Gaulle government or the Catholic Church. Several attempts were made to ban the magazine; intellectuals like Simone de Beauvoir and Jean-Paul Sartre fought for its survival. When it was censored in 1970 (after having joked about Charles de Gaulle's death) its authors spontaneously published their content in a new magazine they called *Charlie Hebdo* (pun intended). Hereafter, all the translations in square brackets are my translations.

[2] Fischer also published the German compendium *Die vollständige Maus* [The Complete Maus] of Art Spiegelman's autobiographical graphic biography about his father's Auschwitz-Survival (initially published in the art magazine *Raw* from 1980 to 1991) in 2008 and, more recently (in 2018), a comic book adaptation of Anne Frank's diary by Ari Folman and David Polonsky. The fact that Fischer only has a handful of comic books in their portfolio underlines the singular importance of those titles. Obviously, the rare examples deal with topics that are of undeniable socio-political and historical significance.

German translation, using different notions of the word that Jacques Derrida polysemantically exploits in the above-quoted article. Interestingly enough, the comic has not been translated into English until now. In this article, I attempt to find out (*re-lever*) how far the German translation is both revealing as well as relevant for the general controversy about *Charlie Hebdo*.

How did the translators proceed? How far are the translations literal, to what degree are they literary? Can the mistranslations identified be considered as a form of "cultural errors in translation", like those that have given the name to the present volume? And if so: where do the cultural mistakes come from; more precisely: what kind of cultural background do they reveal? To analyse and assess the relevance of the German translation, we first need to take a close look at two domains that are directly related to the question of this specific translation. I shall therefore first consider the challenges of comic translation in general (and comic autobiographical/memoir translation in particular) and, secondly, I will retrace and reflect upon the critical reception of *Charlie Hebdo* (and the reaction of author Luz) after the attack – as cultural errors are partly responsible for the criticism. This criticism, as I hope to demonstrate, has had an impact on the circumstances of publication as well as on the para- and intratextual content of the translated edition.

1. Comics and translation

> But do we not generally regard that which lies beyond communication in a literary work – and even a poor translator will admit that this is its essential substance – as the unfathomable, the mysterious, the "poetic"? And is this not something that a translator can reproduce only if he is also – a poet?
> Walter Benjamin, "The Task of the Translator" (75)

Comics – and, most of all, those labelled as "graphic novels" – have become a recognized part of the literary market. Examples of the *neuvième art*, an expression coined by the French journalist and scholar Francis Lacassin in 1971, are not only discussed in the newspapers and other media of the dominant comic cultures like France, Belgium and the US but also in Germany.

Cultural and scientific canonization go hand in hand; comics have entered bookshops, museums and even universities. Multiple English, French and a growing number of German works deal with the artistic, semiotic and narratological specificities of the hybrid medium, which combines word, image and sequence to entertain, to instruct or to disturb the reader. Prominent comic studies monographs (in English, French and German) include the work of comic scholars as Bart Beaty, Charles Hatfield, Scott McCloud, Benoît Peeters, Thierry Groensteen and Martin Schüwer. Much has been said (and is still being said), in those and other scientific productions, about the never-ending potential of the medium to approach any kind of topic from light-hearted jokes to politics using a variety of different styles and materials, from classic cartooning to abstract minimalism, from woodcuts to digital web comics.

The medium has thus been the object of literary, cultural and media studies, as well as a topic of didactic reflections in history and social science classes. Despite the fertile dynamics that result from the mixture of text and picture, the topic of comic translation is still somewhat neglected in the field of comic studies. The *Bonn Online Bibliography of Comics Research* lists 225 works that are tagged as dealing with "translation", "traduction" or "Übersetzung".

A closer look at the entries reveals that most of the articles are not explicitly dedicated to the topic of translation but merely touch on it as one topic among others. A few articles examine the translation of Asterix and Disney comics; the number of monographs is extremely low. Two conference proceedings have been dedicated to the specific question of comics and translation: Federico Zanettin is the editor of *Comics in Translation*, which was published in 2008;

Nathalie Mälzer edited *Comics – Übersetzungen und Adaptionen* in 2015. Most of the 21 articles of the latter volume focus on the question of adaptation, which etymologically also represents a translation. It resembles the third group of translations (next to the "intralingual"/ "rewording" and "interlingual"/ "translation proper") identified by Roman Jakobson in 1959 as the "intersemiotic translation" or "transmutation", which is "an interpretation of verbal signs by means of nonverbal sign systems" (*On Linguistic Aspects of Translation* 233). In this case, the content becomes translated into another medium. The remarks made regarding the *Bonn Online Bibliography* research results could also be applied to the other two volumes as well: apart from the introductory articles by the editors, the analysis of specific primary literature represents the bulk of the two volumes. I could not find any literature at all on the translation of autobiographical comics, which seems especially interesting in the given context. For that reason, I will outline the questions that seem most crucial to me.

1.1 Sign system abundance and limited space: translation of image and text in (autobiographical) comics

As stated above, comics combine two sign systems, the verbal and the visual. This distinctiveness has impact on the issues that have to be addressed regarding the challenges and potentials of translation. It is medium-specific, so that one of the two sign systems (the visual) can be understood without many obstacles: in most cases, drawings do not have to be changed, even though certain national norms might sometimes ask for censorship (for example in the case of depiction of nudity or violence). The panel order might be changed as well (but rarely is) for instance if the publication format or the reading direction (for instance in Japanese Manga) differs from the original.

The well-known proverb "A picture is worth a thousand words" (which also exists in French and German) can be cited here to stress the smooth translatability of pictures, especially in the case of autobiographical comics. No matter how mutilated the original may feel due to the impossibility of textual translation (Derrida,

"'Relevant' Translation" 178), the picture remains as a trace of the original author. Elisabeth El Refaie argues in her monograph entitled *Autobiographical Comics: Life Writing in Pictures* that hand-drawing is perceived as especially authentic. One could assume that the same effect would be produced with regard to the (hand-written) lettering done by the autobiographical author. However, in the translation of an autobiographical work, the literal *corporal* trace is lost. Even if the original's author's handwriting is imitated, it will probably look less spontaneous and dynamic because *it is* less spontaneous and dynamic. This leads us to a feature peculiar to comic translation: "They [comics] are limited spatially in that translations must fit into balloons or panels, and in that they have a specific objective" (quoted in Celotti, Grun and Dollerup 198).

As a result, the letterers have to take great care to imitate the curves of letters and the movement of another person's handwriting. Moreover, the spatial problem also affects the translator: he/she not alone needs to find the right words but also the right words with the right number of letters to fill the frame or bubble. The challenge to combine register, length and rhythm harmoniously in comic translation resembles the task of translating song lyrics or poetry. The difficulty is exacerbated when the text is written in verse. Translators may be obliged to use free verse instead of imitating the rhyme pattern (Luz 72).

1.2 Dialogue and dialect, colloquialism and humor

Comics can be described as a medium largely based on dialogue. Obviously, this has an impact on the role of the translator. He/she has to be able to understand and communicate the colloquialism of oral language, including dialect, accents, youth slang, (intra-)cultural jokes, puns, etc. Great expertise of literary and standard French does not suffice to carry out the task of comic translation. The translator needs to be in constant touch with the latest linguistic and cultural developments of both target cultures. Of course, cultural knowledge is also required in standard prose translation but there is usually less dialogue. In comics, humour is not always conveyed by the text or by the image alone. In some cases, verbal puns are only revealed or explained with the help of the picture. This means that the translator also needs to be in possession of a high degree of visual literacy (especially with regard to popular culture). Otherwise, he might simply not understand the jokes and nuances.

Aspects mentioned in this brief outline have hinted at multiple occasions on which cultural errors can occur in comic translation. This list will help to analyze the "relevance" of the translation of Luz' autobiography. How relevant (well suited/ important) is the translation, where does it come (*relève*) from? One last point should be stressed, especially with regard to the case of autobiographical writing in comic book form – both the drawing and the language are seen to form part of a testimony of intimate identity. Comic scholars tend to neglect the stylistic analysis of the textual part and concentrate on the interplay between text and image. Translation analysis can help to foreground the language in order to show that textual style and register matter and are not substituted by (the combination with) the drawings.

Luz' autobiography and its translation cannot be judged without some contextual knowledge with regard to the *Charlie Hebdo* affair. Cultural errors also result from a different cultural and/or national background. A different (or missing) comic cultural (or other subcultural) background can also lead to cultural misunderstandings.

2. The reception of *Charlie Hebdo*

Katharsis is the first comic by Luz to be translated into German (he published numerous works in French). To understand why *Katharsis* was published in Germany (by a publisher without any particular expertise with comics), and why it has *not* (yet?) been published in English, and why it is translated the way it is (by translators who are not specialized in the translation of comics), we need to take a closer look at the socio-political background of the reception of *Charlie Hebdo*.

Very soon after the attacks of 7th January 2015, two dichotomous camps emerged in German conversations about *Charlie Hebdo*. One shouted "Je suis *Charlie*" [I am *Charlie*] while the other maintained: "Je ne suis pas *Charlie*" [I am not *Charlie*]. The former supported the freedom of the press and an unconditional right to free speech (including a right to blaspheme)³. The latter also condemned the attacks, but criticized the unconditional expressions of support. This group justified and illustrated its position with a selection of particularly provocative *CH*-covers. The article by Jacob Canfield⁴, published on the day of the attacks, can serve as an example.

Canfield's article was widely discussed and its line of reasoning and selection of images served as inspiration for subsequent articles and blog entries. What was largely missing, however, was the context in which the images were published: The *CH*-critics disregarded (purposefully or for lack of better understanding) the cultural and legal specificities of the French situation; the French political discourse, without which some of the caricatures are simply incomprehensible, was never explained. The general tone went as follows: one does not need detailed knowledge of the magazine, nor does one

---

3   The unfortunate side-effect of every discourse connected to the topic of Islam is that right-wing-populists tend to exploit it for their very own purpose. In a perfidious strategy the German Pegida-Movement used the attack to present itself as a victim of free speech opponents carrying posters with "Je suis *Charlie*" and, even worse, "Pegida = *Charlie*"-slogans.

4   Canfield calls the cartoons racist and argues that the horrible event should not prevent people from judging *Charlie Hebdo* critically. In their argumentation, Canfield and others do not only refer to the Mohammed-caricatures but also concentrate on a cartoon depicting Christiane Taubira (the French Minister for Justice at the time) as a monkey as well as on the representation of pregnant Boko-Haram sex slaves. The impact of Canfield's post can be viewed not only in the comment column under the article: established publishing organs like the *New York Times* did not print the criticized cartoons and pointed at Canfield's article in their justification to do so (Schuessler). To get an appropriate idea of pictures, you need to see them and you need to know about their context. To know more about the original stories (Moneyron).

even need to read French in order to recognize an Islamophobic and racist humor that targets minorities and escalates existing tensions (Parkhill). On the basis of a small selection of covers, some observers arrived at the following conclusion: *Charlie Hebdo* is crude, brutal and full of black humour. Below the belt. Tasteless.

Knut Rio discusses the economic incentives for criticizing Islam and summarizes, in passing, his view of *Charlie*: "From random nonsense and obscene mockery of politicians and celebrities, it suddenly touched on something of a whole other order: an indefinable terrain of massive popular interest, an intimation of danger, of stepping across a line" (18). And: "Puerile Grobheit ist der Standardstil von *Charlie*" [Puerile crassness is the standard mode of *Charlie*] writes novelist Ulf Erdmann Ziegler towards the end of January 2015 on the German literary criticism website *perlentaucher.de*.

Even where the analysis concentrates on the political dimension of the events and the sole focus on the Mohammed-caricatures could be justified, academic publications are often content to point out that the quality of the drawings and the magazine hardly passes muster, and consequently do not refrain from a predominantly "aestheticist reaction" (Chervel). Even the American cartoonist Gary Trudeau embellishes his criticism of the content with a deprecation of its form: "By punching downward, by attacking a powerless, disenfranchised minority with crude, vulgar drawings closer to graffiti than cartoons, *Charlie* wandered into the realm of hate speech, which in France is only illegal if it directly incites violence". He labels the authors "free speech absolutists" and suggests they are their own kind of fanatics: "at some point free expression absolutism becomes childish and unserious. It becomes its own kind of fanaticism".

Reacting to these accusations, academics and journalists, such as Josselin Moneyron in *The Hooded Utilitarian*, demonstrated that "Islamism" ranks rather low among the topics addressed by *Charlie* (in 2014, only one cover among 52 addressed religion, eight alluded to jihadism). The fight against the Front National, on the other hand, figures prominently in its pages. Moneyron's stated intention is to use the corpus to investigate representations (and discriminations) of minorities, but her doubts about the accuracy of the widespread opinion about *CH* are implicit:

> The hope is that, with a segment this size, we can investigate the techniques used to represent racial minorities, and especially the Muslim community. After all, they have been constantly under attack, haven't they?

The reactions tend to the extremes, from premature identification on the one side to premature condemnation on the other side. The omnipresent digital communication invites knee-jerk reactions. The virtual community of grief offers a feeling of belonging and protection. The public vaunting of a more differentiated opinion is often equally close-minded and self-satisfied: *political correctness*, which sometimes is *not* politically correct, turns into an *ersatz*-religion of those who crave dogma and *doxa*. Empathy loses its innocence when it results from an unthinking behavioral code. The result is a low tolerance for ambiguity and a diffuse subsumption of the whole magazine under a range of catchwords: "obscene", "raw", "crude", "vulgar", "brutal", "childish", or "puerile". One can conclude that different groups made *Charlie Hebdo* into a symbol that was instrumentalised to ulterior ends. Images were taken out of context and distorted to carry pre-existing perceptions and worldviews: *Charlie* as a martyr of freedom, as a valve for populist propaganda, as a stand-in for quotidian racism, as a call-to-arms against an essentialized Islam.

The (selective presentation of) covers, for the most part, served as illustrations of a standpoint – predominantly the Mohammed caricatures. The context, however, was rarely supplied. Other covers that mock(ed) Catholic pieties or the majority of covers that criticize(d) the French shift to the right did not feature. Neither did the actual content of the magazine, which offers an intellectual take on cultural issues, environmental protection, or psychoanalysis (and not based on cartoons or caricatures). People also ignored the diversity of styles and voices within the magazine; the magazine's leftist-secular roots; its auto-ironic self-identification as the successor to *Hara-Kiri*, which used the authorities' criticism as a subtitle: "Journal bête et méchant". And, as the aforementioned list implies, the magazine's humour is also rarely picked up.

What is lacking is a competence to decipher (and translate!) this humour also in its caricatures. It is no secret that humour largely depends on socialization, education and the cultural environment. Pierre Bourdieu, in *Distinction*, counts *Charlie Hebdo* among the productions of the *counter-culture*, "which offer the products of the intellectual avant-garde in journalistic form" (85). This, in his estimation, is primarily consumed by autodidacts, who are well educated but do not come from a background of "high culture". Building on Bourdieu, Giselinde Kuipers concludes in her sociological study *Good Humor, Bad Taste* that

> humor will never completely belong to great art, high culture or pure beauty: even the highest humor will always be a bit low. A common glint and tarnished glow, with all their positive and negative associations will continue to emanate from all humor, even from genres many times more refined, restrained, sophisticated, witty and creative than the joke. Good humor always implies some bad taste (248).

The respondents in her study associate "good" *highbrow* humour with just those adjectives that were used to deprecate *Charlie Hebdo*: "good" humour is often "sharp" and "coarse" – not facile, not just focused on the punch-line, not smooth, not moralizing, not empathetic, not kitschy.

2.1 No offense?! Is Charlie's humour non-translatable to a non-charlie-esque-readership?

In his posthumously published Lettre aux escrocs de l'islamophobie qui font le jeu des racistes [Open Letter – On Blasphemy, Islamophobia, and the True Enemies of Free Expression], Charb argues against the accusation that *Charlie Hebdo*'s drawings are Islamophobic. According to him, it is the critic's own racism that is exposed in the interfering and overprotective supposition that every Muslim is offended by a caricature of Mohammed. This argument is plausible, but it does not solve the question of how to deal with caricatures that serve as stand-ins in complex political debates, particularly in volatile times. In face of the violent reactions to the magazine, it is legitimate to ask whether we can plead, as Trudeau does (irrespective of his implicit deprecation of the magazine's content), for a more responsible handling of free speech. The call for de-escalation faces a call for more satire, as moderation runs the danger of legitimizing violent reactions in retrospect.

This could endanger not just free speech but the freedom of artistic expression and its inherent ambiguity. Good art, like good humour, is often double-edged, ambiguous, and therefore prone to misunderstanding. It should generally be questioned if pragmatism ("Do not fan the flames!") is a valid response in this context at all. Invoking Salman Rushdie's *Satanic Verses*, Slavoj Žižek warns against the side-effects of over-hasty obedience:

> The result of such a stance is what one might expect: the more Western liberal Leftists probe their own guilt, the more they are accused by Muslim fundamentalists of being hypocrites who try to conceal their hatred of Islam. Such a paradigm reproduces the paradox of the superego to perfection: the more you obey what the pseudo-moral agency demands of you, the more guilty you are.

2.2 Charlie *as a symbol – Luz' reflections on attributions and self-image*

> But one should never speak of the assassination of a man as a figure, not even an exemplary figure in the logic of an emblem, a rhetoric of the flag or of martyrdom. A man's life, as unique as his death, will always be more than a paradigm and something other than a symbole.

This is how Jacques Derrida puts it in *Specters of Marx* (xiv). Luz himself commented on *Charlie* becoming a symbol three days after the attacks in an interview with the magazine *Les Inrocks*:

> The media made a mountain out of our cartoons, when on a worldwide scale, we are merely a damn teenage fanzine. This fanzine has become a national and international symbol, but it was people that were assassinated, not the freedom of speech! People who sat in an office and drew cartoons. (Luz, Laffeter)

Now that we have an overview of the background to *Charlie Hebdo* and the complex political situation that ensued from the terror attacks, it is time to deconstruct the symbol of *Charlie* itself in order to let those who were killed and those who survived speak for themselves. Charb, one of the caricaturists killed in the attacks, in interviews ("Entretiens") repeatedly expressed his concern about the status of the caricature.

He decried a form of illiteracy on the part of those in charge of newspapers, who no longer knew how to read a caricature and therefore set very rigid limits. Despite this illiteracy, *Charlie Hebdo* could continue to joke, as the publication, contrary to the daily papers, offered the requisite space for a specific readership. As Luz highlights, it was not the intention of the artists to become a symbol.

Like Charb, he deplores the inability of readers (especially those to whom the magazine was not addressed) to comprehend the images in their ambiguity:

> Since the cartoons of Muhammad, the irresponsible nature of cartoons has gradually disappeared. Since 2007, our cartoons are read literally. People or cartoonists, like Plantu, believe we shouldn't do drawings on [sic.] Muhammad because they go viral on the Internet. Therefore, we have to be careful what we do in France as someone may react in Kuala Lumpur or somewhere else. It's unbearable.
> (Luz, Laffeter)

The literal reading of a cartoon can be seen as a result of a cultural error, which corresponds to the inability to translate the ambiguity of visual signs. According to Luz, the "irresponsible nature" is precisely the feature that stands out in the cartoons and caricatures published in *Charlie*. His explanation helps filter out the common denominator among *Charlie's* contributors, which is not obscenity, but a pluralism of styles in a humoristic reaction to the horrors of the real world.

> Sometimes goofy, other times crass, punk for sure. Sometimes it doesn't work, other times it's simply beautiful. *Charlie* is the combination of a group of very different people, who all draw cartoons. The nature of the cartoon changed depending on which cartoonist was working on it, using his or her style, drawing on previous political or artistic influences. But this modesty and diversity of expression no longer exists. Each cartoon is seen to having been done by all of us. (Luz, Laffeter)

Luz's puzzlement about the appropriation of *Charlie* by the media, politics and the public reveals a central characteristic of the magazine. As mentioned, a critique of the Church and of authority has always been a central feature. Luz not only points to the diversity of voices and styles that expressed this critique in pictorial "modesty". He also implicitly describes the ethos behind this pluralism: "The symbolic weight is exactly what *Charlie* has always worked against: destroying symbols, breaking down taboos, bursting bubbles of fantasy" (Luz/Laffeter). The magazine employed the *inspirational, emancipatory* and *enlightening* potential of images, squibs and cartoons in order to question doctrines, deconstruct symbols, brake taboos and dispose of tired clichés: religious dogma, right-wing populism, stereotypic role-models were drawn, caricatured and deconstructed.

3. Luz' *Catharsis* and (comic-)cultural errors?

The controversy described and commented on above is probably the reason why no English translation has seen the light of day until now. The politically incorrect connotations disseminated in the (Anglo-American) media might have discouraged potential publishers, regardless of the actual content. Luz' *Catharsis* is a compendium of thirty autobiographical fragments, in which the author deals with the *Charlie Hebdo* events in very different ways (desperate, funny, poetic...). He tells about his life and relationship after the attacks, tries to find images for the attack itself (for instance a wordless macabre ballet of Kalashnikov-equipped dancers), pays verbal and visual homage to the lost members of his tribe, imagines a meeting with the Kouachi-brothers (when they were children), retraces his beginnings at *Charlie Hebdo* – in short, he tries to find a way to deal with the trauma and to regain (artistic) agency. As the title implies, the aim is to obtain catharsis. The (hand-written!) prologue indicates the theme:

> Un jour, le dessin m'a quitté. Le même jour qu'une poignée d'amis chers. À la seule différence qu'il est revenu, lui. Petit à petit. A la fois plus sombre et plus léger. Avec ce revenant,

j'ai dialogué, pleuré, ri, hurlé ... Ce livre n'est pas un témoignage ... mais l'histoire de retrouvailles entre deux amis qui ont failli un jour ne plus jamais se croiser.

[One day, drawing left me. The same day as a bunch of good friends. The only difference was that the drawing returned, little by little. Both darker and more light-hearted. With this returning ghost, I talked, cried, laughed and screamed ... This book is not a testament ... It's the reunion of two friends who might never have run into each other again.] (*Catharsis* 3)

The German version of the prologue can serve to illustrate two important aspects, which were mentioned in the introductory section on comics in translation – first, as I mentioned earlier, we immediately notice that the (very well done) hand lettering is still a little less spontaneous than in the French version. Second, we can assume that the translators missed the personification of the drawing, which Luz introduced in the first sentence because of the fact that they are translating a comic and have thus paid less attention to the weight of every single word (perhaps relying too heavily on the word-image-balance?). In the original the drawing actively leaves ("quitté") the author to return as a friend ("revenu", "retrouvailles entre deux amis") in the end (of the prologue and the book). In the German translation, the drawing is "abhandengekommen" ("lost") which omits the notion of the drawing's independent and organic *existence*. This literary game (with the drawing being one active player) is performed in the entire preface to the French version.

It is especially worth noting the omission in this case as the translators of the German version, Uli Aumüller and Grete Osterwald, do not normally work as comic book translators but have translated the works of Albert Camus, Simone de Beauvoir, Jean-Paul Sartre and the likes. An online-interview (Aumüller, Osterwald) with the German publishing house, Fischer, shows that the medium (which the interviewer, and that is telling as well, keeps on calling a "genre") is new to both translators, who state that they appreciated the distraction "from more complex literary works"[5].

The interview is quite revealing in general: Aumüller stresses the fact that *Katharsis* is not a normal comic because it is not funny. Subconscious prejudices against comics (which are already implicitly implied in the expression genre) can be identified despite all the euphoric statements. They can partly explain why cultural errors occur in the comic book translation. With a variation on Derrida and, here even more, on Walter Benjamin we could ask about the dangers of irrelevant translation: "And is this not something that a translator can reproduce only if he is also – a *connaisseur* of comic culture?"

---

[5] "sehr anregende Abwechslung von den oft sehr umfangreichen und literarisch anspruchsvollen Büchern, die wir sonst übersetzen" (Aumüller, Osterwald).

Luz (9)

Luz (10)

Two pages are shown here to exemplify the translation problems; other examples are summarized in the following list. The extract shows how the (metaphorically) wounded and bleeding Luz portrays himself imagining an editorial meeting and juggling with ideas. The size and form of the speech bubble corresponds to the French original. The extract demonstrates the challenges of the formal constraints of comic book translation. In the last speech bubble, Luz is shown expressing his confusion: "Mein Kuchen is weg". The number of letters (16) is nearly similar to the number in the original version, where the statement "J'ai perdu ma galette" consists of 17 letters. The literal translation and the didactic/explanatory version would have demanded a lot more letters (27 letters for "Ich habe meinen Kuchen verloren" and 36 letters for "Ich habe meinen Dreikönigskuchen verloren"). A look at the size of the final bubble typifies the problem caused by issues of space: it would have been difficult to squeeze the sentence into the bubble without making it unreadable. The formal constraints can explain some of the mistranslations that are observed in comic translation. But why choose "Kuchen" instead of "galette"?

Let us take another look at the content of the scene depicted. As in real life (on 7th January), Luz brought a *galette* (a special cake which is eaten in France on the feast of Epiphany) to the office because it was his birthday the day before. The cultural context is lost in the German translation, where the *galette* is translated simply as "cake". This may seem a minor detail but it is not. The tradition of sharing a *galette* is an especially joyous French ritual; the innocence of this tradition makes the scene look all the more grotesque.

As his colleagues do not react – for obvious reasons – Luz addresses them: "Putain, vous êtes amorphes aujourd'hui. Vous vous êtes tous engueulés ou quoi?" [Fuck it, you're lifeless today. Have you been fighting or what?]. In the German version, the register does not correspond to the original style: *sich fetzen* is an outdated way of saying "to fight". It could best be described as a result of: "How older people imagine younger peoples' slang".

It is also difficult to explain why the "lifeless" (*amorphous*) has been erased and replaced by *schlapp* ("weak"); "être amorphe" [to be lifeless] is not a proverbial saying but originates in the author's idiolect. In so far it is much more original (in both senses of the word) as the translation. Again (as in the preface) the individual literary style is lost and the text is somehow flattened. Similar examples can be found in the rest of the book as the following list shows:

Catharsis (French)	***Katharsis*** (German)	English Translation, meaning, comment (translation error)
picolé (9)	gepichelt (9)	Both mean to drink alcohol, but "gepichelt" sounds far more old-fashioned (register/ idiolect), cf. analysis
Galette (9)	Kuchen (9)	Cf. analysis
amorphes, engueulés (10)	schlapp, gefetzt	Cf. analysis
Tu avais du rouges à levres? (26)	Hattest Du Dir die Lippen rot gemalt? (26)	"Did you wear lipstick?" German translation: less familiar, more literary ("Did you colour your lips red?") (register/idiolect)
T´écris une lettre à ta fiancée? (31)	Schreibst Du einen Brief an Deine Braut? (31)	"Are you writing a letter to your girl/woman?" Deine Braut [your bride] sounds like artificial (outdated) slang (register, idiolect)
et c'est le bordel (34)	Schon macht ihr Rabatz (34)	"And it gets chaotic immediately." "Rabatz" is a (very) old-school term for chaos which is usually not (seriously)

			employed by people of Luz' generation (register, idiolect)
- être aussi zen - ma vieille - quelque part (38)	- gelassen - meine Alte - irgendwo (38)		- You would more likely use the literal translation "to be zen" in German "Zen sein" - "ma vieille" is a term of endearment in the given context, "meine Alte" [my old] in German is not "meine Gute" [my dear] would work better - "quelque part" can mean "somewhere" ("irgendwo") but here it means "somehow" ("irgendwie") (register/colloquialism)
j'ose pas (47)	Ich wage nicht mehr (47)		"I don't dare" (the French version is more colloquial, omission of the negation particle "ne") (register)
se bidonner comme un sale gosse (49)	Wie er sich vor Lachen gebogen hat (49)		"that stupid guy was convulsed with laughter", more vulgar and colloquial in the French version (register)
Tu nous traites pas de Juifs! (54)	Wir lassen uns nicht Juden schimpfen! (54)		"Do not insult us by calling us Jewish!"

		"Jmdn. etw. Schimpfen" [to insult s.o. as s.th.] is a very outdated expression (register)
-Allez, on va pas y passer des heures … ! - sur Wikipedia (68)	- Na los, dass wir hier nicht versauern! - in Wikipedia nachsehen (68)	- "We don't need to spend hours on this. " "Versauern" as a verb is quite outdated. - "in Wikipedia", even though "in" is probably the correct preposition, most youngish Germans would use the preposition "auf". (register, youth language)
et putain, mon salaud (70)	und verdammt, Himmelarsch… (70)	The German translation of the French cursing is not vulgar enough, it is like employing "Heck!" instead of "Fuck!" (register, vulgarity)
t'es con (71)	Du Knalltüte (71)	Same problem as in the example above: "T'es" con means "You're an asshole" not "a goofball" (register, vulgarity)

The above selection of translation problems and the cited pages are representative for the general tone of the translation, which inspired the pun in this chapter's title: "Too graphic a novel?!" Being less vulgar, the Luz-character of the German version gives the impression of being a "little less *Charlie Hebdo*" and a little more harmless instead. To explain the lack of (the corresponding degree of) vulgarity, several reasons can be named, that are partly caused by cultural errors. The second section of this paper dedicated to the *Charlie Hebdo* controversy retraced the debate, which presumably prevented the publication of an English translation.

It could be argued that "downgrading vulgarity" is a good way of softening the potential blow, rendering the text more politically correct and sparing the German readership, especially a cultivated readership (but not necessarily *comic-cultivated*) targeted by the Fischer Verlag. However, my assumption is that the more faithful translations do not come from the attempt to make *Charlie Hebdo*-humour bearable for a readership with another cultural background (more *German*, more mature, and more cultivated). As the paratextual statements show, Aumüller and Osterwald are new to the comic book business, to the humour and the language of *Charlie Hebdo*: they say so themselves.

Their register differs a lot from Luz' language in *Charlie Hebdo*; they might be less used to contemporary everyday language – though they are nevertheless motivated and enthusiastic. This difference in register is especially striking in an autobiographical comic book, where the idiolect needs to feel authentic. The publishing house's decision to employ two prestigious literary translators (instead of translators who specialize in comics) might also be a result of the debate discussed in section two. When issues of reputation are at stake for both the satirical journal *Charlie Hebdo* as well for comics as a genre, translators associated with canonical literature can seem to be a simple solution. However, as I have shown, comic book translation should not be underestimated. The images do not render the text any easier; it still has to be relevant in all senses of the word.

Works cited

Beaty, Bart. *Comics versus art*. University of Toronto Press, 2012.

Benjamin, Walter. "The Task of the Translator". *Walter Benjamin: Selected Writings Volume 1*, edited by Marc Bullock and Michael Jennings. Harvard University Press, 1996, pp. 253-263.

Bourdieu, Pierre. *Distinction: A Social Critique of the Judgement of Taste*. Harvard University Press, 1984.

Celotti, Nadine. "The translator of comics as a semiotic investigator". *Comics in Translation*, edited by Frederico Zanettin, St. Jerome, 2008, pp. 33-49.

Charb [Stéphane Charbonnier]/François Forcadel. "Entretien". *Quel avenir pour le dessin de presse?* 2009, pp. 20-41.

Charb [Stéphane Charbonnier]. *Lettre aux escrocs de l'islamophobie qui font le jeu des racistes.* Les Échappés, 2015.

Charb [Stéphane Charbonnier]. *Open letter: On Blasphemy, Islamophobia, and the True Enemies of Free Expression*. Little, Brown and Company, 2016.

Derrida, Jacques. *Specters of Marx: The State of the Debt, the Work of Mourning and the New International*. Routledge, 1994.

Derrida, Jacques. "What Is a 'Relevant' Translation?", translated by Lawrence Venuti. *Critical Inquiry*, vol. 27, no. 2, 2001, pp. 174-200.

Eco, Umberto. *The Search for the Perfect Language*, translated by James Fentress. Blackwell, 1995.

El Refaie, Elisabeth. *Autobiographical Comics*. University Press of Mississippi, 2012.

Groensteen, Thierry. *Système de la bande dessinée.* PUF, 1999.

Hatfield, Charles. *Alternative comics: An emerging literature*. University Press of Mississippi, 2005.

Jakobson, Roman. "On Linguistic Aspects of Translation". *On Translation*, edited by Arthur Reuben Brower. Harvard University Press, 1959, p. 232-239.

Luz. *Catharsis*. Futuropolis, 2015.

Luz. *Katharsis*. Translated by Uli Aumüller and Grete Osterwald. S. Fischer Verlag, 2015.

McCloud, Scott. *Understanding Comics: the Invisible Art.* 1. Harper, 1994.

Mälzer, Nathalie (ed.). *Comics – Übersetzungen und Adaptionen*. Frank & Timme, 2015.

Peeters, Benoît. *Case, planche, récit: Comment lire la bande dessinée.* Casterman, 1998.

Rio, Knut. "The *Barbariat* and democratic tolerance". *The Event of Charlie Hebdo. Imaginaries of Freedom and Control*, edited by Alessandro Zagato, Berghahn Books, 2015, pp. 12-23.

Schüwer, Martin. *Wie Comics erzählen: Grundriss einer intermedialen Erzähltheorie der grafischen Literatur.* WVT-Handbücher und Studien zur Medienkulturwissenschaft, 2008.

Zanettin, Federico (ed.): *Comics in Translation*. St. Jerome, 2008.

Webography

Aumüller, Uli/ Osterwald, Grete. "Trauerarbeit mit dem Zeichenstift. Interview", [2015], *Hundervierzehn. Das literarische Magazin des S. Fischer Verlags.* https://www.hundertvier zehn.de/artikel/trauerarbeit-mit-dem-zeichenstift_1056.html. Accessed 14 January 2019.

Canfield, Jacob. "In the Wake of Charlie Hebdo, Free Speech Does Not Mean Freedom From Criticism", 07.01.2015, *The Hooded utilitarian.* http://www.hoodedutilitarian.com/2015/01/in-the-wake-of-charlie-hebdo-free-speech-does-not-mean-freedom-from-criticism. Accessed 14 January 2019.

Chervel, Thierry. "Figur der Opfermediokrität", 27.01.2015, *perlen taucher.de. Das Kulturmagazin.* https://www.perlentauche r.de/blog/2015/01/27/figur-deropfermediokritaet.hatml?highlight=Charlie+Hebdo. Accessed 14 January 2019.

Le Saux, Laurence. "Portrait: Luz. Survivant à Vie'", 31.05.2015, *Télérama.* http://www.telerama.fr/livre/luz-survivant-a-vie, 127150. php. Accessed 14 January 2019.

Luz [Renald Luzier]/Laffeter, Ann. "Luz: All eyes are on us. We've become a symbol'". Translated by Nick Haughton, 10.01.2015, *Les Inrocks.com.* http://www.lesinrocks. com/ 2015 /01/10/actualite/luz-eyes-us-weve-become-symbol-11545 347/. Accessed 14 January 2019.

Moneyron, Josselin. "A Year in the Merde", 17.01.2015, *The Hooded Utilitarian.* http://www.hoodedutilitarian.com/2015/01/a-year-in-the-merde. Accessed 14 January 2019.

Parkhill, Chad. "The Problem with #JeSuisCharlie", 09.01.2015, *jun kee.com.* http://junkee.com/the-problem-with-jesuischarli / 48456. Accessed 14 January 2019.

Schuessler, Jennifer. "Charlie Hebdo Attack Chills Satirists and Prompts a Debate", 09.01.2017, *The New York Times.* https://www.nytimes.com/2015/01/10/arts/an-attack-chi lls-satirists-and-prompts-debate.html. Accessed 14 January 2019.

Trudeau, Garry. "The Abuse of Satire", 11.04.2015, *The Atlantic.* https://www.theatlantic.com/international/archive/2015/ 04/the-abuse-of-satire/390312. Accessed 14 January 2019.

Ziegler, Ulf Erdmann. "Charlie. Ein Missverständnis",26.01.2015, *perlentaucher.de. Das Kulturmagazin.* https://www.perlen taucher.de/maluma-und-takete/charlie-ein missverstaendni s.html.

Žižek, Slavoj. "Are the worst really full of passionate intensity?", 10.01.2015, *New Statesman*. https://www.newstatesman.com/world-affairs/2015/01/slavoj-i-ek-charlie-hebdo-massacre-are-worst-really-full-passionate-intensity. Accessed 14 January 2019.

The End of Eddy, The End of France?

Clíona Ní Ríordáin

> The meaning of texts change when they hook up with different interpretative communities.
> Rita Felski (15)

Introduction

Rita Felski's text on *The Uses of Literature* is invaluable as an aid to explore one aspect of cultural errors in translation: that of the reception of the translated text. A translated text leaves the sphere in which it was written, and its reception in the target culture is always difficult to determine in advance. Among the factors that influence its reception are the obvious ones, like the quality of the translation in the target language. However, in this chapter, I will argue that other factors are also key to the way in which a book is received, chief among them are the means of production, i.e. networks of distribution, promotion, and above all the spatio-temporal frame of the publication. This view is in keeping with what Felski has called "a historically attuned approach" (15) to the production of a literary text. My study is thus squarely set in the field of the sociology of translation. Following on from the theories of Bourdieu (*La Distinction*), it will examine how one text is invested with a degree of symbolic power (Blommaert 223) in the target culture and is used to justify a perspective, that suits the system into which the text is received, examining the embedding and the articulation of the text once it enters the target system.

The focus for my study is the novel *En finir avec Eddy Bellegueule*, published by Le Seuil in France in 2014. In the English language (translated by Michael Lucey), it appeared in 2017, under the Farrar Strauss and Giroux imprint in the US; while in the UK it was published by Harvill & Secker. I contend that the reception of the translation of this novel was influenced by the period of publication (2017), and the socio-political movements that traversed the Anglosphere at that juncture in time. I refer specifically to the UK's referendum on Brexit (23 June, 2016), closely followed, in November of that same year, by the election of US President, Donald Trump. As Michaela Wolf underlined in her introduction to *Constructing a Sociology of Translation*:

> Any translation, as both an enactment and a product, is necessarily embedded within social contexts. On the one hand, the act of translating, in all its various stages, is undeniably carried out by individuals who belong to a social system; on the other, the translation phenomenon is inevitably implicated in social institutions, which greatly determine the selection, production and distribution of translation and, as a result, the strategies adopted in the translation itself. (1)

I will argue that those events, which have had a profound effect on both social policy in general in the UK and the US, and on the self-perception of those states by the literary elite in particular, have led to both a form of self-questioning, and a desire to find events that mirror those phenomena elsewhere. This in turn, I contend, leads to the form of cultural error that I will examine in the present case-study.

1. Context

Edouard Louis, author of *The End of Eddy*, comes from a poor working-class family in a rurally deprived corner of the province of Picardy, in the North-East of France. Statistics for the region[1] indicate that the percentage of school-leavers departing formal education without any formal qualification are more than 5 percentage points higher than the national norm. Unemployment figures for the region, at the time of the publication of the novel, were also higher than the national norm, with some areas of Picardy displaying figures that were 4 points higher than the national average[2]. The statistics also indicate a high proportion of workers who are dependent on short-term (interim) contracts; with more than 30% of the active population in the 2012 census who identified as *ouvriers*, that is to say blue-collar workers.

Edouard Louis' novel, set in the rural village of Hallencourt (Somme), is autobiographical, and can be seen as a form of auto-fiction. It tells the story of his upbringing, as a young effeminate boy in a community wracked by violence, born of despair, and which is directed against all those who deviate from the perceived norms of that society. A double narrative strategy is employed. The empirical voice of the omniscient narrator outlines the events of his life in sociological terms, often using learned vocabulary. The voice of his subjects (parents, siblings, classmates, tormentors) is italicized, purporting to be the direct transcription of the voices of his milieu, the voiceless individuals, whom François Hollande, President of France at the time of its publication, is said to have called *les sans dents* [the toothless masses][3]. Hollande's alleged nickname for the French underclass takes on a particular poignancy in the case of Louis' narrative as the poor state of his teeth leads him to invent stories of

---

[1] http://hauts-de-france.direccte.gouv.fr/sites/hauts-defrance.direccte. gouv.fr/IMG/pdf/chiffres_cles_edition_2015-2.pdf. Accessed 18 February 2019.
[2] See figures from the following report https://www.insee.fr/fr/statisti ques/2018336?sommaire=2018349. Accessed 18 February 2019.
[3] This was the claim made by Valérie Trierweiler in her memoir written after her break-up with the President and largely reposted in the press. See for instance the following account in *Les Echos*: https://www.lese chos.fr/03/09/2014/lesechos.fr/0203746205048_valerie-trierweiler-sans-dents-et-sans-decence.htm. Accessed 18 February 2019.

neglect by airheaded intellectual parents (12) when he leaves his social class; later in the novel (68), he tells the story of his aunt who, while drunk, would pull out her own teeth for fun.

The novel depicts the violence of Louis' home and his community, what Bourdieu refers to as a sociological subject's *habitus*. The use of sociological terminology here is appropriate as it is through sociology, and initially via a theatre option at high-school, that the young Eddy Bellegueule [literally "Eddy Handsome Mug"[4]] manages to escape from his social class. Edouard Louis is the name that the young author takes (his last name is changed by deed-poll to Louis) before the publication of his first book: a volume of essays that he edits entitled *Pierre Bourdieu: L'insoumission en héritage* published by the venerable publishing house, les Presses Universitaires de France. The French reception of Edouard Louis' novel focussed primarily on the author's homosexuality and on the violence and poverty endemic in a predominantly white underclass.

2. Reception

The violence and poverty become the backdrop to a tale of academic success. This is how the novel was received by Catherine Simon in *Le Monde*, the French newspaper of reference:

> Rossé et humilié quotidiennement au collège, menacé par un frère alcoolique, raillé par un père infantile et tyrannique, montré du doigt par tous et toutes, « Bellegueule, la pédale » finit par rompre avec les siens – et fuir. À Amiens d'abord, où il achève ses études secondaires, puis à Paris, où il est admis à l'École normale supérieure de la rue d'Ulm. Chaque fois, des enseignants – qu'ils soient bénis ! – l'encouragent et l'aident à se sauver lui-même.

---

[4] All translations that follow are mine, with the exception of the translations excerpted from the English version of *Pour en finir avec Eddy Bellegueule* (2014), which are taken from Michael Lucey's translation, *The End of Eddy* (2017).

[Beaten and humiliated on a daily basis in middle school, threatened by an alcoholic brother, railed at by an infantile and tyrannical father, and mocked by one and all as "Belleguele, the poof", the author breaks with his family and runs away. To Amiens first of all, where he finishes high-school, and then to Paris where he gains entrance to l'École normale supérieure in the rue d'Ulm. At every turn, it is teachers – they deserve his gratitude – who encourage him and help him to save himself from himself.]

The cultural references are key here in understanding the power structures in which this novel is inscribed. L'Ecole normale supérieure de la rue d'Ulm (ENS) is the holy of holies in the French academic system. Admission to the school comes after two years of intense study for a competitive post-high-school exam, which is notoriously difficult. *Normaliens* are paid a salary while they study, and the school opens doors to the highest echelons of French life. The school is the stomping ground of French intellectuals, Nobel prize winners from all fields, novelists, politicians; in Bourdieusian terms, it is a locus for those who are, or who go on to become, *les héritiers* (*La Distinction*), or to refer to the work used by Louis in his book of essays on Bourdieu, many of them come to embody *Homo academicus*. The newspaper article in *Le Monde* is illustrated by a photo of Edouard Louis taken in the entrance hall to the ENS. It shows a very preppy blonde-haired youth in a crew neck sweater who looks totally at ease in his environment.

Le Monde's article makes reference to the language of Louis-Ferdinand Céline: "*En finir avec Eddy Bellegueule donne à entendre la violence presque célinienne de la France des laissés-pour-compte*" [*The End of Eddy* allows one to overhear the Céline-like violence of France's abandoned people]. The literary references are clear, *Le Monde*'s phrase suggests that this is a novel that can be inscribed into French literary history; although Edouard Louis himself, in a short interview filmed for Mollat, a bookshop in Bordeaux, argues that he deliberately writes against Céline's impulse to estheticize the language of the proletariat.

In 2014, the critical reception in France made much of Edouard Louis' attempt in his childhood to correspond to a certain butch conception of masculinity. *Le Monde* again underlines this fact:

> Pendant toute son enfance, Eddy essaye « d'être comme tout le monde » : devenir « un dur », grossier, couillu, un bagarreur. Il se force à draguer les filles, à aimer le football, à s'empiffrer de frites trop grasses, une « bouffe d'homme qui tient bien à l'estomac, a décrété le père, pas comme dans les trucs de bourges où plus c'est cher, moins t'en as dans l'assiette ».

> [Throughout his childhood, Eddy will try "to resemble everyone else": to become "a tough guy", vulgar, ballsy, a fighter. He will force himself to flirt with girls, to like football, to stuff his face with very greasy chips, " a man's food grub that sticks to your ribs", his father decreed, "not like that fancy rich people crap where the more it costs the less you have on your plate".]

The focalisation on forms of masculinity can be explained by the tensions that were apparent in France the year before the novel was published. On 23 April 2013, the French parliament voted a law that permitted gay marriage. In the months that preceded the parliamentary vote, demonstration and counterdemonstration argued vocally in favour of and against the legislation. La manif pour tous [Demo for all] was vehemently opposed to in vitro fertilisation for gay couples and was against gay marriage[5].

---

5   See for instance the coverage of the march in the centre right newspaper *Le Figaro* http://www.lefigaro.fr/actualite-france/2013/01/13/01016-20130113ARTFIG00217-mobilisation-historique-contre-le-mariage-pour-tous.php. Accessed 18 February 2019.

As we see in what follows, the reception of the novel in the Anglosphere took a different slant. And this despite the fact that it was translated by Berkeley professor of French and comparative literature, Michael Lucey. Lucey, who had previously translated the memoir of Edouard Louis' sociologist mentor, Didier Eribon, *Retour à Reims* [Return to Reims], is a gender studies specialist and founder of the Centre for the Study of Sexual Culture. Lucey's *démarche* as a translator could be conceived as forming part of a network of empathy, along the lines suggested by André Dussart in his article on empathy in translation studies (2002), which builds on work by Kelly (1979) and Wuillmart (1990). It could thus be viewed as part of a strategy to develop an audience for gender studies *à la française* on an international stage. Nonetheless, many of the critics outside of France chose to use the story of Eddy Bellegueule as both a metonym and a metaphor for the state of France.

The following example, taken from the Canadian paper *The Globe & Mail*, is typical of the metonymic/metaphorical approach adopted:

A lot of countries are haltingly, painfully coming to terms with the fact that they're not what they thought they were ... And the French, with their Revolution and Napoleonic Code, the national incarnation of modern sophistication, are on the verge of making Marine Le Pen theirs, against a backdrop of racial violence and an increasingly general intolerance – of immigrants, of Muslims, even of other Europeans.

With headlines blaring: *"The End of Eddy* shows a different side of France", the article goes on to proclaim "This is a story of France today, the France outside the dozen or so Paris *arrondissements* that foreigners and French alike have been using metonymically for far too long, long enough to let Louis's characters vote Le Pen to the brink of the presidency". The critic, Ben Archer, concludes by reinserting the novel into French literary history, while simultaneously identifying it as part of a wider global phenomenon:

> This is Zola without the sense of justice, Rabelais without the need for monsters, Genet without the ability to find anything beautiful about getting badly beaten up. It's the ground-level story of a new subversive force in the West, born of an abandoned working class, that's fuelling a whole new kind of revolution.

Archer's review is marked by a form of *Schadenfreude*. A smug smirk is to be detected in the fact that despite what the author sees as the trappings of French sophistication (interestingly defined in relation to convulsive moments in French history: the revolution and Napoleon's first empire during which his code came into force as France's civil code). France has been outed as being just like everyone else.

It is interesting in this context that the late Eileen Battersby, literary correspondent of *The Irish Times*, chose to view the novel primarily from the perspective of gender, highlighting what she calls "the perverse cult of masculinity". Ireland in 2015 had also voted for gay marriage, contrary to France, it was established via referendum (62% voted in favour of the modification to the constitution). It was preceded by an intense debate on constructs of gender. Again, this in keeping with Rita Felski's notion of perceiving the reception of text as a result of their place within the social world (13).

Elsewhere, in the *New York Review of Books*, another Irish writer, and New York resident, Colm Toibín is quick to identify Édouard Louis' immediate forerunners in Annie Ernaux and Didier Eribon. Eribon, as we have seen earlier, is the sociologist and mentor of Louis, whose *Retour à Reims*, had such an influence on his own writing. Annie Ernaux, born to a family of petit-bourgeois shopkeepers in Normandy, has devoted many of her loosely autofictional novels to accounts of her painful extraction from her original social class. And it is this to which Toibín alludes in his introduction, offering an empathetic reading of Louis' novel. Yet, once again, Toibín insists on inscribing Louis' novel within a meta-perception of France, suggesting that Louis not alone offers a different image of France, but sculpts it in his own image:

> Like Annie Ernaux and Didier Eribon, the war Édouard Louis is waging is not against his own background, but against an image of France as comfortable, settled, at ease with itself, an image that has fully excluded him and made him feel shame … In *The End of Eddy*, which has been a best seller in France, Louis enacts a sort of homecoming as he offers his compatriots a new version of their country, a version that he has chiseled with considerable skill, thus remaking France in his own image, with his own unsparing gaze.

Toibín's analysis is complex, suggestive of a form of narcissism in the phrase "remaking France in his own image". France has had no shortage of gay icons, from Jean Genet to Michel Foucault, to Roland Barthes. Thus, it would seem that rather than dwelling on the issue gender, it is again a question of class that is central to Toibín's reception of the text; an intuition confirmed by the title of his review: "The Class Renegade".

Jennifer Senior in a review published in the *New York Times* immediately claims that *The End of Eddy* is the *Hillbilly Elegy* of France. In making a parallel to JD Vance's memoir, she is offering Louis's text as the key to understanding contemporary France, much as Vance's book functioned as an explanation for the election of Trump:

> Both Louis's deeply autobiographical novel and J. D. Vance's memoir are stories by precocious young men about the sa-

vagery of their childhoods. Both explore cultures of spectacular violence. Both are set in decaying manufacturing towns – places where the men and women scuff and strain against economic morbidity, class invisibility and narcotizing boredom. Yet these same men and women have a paradoxical relationship with the government, at once resenting its power and depending on its largess. Welfare is as common as rain.

Yet, despite the parallels, Senior admits the major difference in the social circumstances of the two men:

France is a social democracy, extending to its citizens benefits Americans would find unimaginable; the United States remains, as ever, enthusiastically capitalist, with an instinctive distaste for big government.

However, once Senior has acknowledged this fundamental difference, she returns again to the question of similarities, outlining common characteristics that range from bad teeth, to obesity and the omnipresence of blaring TV sets.

Senior's recognition of the difference of the social systems into which Vance and Louis were born is vital in understanding the cultural error in the reception of the book in the Anglosphere. France's revolution, with its key phrase "liberté, égalité, fraternité" [liberty, equality, fraternity] inscribed on the front of every school building, and town hall, in the French republic is a constant reminder of the standards to which the French nation wishes to aspire.

3. Perception

Yet, as I will argue, outside France, *The End of Eddy* continues to be viewed in terms that ignore this radical equality, which remains at the heart of France's preoccupations and self-image. Far from being an empty catch phrase, the key concepts of the French republic influence social policy, dominate political thinking, and lead to phenomena like *Nuit debout* [Up All Night], a three-month-long nightly debate that emerged from the opposition to a reform of the labour code[6]. The radicality also explains campaign promises, like that made by François Hollande, to increase the income tax paid by wealthy people, *l'Impôt sur les grandes fortunes* (ISF)[7]. The abolition of this tax by his successor, Emmanuel Macron, is one of the demands that the *gilet jaune* [yellow vest] protestors have made. Of which more later…

French philosophers, such as Jacques Rancière, continue to contribute to the political debate in the country, with, for instance, his key concept of *le partage du sensible* (2007), [the distribution of the sensible]. Rancière argues in favour of a rethinking of the relationship between art and politics. Renewing the debate initiated by Bourdieu, Rancière's ideas seem especially relevant in terms of the reception of Louis' text. Rancière argues in favour of a reconfiguring of the organs of perception. He argues that people need to reevaluate their opinion on the objects worthy of perception. This, in essence, is what Edouard Louis is doing in his novel, drawing our attention to those whom he deems to be ignored because they are unworthy of society's gaze.

It is in the context of the understanding of the French social system, and the inability to measure the continuing distance between it and the *régimes* in force in both the UK and the USA, that ensure that even the otherwise excellent Toibín errs in his analysis. Describing Louis' escape via education he states:

---

[6] For an assessment of the impact of the movement see Catherine Vincent's article "Un an après, nuit (toujours) debout ?" https://www.lemonde.fr/idees/article/2017/03/30/toujours-debout_5103350_3232.html. Accessed 18 February, 2019. Accessed 18 February, 2019.

[7] For the impact of this measure see Emmanuel Lévy's article in Marianne : https://www.marianne.net/economie/les-riches-fuient-la-france-d-hollande-info-ou-intox. Accessed 18 February, 2019.

When he finally gets away, into a world he has dreamed of, he notices in his boarding school, to which he has won a theater scholarship, the gentle manners of the other boys and says to himself, as though he is still the son of his father: "What a bunch of faggots, " and then muses, "maybe I'm not gay, maybe things aren't the way I thought they were, maybe I've just always had a bourgeois body, trapped in the world of my childhood".

Toibín's error comes from his misinterpretation of the term "boarding school" in Louis' text. Boarding school and the allied concept of "winning a theater scholarship" can be understood in a network where boarding schools are seen as a symbol of privilege. Allied perhaps to images of public schools, such as Eton or Marlborough in the UK, or Andover in the US; the reference extracts Louis from the French egalitarian school system and places him in a profoundly unequal one where scholarships for promising poor children are seen as a lever to social success, and a sop to social justice. Toibín's understanding of the school within this system is further compounded by his juxtaposition of this information with Louis' own reflection on his body, and his potential perception of himself as being *déclassé* or perhaps more accurately, *méclassé* as a bourgeois body within a proletarian sphere.

The interest in Louis's novel in the anglophone world was at its most acute in the run up to the French presidential election. His work was offered as a way in which to account for the rise of Le Pen. The date of publication of the article by Ben Archer in the *Globe and Mail* was 5 May 2017, it could be seen almost as a curtain raiser for the potential election of Le Pen on 7 May. Yet, two days later it was Emmanuel Macron who was declared the victor. Toibín's article was published very symbolically on 13 July 2017, on the eve of Macron celebrating his first Bastille Day in office.

Toibín's article contains within it, as I have argued, the significant kernel of cultural misunderstanding that explains Macron's election, the misreading of the French system and an attempt to apply a frame of reference in which capitalism continues to be the dominant economic narrative. The French school system, in the case of Edouard Louis, as in the case of so many writers before him, continued to operate as *un ascenseur social*, an engine of social promotion. Louis' school was not the boarding school to which Toibín alludes, but a residence for students *un internat* (Louis 144), attached to the Lycée Madeleine Michelis. The Lycée in question is a French state high-school, where schooling is free. It offers specialised teaching in dance, music and theatre. Louis had no tuition fees to pay, and the scholarship alluded to comes from the fact that Louis was a *boursier*. In other words, his family's income was below a certain fiscal threshold. These *bourses* are not granted on the base of any particular gifts displayed by a student, as would be the case of a "theater scholarship" alluded to by Toibín, rather they are a right to which every child in France can have access[8].

It is this misreading and misinterpretation of cultural allusions that has led to a partly flawed cultural reading of Edouard Louis' work. For although *The End of Eddy* displays a profound awareness of social injustice, expressed clearly in very Bourdieusian terms, it is only by reading *The End of Eddy* within the French social network and norms that the novel can be fully comprehended. This underlines the fact that comprehension of cultural references and the systems from which they emerge are vital if texts from a source culture are to be understood within a target culture.

Toibín's interpretation is of course linked to Lucey's choice of terminology. For it is the translator who chose "boarding school" as a term that equated to *internat*. The inadequacy of the term

---

[8] The fiscal threshold is also applied to a range of other activities and services from school dinners, to municipal creches, to music and dance classes in the national and local Conservatoires. A healthcare system, which is already viewed as being generous, extends universal health care to all those resident in France not covered by the social security system. See the effects of this system in the article by Elise Barthet in *Le Monde* https://www.lemonde.fr/societe/article/2009/09/09/en-dix-ans-la-cmu-a-reduit-les-inegalites-dans-l-acces-a-lasante_1238143_3224.html. Accessed 18 February 2019.

becomes apparent on the following page (188) when the word "dormitory" appears as a synonym for "boarding school", and later on the same page, when Louis is told that he will have a room to himself in the dormitory. Networks of meaning collide "une chambre dans un internat" [a room in a student residence] is a compact logical sequence of signifiers. A boarding school, which then becomes a dormitory in another part of town, where the student has his own room, jars. There is a friction between the meaning of the discrete parts of the chain of signifiers. This is clearly where the two cultural systems, the French and the American, come into conflict, and where the terms from one system are not adequate to explain the other. The only recourse in this instance would have been a footnote, or perhaps an *explicitation*, where the French term would remain in the text in italics, signalling that French reality cannot always be explained by English words.

As we have seen, an understanding of the reception of *The End of Eddy* is possible when one views its publication, in France and in the Anglosphere, as occurring within two opposing fields of power. The opposition is most visible between the American *habitus* of the translator Michael Lucey and the French one of Edouard Louis. The societies in which they live are constructed on different value systems. The book in its French and American incarnations plays a role in the soft culture promotion of France. Yet, in a way, the translation errors in the book can be viewed as collateral damage in the culture wars between the two systems it seeks to mediate between.

Louis and Lucey are agents of mediation between the two worlds in their respective roles as writer and translator. It is other agents of mediation (i.e. the critics in each space, who received the text), who have played their part in this "soft-culture struggle". This is because the critics have not concentrated on the book's value as a purely literary object, a stance facilitated, or compounded, by the auto-fictional status of the text. The proximity between Edouard Louis' life story and his novel, enabled the critics to disregard the desire on his part to create a literary artefact. Instead, the economic, historical and sociological forces that operate in the critics' respective spaces shaped their understanding of the text. And so it was that critics in the Anglosphere saw the forces of populism massing within the pages of Louis' work and believed they would triumph in France, as they had elsewhere. Instead, the presidential election saw the triumph of another youth from Picardy, Emmanuel Macron.

Conclusion

Ironically, Macron's France is convulsed today by a populist movement, the *gilets jaunes* or yellow vests. The protests and general discontent with the president result from the widespread perception that he putting in place measures, which in their Thatcherite inspiration, will lead to the dismemberment of French society in its present form[9]. And Edouard Louis has issued another text, *Qui a tué mon père*. Interestingly, he has entered the fray in person explaining the parallel for himself in the pages of *Les Inrockuptibles* in a text entitled "Chaque personne qui insultait un gilet jaune insultait mon père" [Everyone who insulted a yellow-vest protestor insulted my father].

Perhaps Louis' willingness to intervene in the political debate is linked to a desire to seize control of his text for himself, and thus avoid all potential cultural errors in the interpretation of his work?

---

[9] See the article by Solenn de Royer in *Le Monde* where this comparison is made explicit, notably via a mention of the Miners' Strike : https://www.lemonde.fr/politique/article/2018/02/26/macron-la-re forme-au-pas-de-charge_5262648_823448.html Accessed 18 February 2019.

Works cited

Blommaert, Jan. "Bourdieu The Ethnographer". *The Translator*, vol. 11, no. 2, 2005, pp. 219-236.

Bourdieu, Pierre. *Esquisse d'une théorie de la pratique*. Seuil, 2000 [1972].

Bourdieu, Pierre. *La Distinction*. Minuit, 1979.

Bourdieu, Pierre. *Homo academicus*. Minuit, 1984.

Dussart, André. "L'empathie, esquisse d'une théorie de la reception en traduction". *Meta*, vol. 39, no. 1, 1994, pp. 107-115.

Felski, Rita. *Uses of Literature*. Blackwell, 2008.

Kelly, Louis G. *The True Interpreter: A History of Translation Theory and Practice in the West*. Blackwell, 1979.

Louis, Edouard. *En finir avec Eddy Bellegueule*. Seuil, 2014.

Louis, Edouard. *The End of Eddy*, translated by Michael Lucey. Farrar Strauss Giroux, 2017.

Louis, Edouard. *Qui a tué mon père*. Seuil, 2018.

Rancière, Jacques. *Le partage du sensible*. La Fabrique éditions, 2000.

Vance, James David. *Hillbilly Elegy*. Harper, 2016.

Wolf, Michaela, *Constructing a Sociology of Translation*. John Benjamins, 2007.

Wuilmart, Françoise. "Le Traducteur littéraire: Un marieur empathique de cultures". *Meta*, vol. 35, no. 1, 1990, pp. 236-242.

Webography

Louis, Edouard. "Interview. Librairie Mollat". https://www.youtube.com/watch?v=RsJznxDpCLA. Accessed 18 February 2019.

Louis, Edouard. "Chaque personne qui insultait un gilet jaune insultait mon père". *Les Inrockuptibles,* 04 December, 2018.

https://www.lesinrocks.com/2018/12/04/actualite/edouard-louis-chaque-personne-qui-insultait-un-gilet-jaune-insultait-mon-pere-111149208. Accessed 18 February 2019.

Senior, Jennifer. "*The End of Eddy* Captures a Savage Childhood and a Global Movement", *NYT*, 17 May, 2017. https://www.nytimes.com/2017/05/17/books/review-end-of-eddy-edouard-louis.html. Accessed 18 February 2019.

Simon, Catherine. "Eddy se fait la belle". *Le Monde*, 16 January 2014. https://www.lemonde.fr/livres/article/2014/01/16/eddy-se-fait-la-belle_4348681_3260.html. Accessed 18 February 2019.

Toibín, Colm. "The Class Renegade". *NYRB*, 13 July, 2017. https://www.nybooks.com/articles/2017/07/13/end-of-eddy-class-renegade. Accessed 18 February 2019.

Walker, Ben. "The End of Eddy by Édouard Louis shows a different side of France". *Globe and Mail*, 5 May 2017. https://www.theglobeandmail.com/arts/books-and-media/book-reviews/review-the-end-of-eddy-by-edouard-louis-shows-a-different-side-of-france/article34905597. Accessed 18 February 2019.

Translation Errors in Higher Education

Gundula Gwenn Hiller

Introduction

The number of academic documents that need to be translated is growing due to an increase in the number of bicultural university cooperation agreements. In this article, I shall firstly give an overview of the situation pointing out the difficulties for academic staff and translators to figure out equivalents for terms depicting academic programs, positions, and institutions and then, I shall show how different university systems and disciplines sometimes render exact translations impossible. As a theoretical framework, I will introduce the concept of "rich points" (Agar, *Language Shock*) and "hotwords" (Heringer), based on the notion of "languaculture" (Agar, *Language Shock*).

In relying on the examples of the "hotwords" *Wissenschaft* [usually translated as "science" in English and French and the composite term *Kulturwissenschaften* usually translated as "cultural studies" in English, and *études culturelles* in French], I shall show that university terminology is often deeply culture-specific and that translation can be no more than approximate. The result is that a large number of ambiguous translations have been institutionalized, and that these translations simulate correspondences which do not exist, or may even lead to serious intercultural misunderstandings.

1. Terminological confusion as part of internationalisation in higher education

Internationalisation has been gathering speed in the German higher education sphere over the past decades. Although Teichler already revealed in 2007 that a high-quality internationalisation process required intercultural competences (besides ever growing numbers of cooperation and lessons taught in English), intercultural training for academic faculty and staff is still in its infancy (Hiller). My work as a trainer in this area has shown that faculty and staff, even when internationally experienced and open-minded, often are not aware of the subtle differences in academic systems, concepts and language use. These three dimensions are intertwined, and they can be seen as a manifestation of cultural differences. Thus, the following explanations can be seen as potential topics for discussion in intercultural training in higher education. Let us start with two empirical examples:

Example 1:
Recently, an important conference was held at the Technical University Berlin (TU Berlin), which was dedicated to the "Internationalisation of the curricula" (ICM 2018, www.tu-berlin.de). In his keynote lecture about "international compatibility in STEM-disciplines", the Vice President of TU Berlin talked about his practical experience and pointed at the numerous incompatibilities of the university systems that make life difficult for him. He attracted attention to the general confusion regarding equivalences and mentioned issues involving institutional settings, contents, and the names of disciplines and degrees. He said that in the case of international applications for Masters programmes, for instance, it is often not possible to assess what competences are hidden behind the names of the degrees on the certificates. Faculty and staff are faced with numerous problems, especially when it comes to evaluating academic profiles and the naming of programmes. The following 2 slides from his PowerPoint presentation illustrate this:

Diversität von Profilen

Research orientation   Application orientation

High specialisation
Dual education programs
Blended Learning
Classical teaching
Undergraduate programs

Consecutive programs
Distance Learning   Postgraduate programs
Regional orientation
Conversion programs
Continuous education programs
International orientation

Fig. 1: Slide Heiss 2018, title: "Diversität von Profilen" [Diversity of Profiles][1], ICM 2018, www.tu-berlin.de

This slide shows the variety of terminology in academic profiles, which outline different features and orientations of the programs, often not having equivalences in other education systems. The here-listed terms refer to special *foci* of study programmes, which might be not understandable for people from another system, like for example "dual education program", which refers to specific features of a professional training track which exists in Germany, giving students the possibility to be student and trainee in a company at the same time.

---

[1] The following translations in square brackets are my translations.

Diversität von Programmen innerhalb eines Fachs

Scientific Computing   Computer Science
          Software Engineering   Computer Visualistics
Information Management   IT Security
                                   ICT Innovation
     Communication Systems   Computer Engineering
                                   Informatics   Geo-Informatics
     Information Systems
                          Embedded Systems   Business Informatics
          Media Informatics   Computational Neuroscience
Computational Media   Web Science
                                   Information Engineering
          Bio-Informatics   Data Science

Fig. 2: Slide Heiss 2018, Title: "Diversität von Programmen innerhalb eines Fachs" [Diversity of Programmes within the Same Discipline], ICM 2018, www.tu-berlin.de

This slide shows the different denominations of programmes within the same discipline, the example cited is taken from Computer Science, in which students who apply have acquired their degrees. While some denominations seem to be clear, others might be not clear at all. This is the case for instance for "computational media".

Students and candidates for academic jobs who send in their CVs to the Technical University Berlin have studied all over the world. Accordingly, many of the courses they have taken are translated into English or German, and the translations may not always be adequate translations, but rather less-then-ideal translation solutions. This shows that even in science, where scholars might think that there is more clarity concerning programme names and contents, there is a great deal of confusion due to the different structures of universities, university programmes, and even to the division of disciplines within different educational systems.

Example 2:
The previous example showed the confusion, which might happen within an institution which receives applications with different course titles from all over the world. The next example shows a person who has to prepare an application abroad and needs to translate his/her CV and diplomas. This might happen when German scholars or scientists, who would like to apply for a position in France, have to prepare their *dossier de qualification* for the CNU (Comité national Universitaire [the French National Board of Universities]), which is a necessary step to allow one to apply for jobs within the French system. The candidates must translate numerous documents into French, including their CVs. In some cases, this can cause a considerable amount of difficulty, because often neither their disciplinary core qualifications nor their academic positions have equivalents in the French system and thus prove impossible to translate.

The following are some concrete examples of the problem outlined above: a person who works in Germany as a *wissenschaftliche(r) Mitarbeiter/in* [which in a word-to-word translation might be "scientific employee"], or holds a *Juniorprofessur* [junior professorship] or even a *Vertretungsprofessur* [substitute professorship] will have problems to translate the terms, because there are no French equivalents for his/ her actual academic status or for any of the positions s/he had held in the past within the German university system.

If the person holds, for example, a Master's degree in *Romanistik* [Romance languages and literature] and a PhD in *Kulturwissenschaften* [usually translated as "Cultural studies"], s/he will have trouble with the translation because in France there is neither an equivalent for *Kulturwissenschaften* nor for *Romanistik*, the subject in which s/he had received her "Master's" degree (to be precise: when the degree was conferred in the last century *Magister*), both being disciplines that in this form are only to be found within the German speaking academic world (*Romanistik* trains *RomanistInnen*, people who have usually studied two or three romance languages and cultures). Finally, after a discussion with French native speakers who know the German system well, we stated that the substitute professorship could be translated by *suppléant* and *for Juniorprofessur* we would leave the German expression [such as *suppléante de la Juniorprofessur*], while we suggest for *Wissenschaftliche Mitarbeiterin* the French term *enseignant-chercheur* [teaching researcher]. For *Romanistik*, we propose *Romanistique*, and we suggest to leave the German term *Kulturwissenschaften* and to add the French translation *sciences culturelles*.

I will come back to the term *Kulturwissenschaften* further on. To understand the trickiness of its translation and its roots in the very culturally specific setting of the humanities and German academia, we must first take a look at the term *Wissenschaft* which is highly cultural and which I will explore at length in the following sections.

2. Resources: academic glossaries – an overview

The issue discussed in the previous section in turn raises the very practical question of how one should deal with the above-mentioned translation problems in practice: how can we run the risk of inadequate translations when people's careers depend on them? There are only a few dictionaries and manuals that are available for translations in the academic context, and in particular those that might be consulted specifically when translating CVs, module guides or other rather technical texts that contain various culture-specific terms. For instance, the DAAD (Deutscher Akademischer Auslandsdienst [German Academic Exchange Service]) has published some glossaries for this purpose. These volumes consist of glossaries with translations of terms that correspond to the various fields of higher education covered by the exchange[2]. However, in practice, such glossaries have ultimately proved inadequate because they attempt to translate terms, like those shown above, for which there are no institutional equivalents in other higher educational systems. A more explanatory

---

2   www.DAAD.de

approach has been provided by a number of glossary guides issued at European level. Here are some examples:

The Eurydice Network published a series of glossaries entitled *European Glossary on Education* with different volumes dedicated to the following topics:

- examinations, qualifications and titles (1999) (2004)
- educational institutions (2000) (2008)
- teaching staff (2002)
- management, monitoring and support staff (2003).[3]

The analysis of these books shows that they are helpful to understand terms in different academic systems, but when translating an academic CV, for instance, they may be of no help at all. A useful publication to understand the perspective of other systems in the French-German context is the manual *Studieren in Frankreich und Deutschland* [Studying in France and Germany] by Durand *et al.*

In the introduction to the book, the authors outline problems similar to those mentioned in the introduction to the present article:

> It is impossible to present the differences in the form of a list of translated terms, because equivalences cannot always be found at the level of individual terms. There are functional equivalents at a general level. Once the analysis becomes more differentiated, the differences become apparent. (Durand *et al* 14 f.)[4]

---

[3] http://www.eurydice.org
[4] "Es ist unmöglich, die Unterschiede in Form einer Liste übersetzter Begriffe zu präsentieren, denn die Äquivalenzen lassen sich nicht immer auf der Ebene von einzelnen Begriffen finden. Es gibt vor allem funktionale Äquivalente auf einem allgemeinen Niveau. Sobald die Analyse

Instead of a glossary, Durand et al. published a handbook, which explains the specific terms in detail, and a term such as *wissenschaftlicher Mitarbeiter* is explained in a paragraph that is more than one page in length. In this explanation, the authors describe the institutional settings necessary to understand their status (e.g. the fact that *wissenschaftliche Mitarbeiter* very often have limited contracts) in addition to the tasks and typical qualifications.

An organisation such as a university, or a field of science can be considered as a cultural field, as Reckwitz says. This field is "produced by a nexus of (non-discursive and discursive) practices" (258). These constitute social practices and contain, according to Reckwitz, "specific forms of knowledge". These forms of knowledge

> embrace ways of understanding, knowing how, ways of wanting and of feeling that are linked to each other within a practice. In a very elementary sense, in a practice the knowledge is a "particular way of understanding the world", which includes an understanding of objects (including abstract ones), of humans, of oneself. This way of understanding is largely implicit and largely historically-culturally specific – it is this form of interpretation that holds together already for the agent herself (the carrier of the practice) the single acts of her own behaviour, so that they form parts of a practice. This way of understanding is, of course, a collective, shared knowledge – but not in the sense of a mere sum of the content of single minds. (253 f)

As "social fields and institutionalized complexes ... are 'structured' by the routines of social practices" (255), we can conclude that social practices also structure the way careers are constructed, how contents are taught. Moreover, it should be considered that the *habitus*, a term introduced by Pierre Bourdieu in 1972 (164 f), i.e. a set of

---

> differenzierter wird, treten die Unterschiede deutlich hervor" (Durand et al. 14 f.). Hereafter, all the translations in the text are mine.

incorporated habits, skills and structures, is the generating principle of social practices (*La Distinction* 190). According to Bourdieu, *habitus* plays an important role in the academic field; he even dedicated a whole book to the *Homo Academicus*. Taking into account the fact that the roles and professions linked to German academia (students, researchers and teaching faculty) are based on a certain *habitus*, which incorporates the concept of *Wissenschaft*, it is crucial to understand the wider meaning of this term.

Going back to the two examples cited earlier, it can also be highlighted that comprehensive "cultural knowledge" (Bertelsmann-Stiftung 9) is very important when it comes to situations where people's qualifications are evaluated. In other words, the cultural background of specific terms is essential because the well-meant translations and the glossaries in the above-mentioned publications are often misleading. As indicated earlier, a key word which helps to understand the German academic context as a cultural field is *Wissenschaft*. Without understanding what *Wissenschaft* means, one cannot grasp the meaning of the terms *wissenschaftlicher Mitarbeiter* and *Kulturwissenschaften*. The same applies to all the other terms derived from or combined with the term *Wissenschaft*, like *wissenschaftliches Arbeiten* [working scientifically], the distinction between *Geisteswissenschaften* [humanities, see below] and *Naturwissenschaften* [science], and even the term *unwissenschaftlich*, which might be translated by "non-academic" or "non-scientific", a term that is often used in intercultural learning situations, where different academic practices collide.

3. Languaculture, "rich points" and "hotspots"

Before taking a closer look at the term *Wissenschaft* and its culture-rooted meaning, it is important to introduce a conceptual framework which can serve to show that language and culture are intertwined, and help to detect differences in meaning due to culture. In 1994, the anthropologist and linguist Michael Agar coined the term "languaculture" (*Language Shock* 60) to highlight the interconnectedness of language and culture, claiming that

> culture is in language, and language is loaded with culture. It often becomes evident during the process of translation that an expression cannot be explained or translated simply because it is connected to a number of concepts. (Sandel 1)

Thus, when linguistic and cultural frames differ at the same time "rich points" may emerge. According to Agar, a "rich point" is a "Whorfian cliff", a reference to the Sapir-Whorf hypothesis that says that an individual's thoughts and actions are determined by the language or languages which that individual speaks:

> No two languages are ever sufficiently similar to be considered as representing the same social reality. The worlds in which different societies live are distinct worlds, not merely the same world with different labels attached ... We see and hear and otherwise experience very largely as we do because the language habits of our community predispose certain choices of interpretation. (Sapir 69)

In other words, learning or trying to understand another language includes stumbling over "rich points". People realize that a culture is different from their own when they face something they do not understand. "Rich points" start from an outsider's expectations and signal a difference between "source languaculture" and "target languaculture".

Although Agar in 1994 relativizes the strong version of the Sapir-Whorf hypothesis (that is that all human thoughts and actions are bound by the restraints of language) by conceding that an understanding between members of different cultures with different languages is possible.

Drawing from his experience as an ethnology fieldworker, he compared the work with "rich points" to this approach and lists six situations in which "rich points" become apparent:

(1) incomprehension, the famous moment in (ethnographic) research when the researcher realizes that something does not make sense to him or her;
(2) contradiction, the moment when the researcher expects that something will happen but to his or her surprise the opposite occurs;
(3) departures from expectations, which describes the fact that the researcher thinks s/he has figured out a pattern and then something unexpected happens
(4) repetition, when the researcher cannot understand the reason for people doing the same thing repeatedly;
(5) repackaging old forms into something new (also in language)
(6) arousal, when an action arouses anger or anxiety in the researcher while the source group is not similarly aroused ("How to Ask" 687).

Agar suggests that once a rich point has been identified, researchers may explain it to others. He calls them "rich" to express the idea that the notion refers something, tasty, thick, and wealthy" (*Language Shock* 100). All in all, the existence of "rich points" comes from the fact that every expression implicitly refers to various elements that are taken for granted in a certain culture but do not correspond to the elements of another culture (cultural implicitness). Thus, "rich points" are moments in communication where misunderstanding, confusion, or even irritation happens.

Another characteristic of "rich points" is that they lead to "fundamental problems for translation work", so Agar ("How to a Ask" 687). He mentions various examples, "rich points" can be words or terms, but for instance also metaphors, ways of greeting or rituals. Later in his career, in 2006, Agar defined culture as "translation" in relation to his notion of "languaculture". He differentiated then between LC1 ("source languaculture") and LC2 ("target languaculture").

In addition to this, he stated that language users "draw on all kinds of things besides grammar and vocabulary – their biography, the nature of the situation they are in, history, politics" (2). According to Agar, "culture is a lens built for LC1 that focuses on problematic meanings in LC2 and the contexts that render them understandable" (2006). He considers culture as "an artificial construction built to enable translation between them and us, between source and target" (6). Norris and Tsedendamba have developed a model to illustrate Agar's notion of "languaculture" for a study, which aims at explaining Asian students' experiences in the Australian tertiary context.

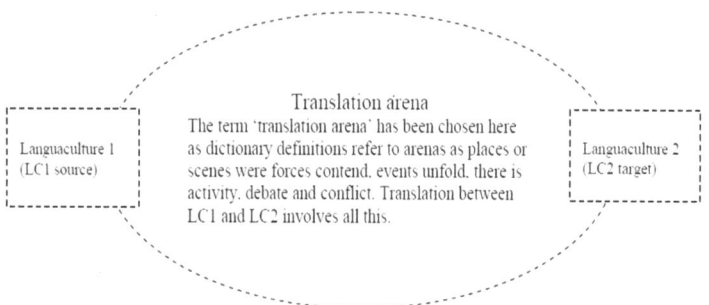

Fig. 3: Agar's languaculture model, developed by Norris & Tsedendamba (205)

In this instance, Agar's concept of "languaculture" as translation between source (LC1) and target culture (LC2) was expanded upon by the addition of the term "translation arena", extrapolated from Agar's original notion of translation because, according to the authors, it "enabled more clarity to be developed around the concept of translation" (205). They consider "translation arenas" as "places or scenes where forces contend, events unfold, and there is activity, debate and conflict" (205). The model can be adapted to the central premise of this article, which wants to show that the translation of academic terms, especially when they are "rich points ", open up an arena for struggling with translation possibilities.

According to Heringer, who revisited and complemented Agar's approach, "rich points" are "rich", because they help us to get deeper insights into another culture and also because they are an aid to reflecting our own expectations, thus reflecting our own communication process (162).

Heringer embedded "rich points" in a larger concept of "hotspots" (areas of communication problems due to culture that can be caused for instance by different use of humor or addresses of welcome, gestures etc.). He added the aspect of "hotwords", which describe single words that represent a hotspot, thus "hotwords are words that summarize a hotspot" (174).

According to Heringer, "hotwords" contain a considerable quantity of culture; they are culturally charged and "hot" because they deal with burning questions of content, because they can be controversial, because they hint at cultural foci, and because they are up-to-date. He argues that it is pointless looking them up in dictionaries to grasp their meaning because dictionaries are inadequate. To understand them one has to dive into the culture of the language: "Only in this way one can attain a true understanding, only in this way one can acquire the necessary communicative competence" (174).

"Hotwords" are condensed terms representing culturally rooted notions that ultimately are not translatable. "Hotwords" show the following characteristics:

- their meaning is difficult to specify
- difficult for strangers to understand
- natives have problems in explaining "hotwords"
- "hotwords" play an important role in the history and the actual discussion of a culture

- o to understand them, you have to know the historical and cultural background
- o sometimes "hotwords" are loaded with emotions, both positive or negative
- o sometimes "hotwords" function as symbols of cultural identity
- o learners face problems with the use of these words
- o you cannot get the meaning by translation.
- o the meaning constitutes a cultural frame. (175)

In this article, I focus on the notion of *Wissenschaft* because it is a key term which is very "rich" and dense (Agar), and "hot" (Heringer). When the characteristics mentioned above are applied to the term *Wissenschaft*, all of them can be validated, so I consider *Wissenschaft* to be a "hotword" par excellence. Thus, *Wissenschaft* is a central "hotword" of German academia, and a key to understand other terms within German academia. It is probable that a culture-rooted understanding of this term will lead to a new understanding of the German academic system.

4. *Wissenschaft* – the quintessential "hotword"

The British historian Denise Phillips states that the German word *Wissenschaft* is an untranslatable term. The German word *Wissenschaft* is a compound deriving from an Indo-European root *Wissen* (from * *weid- see*) and the Old German noun "*scaf (t)*", which means constitution, order, plan, rank (Kluge; Götze). Like many other German compounds with the ending *-schaft*, the word was created in the Middle Ages. Usually it is translated by using the term science (in English and French), however, this term is not an adequate translation of *Wissenschaft*. In French dictionaries, translations like *science, les lettres, la littérature, le savoir, la doctrine, l'érudition* are to be found (e.g. *Le petit Robert, Larousse*).

To stay with the example of the German-French context, I will now point at the wide range of translation difficulties or misunderstandings this causes. Used without a supplement, like in English, the French term "science" only means science de la nature [= natural science], while the German term *Wissenschaft* can be applied to all subjects and disciplines in science and in the humanities: for instance it can be used in mathematics and physics, but it can also be employed in combination with various disciplines to refer to the humanities and social sciences, as for example *Literaturwissenschaften* [science of literature], Sprachwissenschaften [science of language], or *Kulturwissenschaften* [science of culture]. Generally, everything than can studied at university and everything that is done at university is *Wissenschaft*. All social practices in German academia are based on this notion of *Wissenschaft* [which might best be translated in this sense with "academic work"].

Thus, in their self-conception, German scholars understand themselves as *Wissenschaftler/Innen*, and everything that is done at German universities – teaching, learning, and research in all disciplines – is seen as a contribution to *Wissenschaft*. This goes back to the *Bildungsideal* [educational ideal] expressed by Wilhelm von Humboldt, who, in the early 19th century, promoted the ideas of *Bildung durch Wissenschaft* [education through *Wissenschaft*] and the *Einheit von Forschung und Lehre* [unity of research and teaching] (256 f.).

One core part of this German understanding of academia is based on the specific historical development of German academia, which started in the 18th century. Although originally universities were European institutions, national models were developed in the course of the early modern age due to political and religious segmentation, and these were consolidated during the 19th century. From this initial segmentation, national models eventually emerged with their own specific academic practices. In this context, Germany had a special role in generating the first model of a modern research university. This development is attributed to Wilhelm von Humboldt, who laid the groundwork for Prussian educational reform in the early 19th century, introducing a clear division between school instruction and academic teaching.

In the first case, i.e. school education, according to Humboldt, we are dealing with "finished and agreed knowledge"; the second case is *Wissenschaft*, which is described as "something not yet completely found and never completely found" (256 f.). The latter requires completely different forms of teaching and learning, which in the German understanding is a part of *Wissenschaft*. Therefore, what students and professors should do from the very first day at university is summarized as being *wissenschaftliches Arbeiten* [a specific form of academic work].

In this sense, *Wissenschaft* represents everything that refers to university studies, both in science and in the humanities, and there is no conceptual notion of difference between science and humanities or scientists and scholars:

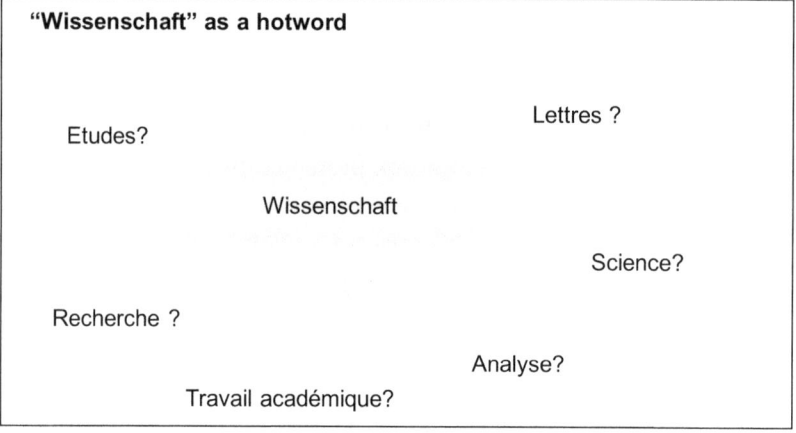

Fig. 4 – Title: *Wissenschaft* as a "hotword" – How to translate the "hotword" *Wissenschaft* into French?

If university lecturers, as is the case in France, are seen as being mediators of knowledge, then it is almost inevitable that there should be a pronounced hierarchy between those who have the knowledge and those to whom the knowledge is to be imparted. In Germany, on the other hand, both students and professors are supposed to do *Wissenschaft* at university. One-way knowledge transfer is traditionally not the primary task of the German university system (and especially not in the humanities), and learning, teaching and assignment methods that focus on mere knowledge transmission and reproduction are criticized as being *unwissenschaftlich* [not academic] or *verschult*, another term which is difficult to translate, it means, rather pejoratively, "like in school" (Hiller, Hippler 2014).

This is one of the main reasons why Germans had major doubts and long discussions with regard to the European Union's Bologna Reform of the higher education system: in their view it put the German ideal of *Wissenschaft* in danger. Empirical research shows many examples of misunderstanding and mutual frustration due to this very specific understanding of academic learning. Studying in Germany is particularly complex for international students because of the very specific German academic system, predominantly in the humanities: because for students in Germany *Wissenschaft* ideally begins at the start of their university career and is not reserved for advanced students alone (Schumann *et al*). The disciplines that in Germany are called philological disciplines are referred to in France as *littéraires*, and instead of speaking of *Wissenschaften*, the French use the *term études*, and *science* is used for the "hard sciences", the *sciences de la nature*.

Thus, we could conclude that implicitly only natural sciences are understood as scientific disciplines. In German, however, all disciplines are considered to be a part of science and very often described with the hyphenated attribute *-wissenschaften*. In France, this distinction begins at the level of the *lycée* [high school], where students determine whether they will pursue a literary or a scientific itinerary.

5. The challenge of translating *Kulturwissenschaften*

The problems with understanding and translating the term *Wissenschaft* continue with all the composites and derivations of this word.

To make this explicit, the difficulties of translating *Kulturwissenschaften* will be discussed at length in what follows. By looking at the historical background, we see that in Germany, at the end of the 19th century, the humanities [*Geisteswissenschaften*] were opposed to the natural sciences. *Geisteswissenschaften* [*sciences de l'esprit* in French, and sciences of the mind/spirit in English] were the disciplines that deal with issues produced by the human *esprit* ["mind" or "spirit"], thus languages, art, etc. Durand *et al* argue that this juxtaposition coincides in part with the French dichotomy of *lettres* and *sciences* [humanities and science] (56-57). This already gives us important clues as to the problem of translating a term like *Kulturwissenschaften* (which is not the same as cultural studies in English) into English or French.

Cultural studies were created in England in the 1950s by scholars from working-class backgrounds (i.e. Richard Hoggart; Raymond Williams, Stuart Hall) to research the distance between canonical cultural knowledge and their own backgrounds, the impact of mass communications towards power and authority. Thus, cultural studies in the Anglosphere are closely linked to questions of politics and society concerning issues of injustice and power relations, whereas in Germany, the field of cultural studies includes interdisciplinary programmes that focus on the challenges of globalisation and technology (Böhme). But even among German scholars the term can be understood in different fashions. Hence, it is important to mention that there can even be a conceptual difference between the use of the singular form *Kulturwissenschaft* and the use of the plural form *Kulturwissenschaften*, as Böhme stated (1). According to him, the former term is often used as a denomination for the "new" discipline, while the latter is rather used as synonym for the ensemble of the disciplines belonging to the *Geisteswissenschaften*.

At the European University Viadrina, the translation problem concerning the *Kulturwissenschaften-Programme* was solved by using the term "Social and Cultural Sciences". The university website describes the program in the following way:

The study of social and cultural sciences is characterized by its interconnection of research and instruction, an innovative interdisciplinary course of study, and an international focus. With our three bachelor programs "Social and Cultural Sciences", ... we offer innovative and interdisciplinary study courses! They are combined with a strong focus on language learning.

Without this description it might be difficult to understand what students learn in this programme, and a translation like "cultural studies" is misleading.

To remain with the German-French example, and to come to a better understanding of the difficulty encountered when translating *Kulturwissenschaften* into French, we must take into account the differentiation between the humanities and the social sciences in France and in Germany. The emergence of new subjects at the interface of humanities and sciences has changed this traditional division in different ways. In Germany, the social sciences became separated from the humanities very early, in the late 19th century, and this happened much more radically than in France, as a result this has led to a tripartite division of subjects into humanities, social sciences and natural sciences.

In France, the distinction that occurred much later between *lettres* [language and literature as well as philosophy] and *sciences humaines* or *sciences sociales*, which arose in the 1970s, does not question the old dichotomy in a radical way. Durand *et al* explain that even the terms *sciences humaines* and *sciences sociales* are sometimes used synonymously (57).

In Germany, the term *Geisteswissenschaften* [humanities] as it is used describes a spectrum of languages and literature, history and philosophy that is distinct from the social sciences. And there is no equivalent to this in French or in English. In French, the term is usually translated with *lettres et sciences humaines*. Thus, institutionally and methodologically, the social sciences are considered to be different from the humanities.

However, in the German university landscape recently a field of studies and research has emerged that questions this distinction, this field of study has been called *Kulturwissenschaften*. The *Kulturwissenschaften* are interdisciplinary forms of study *per se* and are considered to be part of both the *Geisteswissenschaften* and also part of the social sciences, wanting to overcome the traditional dichotomy. In France, there is no equivalent so far.

In other words, the cultural sciences include approaches and subjects which, within the French system, were attributed on the one hand to *lettres, sciences sociales* and *sciences humaines*, an on the other to *sciences politiques*. But how should this be translated? Even when we agree on translations such as *études culturelles*, what exactly this means will not be obvious for a native speaker when s/he is not familiar with the culture into which/from which the term is translated. If we take the English translation as a model, we can translate the term into French as *Etudes culturelles et Sciences sociales*. But would this make sense to a French academic?

And the present paper has ignored the differences between the German and the French understanding of the terms *Kultur* [culture], which could be the topic of another chapter (in short: both French and English languages distinguish much more consequently between culture and civilisation; while the German term *Kultur* includes both aspects. Just to mention one example: Samuel E. Huntington's book title *The Clash of Civilisations*, was translated into French as *Le choc des civilisations* [The Shock of Civilisations] and into German as *Kampf der Kulturen* [The Struggle of Cultures].

Conclusion

By exploring the aforementioned examples, I have discussed the difficulties involved in translating specific academic terms and the limitations of existing resources (dictionaries and glossaries). I concentrated on one term that ultimately belongs to the core of the academic world, namely the German term *Wissenschaft*. With this, I introduced a linguistic concept that takes culture into account: i.e.

the concept of "languaculture" with "rich points" and their derivative "hotwords". This term offers a framework that demonstrates that within every language there exists a wide range of expressions which cannot be translated literally because they unite within their discipline culturally-rooted notions, and the associations and historical background to these disciplines make access to them difficult for people from other cultures.

With the example of the "hotword" *Wissenschaft* and the composite term *Kulturwissenschaften*, I have also demonstrated that university terminology is often deeply culturally specific and that translation can offer no more than an approximation. Neither dictionaries nor specific academic glossaries can help to solve the terminological problem. Ideally, terms should be explained in extended footnotes.

This terminological crux is a big challenge in academia, because the number of academic documents that need to be translated by experts and laymen is growing due to the increase in academic mobility. Students, faculty and staff must not only translate academic contents and thoughts into their own language, but must also study regulations, administrative documents and diplomas which contain expressions specific to each university system. A considerable number of applicants for jobs or study programs must transfer specific expressions into English, French or other target languages, and others have to evaluate their qualifications. The result is that a large number of ambiguous translations have been institutionalized, and that these translations simulate correspondences, which do not exist, and indeed they may lead to serious intercultural misunderstandings. Intercultural training in higher education can serve to make people aware of these kinds of differences and can go some way to providing cultural knowledge about the differences in academic systems and language use.

Works cited

Agar, Michael. *Language Shock: Understanding the Culture of Conversation.* William Morrow and Company, 1994.

Agar, Michael. "How to Ask for a Study in *Qualitatisch*". *Qualitative Health Research*, vol. 9, no. 5, 1999, pp. 684-697.

Böhme, Hartmut. *Kulturwissenschaft. Reallexikon der deutschen Literaturwissenschaft*, vol. II. de Gruyter, 2000, pp. 356-359.

Bourdieu, Pierre. *Esquisse d'une théorie de la pratique précédée de Trois études d'ethnologie Kabyle.* Droz, 1972.

Bourdieu, Pierre. *La Distinction. Critique sociale du jugement.* Éditions de Minuit, 1979.

Bourdieu, Pierre. *Homo academicus.* Éditions de Minuit. 1984.

Bourdieu, Pierre. *Esquisse d'une théorie de la pratique précédée de Trois études d'ethnologie Kabyle.* Droz, 1972.

Durand, Béatrice and Neubert, Stefanie et al. *Étudier en France et en Allemagne. Approche comparée des cultures universitaires.* Presses Universitaires du Septentrion, 2007.

Durand, Béatrice et al. *Studieren in Frankreich und Deutschland. Akademische Lehr- und Lernkulturen im Vergleich.* Avinus, 2006.

Kluge, Friedrich and Götze, Alfred (eds.). *Etymologisches Wörterbuch der deutschen Sprache.* 20. De Gruyter, 1975.

Heringer, Hans-Jürgen. *Interkulturelle Kommunikation.* UTB, 2004.

Hiller, Gundula Gwenn. "Kulturelle und sprachliche Diversität in der Hochschule – am Beispiel von E-Mail-Kommunikation", *Interkulturalität und kulturelle Diversität: Münchner Beiträge zur interkulturellen Kommunikation*, edited by Alois Moosmüller and Jana Möller-Kiero. J. Waxmann, 2014, pp. 233-258.

Hiller, Gundula Gwenn; Hippler, Thomas. "*Studieren* versus *étudier* – aktuelle und historische Perspektiven auf das deutsche und französische Hochschulsystem". *Lendemains. Etudes comparées sur la France*, vol. 39, 2014, pp. 36-55.

Le Petit Robert. *Dictionnaire alphabétique et analogique de la langue française, nouvelle édition Millésime*. Dictionnaires Le Robert, 2011.

Norris, Lindy; Tsedendamba, Nara. "Applying Agar's Concept of 'Languaculture' to Explain Asian Students' Experiences in the Australian Tertiary Context". *English Language Teaching*, vol. 8, No.1, 2015, pp. 205-217, www.researchgate.net /publication/271387516_Applying_Agar%27s_Concept_of_ %27Languaculture%27_to_Explain_Asian_Students%27_Exp eriences_in_the_Australian_Tertiary_Contex. Accessed 20 September 2018.

Phillips, Denise. "Francis Bacon and the Germans: Stories from when 'science' meant 'Wissenschaft'". *History of Science*, vol. 53, no. 4, 2015.

Petit Larousse illustré. Larousse/Bordas, 1999.

Reckwitz, Andreas, "Toward a Theory of Social Practices. A development in culturalist theorizing". *European Journal of Social Theory*, vol. 5, no. 2, 2002, pp. 245-265.

Sandel, Todd L. "Rich Points". *The international encyclopedia of language and social interaction*. Wiley online library, 2015, www.onlinelibrary.wiley.com/doi/10.1002/978111861146 3.wbielsi167. Accessed 1 October 2018.

Sapir, Edward. *Culture, language and personality*. California University Press, 1958.

Schumann, Adelheid. *Interkulturelle Kommunikation in der Hochschule: zur Integration internationaler Studierender und Förderung interkultureller Kompetenz*. transcript Verlag, 2018.

Teichler, Ulrich. *Die Internationalisierung der Hochschulen. Neue Herausforderungen und Strategien*. Campus Verlag, 2007.

von Humboldt, Wilhelm. "Über die innere und äußere Organisation der höheren wissenschaftlichen Anstalten in Berlin", *Werke in fünf Bänden*, vol. IV, *Schriften zur Politik und zum Bildungswesen*, edited by Andreas Flitner and Klaus Giel, Wissenschaftliche Buchgesellschaft, 1964, pp. 256-57.

Webography:

Bertelsmann Stiftung and Fondazione Cariplo, "Intercultural competence – The key competence in the 21st century, Milano 2008", www.ngobg.info/bg/documents/49/726bertelsmannintercuturalcompetences.pdf. Accessed 15 September 2018.

Euridyce, the information network on education in Europe, European glossary on education, Volumes 1-4, European Commisssion, www. publications.europa.eu/en/search-res ults? p_p_id=portal2012searchExecutor_WAR_portal2012portlet_ INSTANCE_q8EzsBteHybf&p_p_lifecycle=1&p_p_state=norm al&queryText=European+glossary+on+education&facet.coll ection=EUPub&language=en&startRow=1&resultsPerPage= 10&SEARCH_TYPE=SIMPLE. Accessed 1 October 2018.

European University Viadrina, Website, www.study.europa-uni.de/ en/kuwi/index.html. Accessed 1 October 2018.

Heiß, Hans-Ulrich, Slides of the keynote presentation "Internationale Kompatibilität von MINT-Studienprogrammen", at the conference "Internationalisation of the curricula" at Technische Universität Berlin, ICM, documentation see www.tu-berlin.de. Accessed 1 October 2018.

Hsu, Hua. "Stuart Hall and the Rise of Cultural Studies". *The New Yorker*. 17th July 2017. www.newyorker.com/books/page-turner/stuart-hall-and-the-rise-of-cultural-studies. Accessed 1 October 2018.

Blind Rice for Lunch?
Cultural Errors and Their Impact on Tourism

Ana-Isabel Foulquié-Rubio, Paula Cifuentes-Férez

Introduction

Spain is one of the most attractive tourist destinations in Europe because of its genuine natural, artistic and cultural heritage, its gastronomy, traditions, and festivals. Moreover, the fact that Spain is located in a temperate zone and thus, has mild weather, allows tourists and visitors to enjoy the country all year round. The Region of Murcia, located in the Southeast, is among the preferred destinations for those tourists looking for beaches, sun and gastronomy. Its coastline is known as the Costa Cálida. The name comes from its nice temperatures and mild weather, throughout the year, with an average temperature of 18ºC and more than 3000 hours of sunshine (*Murcia Turística*). The weather and the sunshine attract not just tourists who come to visit the different attractions and the beaches, but also retired people who find in Murcia the perfect place to live all year round in this region.

The statistics are clear: 82.000.000 million tourists visited Spain in 2017. As shown in the report by *Murcia Turística*, 42.1% of the tourists travelling to the region of Murcia come from the United Kingdom, 15.4 % from France, 10 % from Norway, Sweden and Denmark, 5.8 % from Germany, 5.6% from Ireland, which undoubtedly suggests that tourist texts should be available for tourists, at least in English and French.

Tourists are looking for a positive experience, and when people do not speak Spanish, the positive experience also includes finding the different services in their own language. Therefore, translation services are a critical factor when trying to attract and maintain the area as a destination for tourists from all around the world. There are different quality indicators for tourism, and correct translation aimed at attracting tourism should be one of them. However, this is not always taken into account and translations are published without thinking about the impact they can have on the tourism sector.

This chapter focuses on cultural errors (i.e. errors due to cultural differences between the source and the target cultures) in the translation of Spanish tourist texts, which were created and published for the promotion of the region of Murcia as a tourist destination. With that purpose in mind, we shall deal mainly with examples taken from the official webpage for tourism in the region of Murcia, information brochures, and menus from typical Spanish restaurants.

1. Tourism and its texts

1.1 Tourist texts: definition, main features, and genres

A tourist text could be defined as "any text published by a public or private organisation of any kind intended a) to give information to any kind of visitor or b) to advertise a destination ... and encourage visitors to go there" (Kelly 35). According to Dorothy Kelly, this definition covers a wide range of text types

> from brochures sent abroad to promote a particular destination through brochures available at the destination itself, tourist guides available in the tourist's home country, to menus, information brochures published by authorities responsible for monuments and other places of interest as written guides to them, conference programmes and other conference material, or police warnings regarding dos and don'ts for visitors. (37)

In this way, the topics dealt with in tourist texts are extensive and can include highly specialised areas such as history, architecture, gastronomy, customs, music, among many others.

Now that we have presented the working definition of a tourist text, we shall briefly explain the main features of the language of tourism:

(1) **Linguistic aspects:** these include terminology, syntax and style of the author. The texts are generally brief and concise and aimed at catching the reader's attention (Durán Muñoz, "Analysing Common Mistakes" 4). Creative language is frequently found in these texts with a widespread use of positive adjectivisation, including comparatives and superlatives, and other rhetorical resources, e.g. metaphors, hyperbole, metonymies, etc. Cultural-specific terms are also found in these texts; these terms are semantically very specific and can be employed with a connotative meaning. Another feature is the use of foreign words, especially Anglicisms, either as loanwords such as "charter", "trekking", "overbooking" or *calques* such as *bajo coste* for "low cost" (Durán Muñoz, "Aspectos pragmático-lingüísticos" 55).

(2) **Pragmatic aspects:** Cabré Castellví states that the topic, the users and the communicative scenario are to be taken into account. As far as the topic is concerned, tourist texts are studded with specialised terms from the tourist sector and other disciplines, e.g. history, sports, gastronomy, arts (148-151). Tourist texts are written by professionals, whose audience is also made up of professionals, e.g. international fairs, travel agencies; secondly the topic concerns communication between professionals and non-professionals, e.g. brochures, leaflets, and, thirdly, communication between non-professionals, e.g. travel blogs.

(3) **Functional aspects:** tourist texts serve different functions. The two major functions are referential and appellative, but other functions may be found as well, e.g. the poetic function, the

emotive function (Durán Muñoz, "Aspectos pragmático-lingüísticos" 60).
(4) **Formal aspects:** this concerns the image and the visual aspects of the text. Tourist texts abound with pictures (blue skies, sunny beaches, etc.), tables, charts and drawings. They use different fonts, font sizes and font colours with the sole aim of attracting the reader (Durán Muñoz, "Analysing Common Mistakes" 6).

These features are to be found in most types of tourist texts. Despite the difficulties of providing a clear-cut taxonomy of tourist texts, Calvi ("Los géneros discursivos") distinguishes three main categories:

(1) texts centred on the theoretical analysis of tourism and its features, which can be approached from different perspectives (economy, anthropology, etc.)
(2) texts centred on the management of the tourist sector, such as invoices, catalogues, tickets
(3) texts whose aim is to promote a tourist destination. (18-19)

Kelly (35) also argues that tourist texts can be either promotional (Calvi's third category) or non-promotional (Calvi's first and second categories). Promotional texts aim at selling products and services for one specific destination. Within this category, tourist leaflets and brochures about cities, museums, etc.; catalogues from hotels, travel agencies; reports published in magazines; radio and TV programmes; advertisements on different media; webpages, etc. are to be found. Thanks to the easy accessibility offered by the Internet over the last two decades, tourist texts have evolved and new forms of communication have emerged, such as travel blogs or discussion forums, where users give their opinions and recommendations (Calvi, "Guía de viaje y turismo 2.0"), and which have a mainly informative function.

1.2 Problems, difficulties and recurring errors in tourist translation

High quality translations play a crucial role in the promotion of tourist destinations since both an accurate linguistic translation and a competent cultural transfer one from one language into another is necessary for tourists and visitors to have an enriching experience. In this sense, translation must be considered as a tool for mediating between different cultures; thus it is vital for the translator to take the cultural aspects (i.e. language, values, norms, customs) of tourist texts into account when translating into other languages.

Despite the importance of translation in the tourist sector, as we shall see below, it is quite common to find tourist texts which show a variety of errors, including cultural errors. This seems to come about because of the lack of professionalization in this sector, as the people who translate tourist texts into other languages are, for the most part, not qualified translators (González Pastor, "Análisis descriptivo de la traducción de culturemas" 153; Durán Muñoz, "Analysing Common Mistakes" 111; Soto Almela, "La traducción de términos culturales" 25, 51).

Scholars have identified a number of translation problems and difficulties when it comes to the translation of tourist texts. In very general terms, translation problems are those that translators face irrespective of their expertise, whereas translation difficulties are usually easily overcome when translators have acquired the skills and knowledge to deal with them (Nord, *Text Analysis* 151; Durán Muñoz, "Caracterización de la traducción turística" 106). According to Durán Muñoz, the main problems arising from the translation of tourist texts are:

(a) a lack of information about the function and the audience of the translated text.
(b) ambiguous sentences which, if rendered inappropriately, will lead to information loss in the translated text.
(c) "culturemes", that is, culture-specific terms of a complex semantic and pragmatic nature.

(d) the poetic use of language.
(e) poorly written texts in the original language. (106-109)

With regard to translation difficulties, this article concentrates on those mentioned by Durán Muñoz:

(a) proper names of renowned people, museums, institutions and toponyms (i.e. proper names of towns, cities, etc.)
(b) inverse translations, which occur when translators translate from their mother tongues into their second or third languages, producing texts which may sound unnatural to potential visitors
(c) neologisms, which may sound exotic for the tourist
(d) documentary sources. (109-111)

In addition to these issues, Kelly also notes that another problem is the great variety of specialised terms from areas such as history, architecture, customs, gastronomy, etc. (35).

Besides analysing the main problems and difficulties of tourist texts, scholars working in this field have also examined the main errors that are to be found in them. By way of illustration, Kelly (23-48) points out that in the case of Spanish into English translation of tourist texts, the most common translation errors[1] are due to

(a) a use of figurative language abounding with adjectives, e.g. "estás condenado de por vida a llevar contigo nuestra ciudad" → "you are doomed to take our town with you for live"[2]
(b) the loss of information in the target text when the Spanish culture-specific term or cultureme has been kept without

---

[1] Two types of errors may be found in target texts: translation errors and linguistic errors, which result from the lack of proficiency in the foreign language of the target text: "translation errors" and "linguistic errors".
[2] The examples are also taken from Kelly (38-40).

any further explanation, e.g. Almazara [a traditional place where olives are crushed by round stones so olive oil is obtained] → "Almazara"

(c) no explication in the target text of information which is implicit or known by the audience of the original text, e.g. interchangeable use of "Lorca" and "Federico" to refer to Federico García Lorca

(d) no translation of units of measurement

(e) information overload in the target text, e.g. including a list of traditional dances or typical dishes without further indication of what they are

(f) no information which is culturally relevant in the target texts.

Now that we have discussed the main characteristics of tourist texts, the problems and difficulties of tourist translation as well as the main translation and linguistic errors found in tourist texts, we will examine a number of examples of cultural errors in the Spanish into English/French translation of three types of texts: an official webpage, brochures, and menus[3] from the Region of Murcia.

2. Cultural errors in the Spanish into English/French translation of Spanish tourists texts

Cultural knowledge and cultural differences demand a concerted effort on the part of translators, as they play a crucial role in understanding a tourist text. Therefore, cultural terms have attracted the attention of many scholars over the years, trying to define what they mean when referring to these cultural elements. For example, Baker sees cultural entities as "culture-specific concepts" (18), Robinson

---

[3] As noted by Kelly, the translation of menus are "one of the most challenging translation tasks, given, on the one hand, the enormous cultural differences which exist with regard to eating habits, taboos and so on, and on the other, the tremendous constraints (space) on just how much explanation can be included" (37).

uses the term "realia" (70), while Newmark employs the concept of "cultural words" (173). Nord, on the contrary, coins the term "cultureme" in order to refer to culture specific elements[4]:

> A cultureme is a social phenomenon of a culture X that is regarded as relevant by members of this culture and, when compared with a corresponding social phenomenon in a culture Y, is found to be specific to culture X. (34)

As stated by Nord, "culturemes" do not need any kind of explanation for readers of the original text, but they might require explanations for readers of the translated text. Furthermore, this difficulty is increased in tourist texts, as on many occasions, "culturemes" are not translated with a specific culture or public in mind, but in the framework of a *lingua franca* to be understood by tourists from many different backgrounds.

There are different translation techniques used to translate "culturemes": literal translation, amplification, addition, reduction/implicitation, transposition, omission, borrowing and generalization (Soto Almela, Durán Muñoz, De la Cruz Trainor). Translators should choose the right technique in order to transfer accurately the "cultureme" into a different context.

As we have seen, the translation of "culturemes" can be done by means of a variety of approaches. The main point in the translation of these terms is to provide the reader of the translation with the same information as would be contained in the original term. Soto Almela ("Los términos culturales") analysed different approaches and carried out a survey among the potential English readers of the translated brochures to find out what their response might be to the different ways of translating "culturemes". Soto Almela provided the potential readers of the translated "culturemes" (15 units) with four different translations, using four techniques:

---

[4] In this chapter, the authors have decided to use the term used by Nord in *Translating as a Purposeful Activity*.

amplification, description, generalization and borrowing, and he asked them for their preferred translation. The results of this survey might be used by translators as a guide when translating the type of "culturemes" presented by the author.

When one looks at the different texts analysed, "culturemes" usually refer to specific places, such as *barraca*, gastronomy terms such as *Gazpachos Jumillanos*, or specific festivities such as *Bando de la Huerta*. The examples shown here belong mainly to two of the types of texts defined in the previous section: brochures (either included as part of websites or printed in paper) and restaurant menus. Both types of texts are aimed at attracting tourists to visit the places or to try the dishes advertised by them. As stated by González Pastor ("Como se traducen" 68), due to the lack of equivalents, translating "culturemes" within the field of gastronomy poses many problems for translators.

2.1 Brochures and information in webpages

There are a great number of webpages and brochures aimed at promoting the different aspects of cities and regions. The Region of Murcia is no exception, and due to the fact that it is a region that attracts a large number of tourists from abroad, most information (brochures, webpages and other information for visitors) is translated, primarily into English before offering a translation in other languages.

In this section, and due to constraints of space in this chapter, we have examined just one of the main official websites. The webpage *Murcia Touristica* is the official webpage of the Department of Tourism of the region of Murcia and they produce a high number of texts promoting this region of Murcia. Most of the information of this website is translated into English, French and German, and some parts are also translated into Swedish, Russian and Czech. It provides information about every aspect of life in the region: suggesting what to see, what to do, how to plan your visit ahead, etc. It has to be said that the quality of the translations into English is very good.

As with many other types of tourism texts, there is a very high number of "culturemes", not only related to gastronomy, but to architecture, customs, names of places, etc. In this chapter, some errors in the translation of "culturemes" in the field of gastronomy found on the website will be analysed. In these "culturemes", the term is illustrated with a picture of the "cultureme", this helps the translator to convey meaning and it is followed by description also in the Spanish webpage. The reason for this is that this website is not just aimed at visitors from abroad, but also at visitors from other parts of Spain. As it will be shown below, the "culturemes" are translated using the borrowing technique, i.e. keeping the term in Spanish, and the translation of the description included in the webpage is done using different techniques. However, and as it is shown below, this technique does not work for "culturemes" included in the explanation as they do not convey any meaning to the target reader.

In the case of a typical coffee called *Asiático*, the option chosen here, is keeping the name of the coffee in Spanish, using the borrowing technique. However, the problem arises within the explanation. This coffee is served in a special and characteristic glass called *copa de Asiático*. This poses a difficulty to translators, as there is no equivalent term in the target languages. In this example, the translator into French uses the generalization technique and eliminates the term in Spanish "on le sert dans un verre très caractéristique et original" [it is served in a very original and characteristic glass]. From our point of view, this solves the problem, and this is helped by the fact that there is a picture of this glass. However, when translating this "cultureme" into English, *Asiático* is considered as an adjective for "Asian" and it is translated as such "it is served in a unique glass: the Asian Cup". This could be considered as a cultural error, as there is no such thing as an "Asian Cup" in the target culture and therefore it does not transmit any information to the target reader.

In the case of the description of another typical sweet called *Bienmesabe*, which is kept in all the languages as *Bienmesabe* using the borrowing technique, the cultural error is found this time in the translation into French of one of the terms included in the description of the dessert. The term in Spanish is described as:

"Bizcocho, almíbar, cabello de ángel y almendra son los ingredientes principales de este dulce, mezcla del saber árabe, romano y cristiano". The term *cabello de ángel* in Spanish is transferred into French using the borrowing technique without further explanation. The problem is that "cabello de ángel" does not convey any meaning in French and therefore, the borrowing technique on its own does not work. The translation of the description into French is: "Ses ingrédients principales sont : du gâteau, du sirop, du cabello de ángel[5] et des amandes" [The main ingredients here are: sponge, syrup, cabello de ángel and almonds]. The translation into English reads as follows: "A mixture of Arab, Roman and Christian knowledge, sponge, syrup, sweet pumpkin filling and almond are among the main ingredients of this dish". In this same example, when translating into English, the technique used here is explanation, "sweet pumpkin filling". Here, the translation conveys the meaning of the Spanish "cultureme".

For the description of a drink typical of this region, *Mantelina,* again the name has been kept in English and French, as there is no equivalent in other languages for this "cultureme". The problem appears when translating the ingredients specified in the description of the drink. Here, the term *anís seco* is transferred as *anís seco* in French. This borrowing technique does not render the meaning, as there is an equivalent in French *liqueur d'anis* and that could have been used in this case. In the English translation, there is an attempt to translate the "cultureme", but there is an error, as the term used is "star anise" which refers to a different thing, which is

> "the small brown star-shaped pungent fruit of a Chinese and Vietnamese tree (*Illicium verum*) that has a flavour

---

[5] The published text uses italics for the term "cabello de ángel" in French www.murciaturistica.com.

similar to but stronger than anise and is dried and used whole or ground as a spice especially in Chinese cooking"[6].

Again, there is an equivalent in the target language *anisette*, a sweet liqueur that would convey the meaning without having to resort to the borrowing technique or other type of explanation. Thus, and given there is an equivalent in the target culture, this "cultureme" should not have posed any problems for translators.

As we have seen in this short analysis, the translation of "culturemes" is not easy, and it poses many problems to translators. Official websites seem to start paying more attention to the way the information is translated into other languages and being more aware of the impact that translated texts may have on tourism. Good translations have an influence on how tourists experience gastronomy and bad translations may lead to tourists not being able to taste some products, as their description does not attract them or does not mean anything to them.

2.2 Menus from different restaurants in the region of Murcia

Gastronomy plays a central role in the culture and in the attraction of tourism. Therefore, in this section we will look at how different restaurants translate their typical dishes. One may think that restaurant owners should be attentive to how their dishes are presented in other languages as the function of this type of text is both persuasive and informative: persuasive, as it should attract readers' attention so they will order such dishes, and informative as it should inform readers about what each dish includes. However, when reading most menus in other languages different from the target language, we can argue that, in most cases, they do not fulfill either function.

Restaurant menus are usually full of translation errors of many different types, but the translation of "culturemes" here presents a difficulty that sometimes is not only due to the inability of

---

[6] Definition according to the Merrian Webster Dictionary. https://www.merriam -webster.com/dictionary/star%20anise

the translator to apply the right technique, but also to the limits imposed by the layout of the text.

After analysing the menus of approximately 25 restaurants[7] scattered throughout the whole region of Murcia, many errors were found. We shall concentrate on cultural errors only, but each and every error in the translated text may have a negative impact on the reader, and as a result the reader may not order a certain dish, either because it may appear unattractive or s/he may not understand what the dish includes.

As stated before, "culturemes" within the field of gastronomy are some of the most difficult culture-specific terms to translate as gastronomy differs a lot from one culture to another. Within this group of "culturemes", the difficulty increases when they are not only related to a dish, but to a local and specific preparation, known mostly only to locals. In the menus, the following "culturemes" appear: *a la Jumillana* translated as "to the Jumillana" and *A la Murciana*, which is translated as "to the Murcian". Both published translations do not convey any meaning to the English reader. For both terms, the technique of explanation would work better for the target reader. Thus, *a la Jumill*ana could be explained as "fried with garlic and potatoes" and *a la Murciana* as "baked in a vegetable and wine sauce". Therefore, if terms such as *a la Jumillana* or *a la Murciana* are not explained, this can lead to tourists not feeling as asking for these dishes, as translations such as "to the Murcia" does not mean anything at all in English.

In this same vein, tourists may also encounter problems when trying to understand the different types of sauces used in typical dishes, not only in the region of Murcia, but also in Spain. From our point of view, the translation of these "explanations" included in

---

[7] Examples are taken from two Final Year Projects supervised by one of the authors of this chapter. The Final Year Projects analysed many different aspects of translating menus, but due to the emphasis on culture in the present volume, we are concentrating only on cultural errors. The sample was formed of 25 restaurant menus collected from different parts of the Region of Murcia.

the names of the dishes requires an additional explanation when translating into another language. In the menus analysed, the most widely used techniques are either *calques* or literal translation. We have included them here because the result of these techniques in these cases is that there is a cultural error, because the translation of such "culturemes" does not fulfill the function of the "cultureme" in the original language. In this category, we would include examples such as:

- *Al ajillo* translated with "with garlic" or "garlic food", instead of "in garlic sauce" that would explain better the cooking way.
- *Al ajo pescador* translated with "to Garlic Fisherman". This option, apart from not having any meaning, does not explain the customer how the food is cooked.
- *Al Jerez* translated by "with Jerez". Jerez is a town in Spain but it is also a type of wine. The published translation does not convey any meaning and it would be clearer to the reader if this would use the equivalent in English: sherry, as in "Cooked in sherry wine".
- *Al Pil-pil* appears translated as "Pil-pil sauce". In this case, the borrowing technique does not work because it needs to be explained, as it may happens in most cases in gastronomy translation In this case, a combination of two techniques would render the meaning in a better way, such as "*al Pil-pil* (in garlic and olive oil sauce)".
- *Al ajo cabañil* is translated just as "[rabbit] with garlic". In this case, an explanation would render the meaning, such has "cooked in olive oil and garlic sauce".

Another example of cultural error would be translating *ahumados* by *taramasalata* when the term refers to "smoked fish". There is another very common term used in gastronomy in Spain and this is the term in Spanish *ali-oli*. It was translated by different terms "*alioli*", "garlic sauce" and *"alio oli"*. There are different techniques for translating this term:

- using the borrowing technique: *aioli*
- using the description technique: garlic mayonnaise
- a combination of two techniques: borrowing and amplification: *Aioli* (garlic mayonnaise).

The region of Murcia is located on the Mediterranean Coast and gastronomy in this region includes a wide variety of dishes using rice as their basic ingredient. This again poses a problem for translators, as the name of the dishes do not always reflect their composition and the names given are usually based on tradition and are common knowledge for local people. These are some examples of cultural errors when translating dishes based on rice:

- *Arroz caldero / Arroz en caldero* is translated as "Caldero rice" and "Mediterranean rice and fish hotpot". Both options could be considered as errors as they do not convey the meaning of the dish. In this case, probably a borrowing and an explanation would have worked better, such as "Arroz al caldero (traditional Murcian seafood rice)".
- *Arroz ciego* is translated as "Blind rice". Even though in Spanish the name of the dish is a little bit tricky as literally it translates as "blind rice", it does not mean anything for someone who is not acquainted with Murcian gastronomy, so it would need an explanation. In this case, the best technique would be a combination of two techniques: borrowing and explanation, such as "Arroz ciego (seafood and vegetable paella)".
- *Arroz a banda* appears translated as "Rice to banda". This is a very good example of a cultural error, as *banda* does not convey any meaning for target readers of the translation. In this case, the best way to translate this "cultureme" would

be to borrow, and to explain how the dish is cooked and what its main ingredients are in a concise fashion, such as "Arroz a banda (seafood paella)".

- *Arroz negro* is translated as "Black rice" in the different menus. This would be the literal translation of the Spanish "cultureme", but it does not do justice to the dish. The solution here would be again a combination of a borrowing and explanation, such as "Arroz negro (rice with squid, cooked in squid's ink)".

As we have seen in this analysis, the combination of two translation techniques, borrowing and explanation, seem to be the best ways of rendering the meaning of "culturemes", especially when they fall into the category of gastronomy.

Overall, the field of the translation of gastronomy needs to be developed further in order to attract tourists to local restaurants. It seems sensible that public and private organizations and institutions related to tourism should sit down together and try to look for feasible solutions to the poor quality of translations found in menus in the region. The creation of a glossary for gastronomy would be a step forward and this could be done for other fields of tourism (architecture, music, typical dances, customs, festivities, etc.).

Bad translations may have numerous of potential consequences. If people do not understand what is included in the dish, they might not order it. It can also have negative consequences on a financial level, as a badly translated menu might not attract tourists. Furthermore, if someone is allergic to an ingredient and this is translated in such a way that it is not understood, a person may suffer an allergic reaction. Therefore, restaurant owners should make sure that what is included in the menu in the original language is understood in the target language.

Conclusion

The present chapter intended to emphasize the remarkable importance of translation in the tourist industry and, in turn, to examine the common errors, with a special focus on cultural errors, that are frequently encountered in tourist texts stemming from the region of Murcia. Texts translated for tourists should be attractive and free of linguistic and translation errors, since any mistake could give rise both to the visitor dissatisfaction and to a potential lack of interest in the destination, thus resulting in a negative view of the destination that is being promoted via the tourist text. It is clear that public and private tourist organisations (i.e. administrations, travel agencies, etc.) should be aware of the need for good quality translations of tourist texts and of the positive benefits that quality translations would have in the tourist sector.

As stated by Durán Muñoz (*Caracterización de la traducción turística* 103-112) translated tourist texts frequently abound with mistakes, bad translations and imprecise language. The reason for this is usually that translations are done by non-professional translators and done at the last minute, probably due to the lack of budget allocated for that purpose. Therefore, at this point, we would like to claim that, much as many authors have already argued (Calvi *et al.*), tourist translation due to its particular terminology as well as to its syntactic and textual features should be considered as a type of specialized translation. The complex terminology from the field of tourism and other areas such as gastronomy, history, architecture, customs, music and visual arts, etc. requires this type of translation to be carried out by qualified translators. As we have seen in the analysis of the webtexts, institutions are becoming aware of the importance of translated texts and the impact that it might have in the tourism sector. However, restaurant owners do not seem to be aware of this fact and they do not seem to take into account the impact of cultural errors. Tourism involves direct interplay among cultures. It is culture itself in its many forms, which needs to be rendered properly in high quality tourist texts in order to guarantee satisfactory communication with either real or potential tourists.

Works cited

Baker, Mona. *In Other Words: A Coursebook on Translation*. Routledge, 1992.

Cabré Castellví, María Teresa. *La terminología. Teoría, metodología, aplicaciones*. Antártida/Empúries, 1993.

Calvi, M. Vittoria. *Il linguaggio spagnolo del turismo*. Baroni, 2000.

Calvi, M. Vittoria. "El uso de términos culturales en el lenguaje del turismo: los hoteles y su descripción". *Nuevas tendencias en el discurso de especialidad*, edited by M. Vittoria Calvi & Luisa Chierichetti, Peter Lang, 2006, pp. 271-292.

Calvi, M. Vittoria. "Los géneros discursivos en la lengua del turismo: una propuesta de clasificación". *Ibérica*, vol. 19, 2010, pp. 9-32.

Calvi, M. Vittoria V & Milin Bonomi. "El lenguaje del turismo: de los textos especializados a la Comunidad del viajero". *La comunicación especializada*, edited by Carmen Navarro; Rosa María Rodríguez Abella; Francesca dalle Pezze; Renzo Miotti, Peter Lang, 2008, pp. 181-202.

Calvi, M. Vittoria. "Guía de viaje y turismo 2.0: los borrosos confines de un género". *Simposio Internacional Discurso y Géneros del Turismo 2.0*, 2-4 April 2014, Universitat de València. Keynote address.

De la Cruz Trainor, María Magdalena. "La traducción de textos turísticos: propuesta de clasificación y análisis de muestras". Dissertation. Universidad de Málaga, 2003.

Durán Muñoz, Isabel. "La necesidad de profesionalización en la traducción turística". I Congreso Internacional Translation in the Era of Information, Oviedo, 2008, pp. 99-113.

Durán Muñoz, Isabel. "Caracterización de la traducción turística: problemas, dificultades y posibles soluciones". *Revista de Lingüística y Lenguas Aplicadas*, vol. 7, 2012, pp. 103-113.

Durán Muñoz, Isabel. "Analysing common mistakes in translations of tourist texts (Spanish, English and German)". *Onomázein 26*, vol. 2, 2012, pp. 335-349.

Durán Muñoz, Isabel. "Aspectos pragmático-lingüísticos del discurso del turismo de aventura: estudio de un caso". *Normas*, vol. 4, 2014, pp. 49-69.

Franco Aixelá, Javier. "Culture-specific Items in Translation". *Translation, Power, Subversion*, edited by Román Álvarez; M. Carmen África Vidal, Multilingual Matters, 1996, pp. 52-78.

Fuentes Luque, Adrián. "La traducción de promoción turística institucional: la proyección de la imagen de España". *La traducción en el sector turístico*, edited by Adrián Fuentes Luque. Atrio, 2005, pp. 59-92.

Fuentes Luque, Adrián. "El turismo rural en España: Terminología y problemas de traducción." *Entreculturas*, vol. 1, 2009, pp. 469-486.

González Pastor, Diana María. "Análisis descriptivo de la traducción de culturemas en el texto turístico". Dissertation. Universitat Politécnica de Valencia, 2012.

González Pastor, Diana María. *¿Cómo se traducen los culturemas del ámbito turístico? Análisis de estrategias de traducción (español-inglés)*. Comares, 2018.

Kelly, Dorothy. "The Translation of Texts from the Tourist Sector: Textual Conventions, Cultural Distance and Other Constraints". *Trans*, vol. 2, 1998, pp. 33-42.

Newmark, Paul. "Translation and Culture". *Meaning in Translation*, edited by Barbara Lewandowska Tomaszczyk; Marcel Thelen, Peter Lang, 2010, pp. 171-182.

Nord, Christiane. *Translating as a Purposeful Activity*. St. Jerome Publishing, 1997.

Nord, Christiane. *Text Analysis and Translation*. Rodopi, 2005.

Robinson, Douglas. *Becoming a Translator: An Accelerated Course.* Routledge, 2003.

Soto Almela, Jorge. "La traducción de términos culturales en el contexto turístico español-inglés: recepción real en usuarios anglófonos". *Quaderns. Revista de Traducció*, vol. 20, 2013, pp. 235-250.

Soto Almela, Jorge. "Los términos culturales en el ámbito turístico español-inglés: traducción, manipulación y recepción real en usuarios anglófonos". Dissertation. Universidad de Murcia, 2014.

Webography

Murcia Turística (2018). Resumen cifras de turismo. Región de Murcia. Año 2017. Retrieved from https://www.murcia turistica.es/webs/murciaturistica/documentos/1/DOCUME NTOS_1_2154.pdf. Accessed 18 January 2019.

Murcia Turística (2018). www.murciaturistica.es, Accessed 18 January 2019.

Creative Errors

Cultural Errors and Creativity: How Visual and Textual Triggers Create New Meanings

Costas Mantzalos, Vicky Pericleous

Introduction: towards a definition of cultural errors in visual language

In visual language, the definition of cultural errors remains difficult to determine as even today visual language and visual intelligence lack a strict structure or grammar, by comparison to those available for written forms of language. Unlike written language, visual language has not yet managed to formulate rules and regulations, therefore, it is not always cognitive, as it is mainly concerned with the triggering of emotions rather than with literal understanding. Hence viewers of a visual sign perceive and translate it with diverse degrees of understanding; they bring to their interpretation varied readings which are dependent on their cultural backgrounds.

However, it could be argued that the difficulty in reading images has become less problematic in recent years as a result of the explosion of visual information and, what one might term, the visual revolution. Nevertheless, the translation of this visual form of language is dependent on the recipient's visual intelligence, on their visual literacy and on their level of visual competency. As a result of the combined effects of technological advances and the information revolution, visual language now forms a significant element in every-day life. However, visual intelligence still relies on an individual's understanding and on his or her own perception. As a result, this capacity may vary from one person to another. This is not only the case for the visual arts but also for music or poetry, or many other creative art forms. As Marshal McLuhan said: "The medium is the message"! (7).

This article investigates cultural errors from the perspective of the visual arts and pays particular attention to the significance that art plays in conveying messages and meanings through word play, or the twisting of words to make creative errors in order to translate current socio-political and economic issues. The present study illustrates examples from the art practice of the TWOFOURTWO art group, which uses appropriation in its oeuvre. The co-author of this chapter – Costas Mantzalos – has a dual role here, firstly as a commentator and secondly as an artist/practitioner and co-founder of the TWOFOURWO art group.

The TWOFOURTWO art group has used and reinvented new concepts from numerous industrial signs that came down from bankrupted business as a result of the global – and local – financial crisis. Additionally, the group re-contextualized the work, by twisting the meaning of these signs in order to re-create new names/words that promote a critical view of the current situation of our world. It is the "twisted words" as well as the combination of text and image, which illustrate the daily routine of the world through the concepts of consumerism, greed and megalomania; concepts, which can then be extended into a sociological study which examines identity and belonging. In other words, the TWOFOURTWO art group has created "errors" to project new meanings! "Errors" do not exist in visual language – as one understands the etymology of the word – as they do in written language. It is widely accepted that in art, the notion of trial and error is a positive element, which generates creativity. Errors can often be valuable for encouraging more creative thinking and innovation.

To kick off on the topic of cultural errors, the same words with a different intonation can create chaos and distress. For example, during an accreditation exercise in Lithuania, a team of experts consisting of academics from various countries, used English as the common language to communicate with Lithuanian academics via the aid of an interpreter. At one point, the word "morale" came up as a suggestion to account for the team's shortcomings. The interpreter mistook the sound of the word and translated the word as "moral" instead. The academics showed immediate discomfort and dissatisfaction at this comment and the original intention of the suggestion was transformed from a positive one to a negative one. In the works of the TWOFOURTWO art group, a similar situation occurs since their oeuvre produces diverse meanings for its viewers. TWOFOURTWO uses visual language to generate ambiguity and so error becomes the primary aim, functioning as concept; it projects an uncanny feeling of uneasiness. In the case of the practice of the TWOFOURTWO art group, the "error" is intentional and predetermined, as opposed to the unintentional error in the translation of spoken language, which occurs for example, in the intonation of the word "morale" between French and English, which does not factor in the cultural error.

1. The TWOFOURTWO art group

Over the 20th century, the boundaries of artistic genres became fluid and were constantly changing. Today, it is not rare in the contemporary art scene to find work that requires a whole new platform, which can accommodate a hybrid approach, combining disciplines such as design, architecture, fashion or even literature. The TWOFOURTWO art group embarked on such a voyage of collaboration. From different backgrounds, its members, a visual artist and an architect, explored their common experience, and produced a visual base from which they could communicate, between themselves and with viewers.

The work itself does not pretend to be a traditionally accepted art form but rather it seeks a place in its own right. It was the creative displacement of both parts, which led them to work as a group. Perhaps their being an "artist collective" has resulted in their work taking on multi-fold messages and meanings. This two person collective had to rely on their openness towards the acceptance of and respect for different opinions, and for multiple ideas through their one collective voice. This has resulted in an artistic practice, which fosters ambiguous readings and for whom a form of "cultural error" is central to their creativity.

The TWOFOURTWO art group was formed on 21th of August 1996 in Nicosia, Cyprus by Costas Mantzalos and Constantinos Kounnis. It is an art group that believes in art as an evolutionary institution, which changes over time and mutates with the passing of time. However, like democracy, it believes that art remains a supreme form of power vested in the people and characterized by the recognition of equality of opinions and voices. The work of TWOFOURTWO started from a very personal need to explore the notion of togetherness, the self and the other. Its work evolved and was shaped to investigate the notion of the private and the public space, the personal and the common, the domestic and the international.

As Glyn Hughes said in his comments on the exhibition *Shared Experiences* that took place in 1999 in Nicosia:

> The two artists, Mantzalos and Kounnis, link with overlapping ideas and this "sharing" is fruitful. The admitting of it is almost quietly revolutionary in an art scene where the self usually rules. There's lots of bubbly plastic – the kind which goes "pop" – used as wraps with considerable imagination. The multitude of images are sometimes shielded or "half-remembered" behind these fronts. The elongated architectural forms have intriguing little lighted peep-holes,
> which contain even more intriguing small forms. Some of these are startling. (35)

Often communicating through the Internet, using e-mails and telephone, the members of the group have come to experience each other linguistically. In a sense, the physical dimension was the missing link. And here was the rub which emerged with the obvious concern with the group's presence in their exhibition "Solvent" in Nicosia in 2001.

There are a number of procedures in which a form of human presence is either physically or mentally represented since human qualities are not a mere reflection of our physical existence via the body. It is possible to evoke and manipulate human presence via the body's physical qualities. But this may also be achieved through the mapping of the mental state. In the case of TWOFOURTWO, language is not used to reinforce, contradict, or dismantle the visual. Language is rather the only vehicle for the group's common experience. It is the politics of interaction, which is explored in their work. The participants as individuals are lost, establishing communication as an object of observation in its own right.

The aesthetic characteristic of TWOFOURTWO's visual language remains consistent, marking a territory of industrial or graphic materials and forms. However, the semantics and the rhetoric of their work have shifted into other areas. While the construction of the self and the metaphysics of presence remain of central concern, these issues are now approached differently. The self is no longer evoked by a linguistic undetermined dialogue in the absence of the visual body, but a presence or a concept of the self is redefined through a playful exploration into the mechanics of vision. Using the mirror or mirror-like surfaces, the mental viewing of each other escapes any personal reference, and the viewer becomes observed not only by the other but also by him/herself. The work challenges the borderlines of interaction yet still captures an expressive reaction. The deconstruction and manipulation of the body provokes a new perspective on the self, while there is no effort to bring forth a specific self-identity.

In TWOFOURTWO's work, the body becomes the battle ground where the private narrative, which precedes it and the politics governing it, becomes inscribed onto the body's surface. For the postmodern subject, the body becomes essential for the construction of its identity. But TWOFOURTWO's work highlights the construction of a non-self-identity by visually manipulating the deconstructed and fragmented body. The viewer is no longer the voyeur, who observes the body as the traditional whole figure of another. The subject matter of TWOFOURTWO's work is the suggestion of the body through which one's human nature is best recognized: through one's own body.

In the postmodern period, this is a frequent activity since the solid modernist values of being clear and simple are replaced by principles of complexity and contradiction. The postmodern ethos in the area of Art and Design is characterized by the notion of "polyphony" and allows ambiguity when translating the visual language. Unlike the spoken word, it still remains solid and structural and is still defined and governed by geographical and cultural borders.

Employing distinctly industrial materials, which have been disengaged from the industrial process, makes most of TWOFOURTWO's art appear as "found" art. Here, the design element interacts with the architectural vocabulary of space and volume. The hanging of TWOFOURTWO's work needs to be understood as a whole, and as the sum of its parts, forming a larger installation. It is thus caught between the tendency of the late 80's towards a "return to the body" and the non-referential minimalist view of industrial production. Their work functions on two levels, both as a cultural error which reinforces creativity, and which transmits multiple messages. The non-hierarchical relationships between the light boxes, usually placed in a mathematical grid, form this link. An installation of light is created which interacts and alters the physicality of the space. In this respect the work manipulates fluorescent light in forming installations that literally invade the viewers' space or alter their perception of it.

In general, as in their holistic body of work, the TWOFOURTWO art group negotiates people's interpersonal relationships via the perspective of fusion and the development of a new identity, which is the case with regard to the "THREESOMES" exhibition in 2009. At first glance, these photographic portraits seem to refer to museum portraits. However, after a continuous and more intense examination, they come across to the viewer as a puzzle, or a game, where three different people make up a new portrait, which although familiar, carries a new identity.

The dynamism of these portraits emerges not so much from the portraits themselves as from the process which TWOFOURTWO followed in selecting and associating people in their immediate social sphere. The portraits are the result of the long process of interpersonal relationships, which consciously or unconsciously have formed and informed the cultural, social, geographical, professional and personal behavior of the two members of the TWOFOURTWO art group.

Similarly, the installation of these portraits in the follow up exhibition, which took place at the UN negotiations hall in Nicosia, can be seen as a parallel activity to the process of the negotiations between the two leaders of the Greek and Turkish communities in Cyprus, which sought a solution over the 1974 Turkish invasion to the country. While TWOFOURTWO employs artistic methods which aim to contribute to the development and creation of new identities by merging different personalities into one, the two leaders – Dimistris Christofias, president of the Republic of Cyprus, and Mehmet Ali Talat, the leader of the Turkish Cypriot Community – are conversing about the "melting" of various idiosyncrasies and differences into a reunified country!

Although TWOFOURTWO was engaged in politically inclined art before this exhibition, the presentation of these portraits in this specific location added a new and resolutely political dimension to their work, reinforcing the notion of translation, which relies not only on the works themselves, but which is also governed by the surrounding space and the connotations and politics of each space that the artworks appear in. Thus, one can argue that the conceptual shift in TWOFOURTWO's work, the move from the personal to the political, may be associated with cultural error in translation, where conceptual change can be viewed as a form of translation, and where culture is equal to the space in which TWOFOURTWO's art work is received. When one ignores the significance of space, the meaning of TWOFOURTWO's work does not change, but, when one takes in consideration the "politics" of the space in which the artwork is displayed, the translation of the work takes on a completely new meaning without changing the initial visual signs via the artwork.

For the last 22 years, the work of the TWOFOURTWO art group has been dedicated to the mapping of a personalized cosmos, which attempts to avoid the private. Through their personal visual and, at times, linguistic confessions, the group aims to capture the abstract social practices, which built up and constitute their identity. The body of work entitled *Espace Blanc (White Space), 2011*, remains close to their investigation of mapping personal space, however, visually, it adopts a more formal and austere aesthetic, stripped of any imagery or linguistic references. These works inhabit their surroundings in a cold and minimal manner, qualities that set them clearly apart from TWOFOURTWO's earliest work.

Using the vocabulary of geometric forms, *Espace Blanc* occupies that shared territory where art and architecture explore the politics and rhetoric of interior and exterior space. Architectural spaces always trigger manifold dialogues when it is experienced by the viewer. Architectural spaces can project concepts, indicate and dictate behavior, stimulate cultural or social references or foster psychological and emotional conditions. Architecture, as the mother of the Arts, is translated in exactly the same way as visual language. It needs no grammar, and no syntax, and leaves no room for cultural errors. Architecture is translated by the viewer individually, and is perceived mainly via emotion rather than logic, thus allowing for pluralism in opinions and understanding.

The work of the TWOFOURTWO art group has progressed in recent years towards appropriation and action. In many cases, its latest work has involved a process where the art object became a series of interactive events, allowing audience participation and interaction. Despite this development, and although the visual vocabulary of the work has shifted in a different direction, the TWOFOURTWO art group is religiously following a journey of self-exploration, which can be seen as an autobiographical investigation of interpersonal relationships, governed by personal identity and social behaviour.

The messages that come out of the group's work are stable and consistent, and try to illustrate human relationships, which consciously or not, have determined the cultural, social, geographical, professional and personal behavior for both members of the TWO-FOURTWO art group, as well for those who interact with them in their social sphere. The oeuvre of the TWOFOURTWO art group, like most artworks, can be characterized as "polyphonic" with double-barreled meanings, but the main goal of the group takes into consideration the general concept that in art "errors" provide a creative insight.

2. When images talk

The shift to postmodernity and the development of the multi-disciplinary approach to art, must have seemed like a mark rather than just another doodle on America's avant-garde scene back in the 70's, even if it left the black paint dripping on the walls of the legendary Dwan Gallery. At the beginning of the "ME decade", a term coined by American author Tom Wolfe, "America was moving away from the communitarianism spirit of the 60s to an individualism, and what, at the time, looked like a self-indulgent or, at its best, a self-renewal attitude of the 70s" (27).

Mel Bochner in his seminal work on the exhibition "Language IV" at the Dwan Gallery in New York in 1970, directs the viewer's gaze to his white chalk text, handwritten on the black paint of the gallery's wall. This was an art-gesture that was so immediate that it left its black paint dripping, nearly hitting the floor. It almost resembled a rebel's scribble on a school black board, its bareness and outspokenness hits, not just the gallery floor, but the viewer's perceptiveness: *Language Is Not Transparent* (chalk on paint and wall, 182.9 × 122.6 cm).

Bochner's reflections on Ludwig Wittgenstein's philosophical ideas in respect of language and its visual-perceptual concepts and complex receptiveness and understanding are outlined in the following quotation: "Language is a part of our organism and no less complicated than it. It is not humanly possible to gather immediately from it what the logic of language is" (45). The artistic legacy left by the 60s' and 70s' conceptual artists gradually made way for other relevant work and practices. Art emerged which explores the major concerns of the postmodern period, which called for art to revolve around socio-political issues manifestations and criticism. The shift in artistic practices from Modernist conventions and aesthetics went hand in hand with America's socio-economical turn.

The affirmative shift from the 1960s' industrial economy to excessive prosperity produced by the world of finance, re-shaped attitudes and social inclinations. As Wolfe argued, the newly wealthy American – the *nouveau riche*, to use the European term – would "take his money and run" in order to realize his potential as a human being. This new order produced and increased in an equally excessive manner the desire in everyone, beyond any specific social class, to "take the money and run" – doing so in every possible way. Woody Allen's mockumentary *Take the Money and Run* (1969) about the chronicles of Virgil Starkwell, an incompetent bank robber, highlights this characteristic money lust within society. In the 1970s, the song of the Steven Miller Band with the same title reiterates this exact spirit of the Hoo-hoo era:

> This is a story about Billy Joe and Bobbie Sue. Two young lovers with nothin' better to do than sit around the house, get high, and watch the tube. And here is what happened when they decided to cut loose. They headed down to, ooh, old El Paso.

From the Chicago Boys, an influential network of Chilean economists who performed radical economic practices in the 70s and 80s – most of whom trained at the Department of Economics of the University of Chicago under Milton Friedman and Arnold Harberger – heading south to Chile, all the way to the Old Continent, to the Iron Lady's privatization policies, these neoliberal approaches and practices were gaining ground. America was not the only country to be drumming to the accelerating rhythm of capitalism.

The British Conservative's slogan "Labour isn't working" (taken from the Saatchi and Saatchi advertising campaign for the UK Conservative Party in 1979) would shortly become the hegemonic narrative and the authoritative doctrine across both sides of the Pacific. Shopping malls, chain supermarkets across the globe, globalized museums, brands, corporate companies, – new places and non-spaces – all these entities have been flawed over the years, everywhere.

In 2005, Elmgreen & Dragset created the architectural sculpture *PRADA MARFA* in the Texas desert, about 26 miles outside of Marfa. It was a Prada minimal look-alike shop, with a huge brand sign, PRADA, written large on its façade, which highlights a form of social neurosis. At the same time, the work became a metaphor for the dark side of consumerism and the absurd effects of neoliberal practices and free market movements while, perhaps at the same time, re-enforcing them. The translation of this work can be seen as a manifestation of neoliberalism and it is also deliberately and directly linked to cultural error. It voices arguments about the manipulative essence of neoliberalism. This is a cultural error not in translation but in context; the idea and the ideal of the "free world" and the "opportunities for all" as the new ideology, which eventually became another manufactured dogma of a controlling power over the public.

As corporate entities grew everywhere, multiplying the sense that paradise "is a place on earth", most of their homes became these beautiful – and faraway – havens across the globe: from the Caribbean to Cayman Islands, from the Barbados to the Bahamas, from the Canaries Islands to Malta and Cyprus.

Cyprus, is not a paradise any more. Cyprus can be said to have come down like the Tower of Babel. Communication channels seem to have failed. Everybody seemed to be speaking a different language when the meltdown of the Cypriot economy was announced on the 6th of March 2013, following heart-breaking Euro group meetings. Barbara Krunger's installation on the façade of the Italian Pavilion in the 2005 Venice Biennale still resonates as one of the most trustworthy of all voices in respect of the wider socio-political crisis and its understanding: "Admit Nothing, Blame Everyone" (digitally printed vinyl mural).

In the case of Cyprus and the Euro group meeting of the 6th of March 2013, it became obvious that languages across cultures are not always common, nor are they easily comprehended. One also observes here a new dimension of spoken language, which diverts from culture and goes into the realm of politics. Politicians across Europe, during the financial crisis in Cyprus used a variety of languages. For some politicians (mainly those residing in Brussels) language was quite straightforward, austere and dictatorial. On the other hand, those politicians residing in Cyprus used a milder form of populist language in order to describe to the public the financial situation. The result was a definite cultural error in translation by all politicians on the "both fronts". The aftermath of this was a stricken country. It has become the norm nowadays for politicians to use a type of language and vocabulary, which instead of communicating deliberately manipulates meaning and hides the essence of the matter and the message.

3. *LIKE ORPHANS*

ΛΑΙΚ ΟΡΦΑΝΣ, Installation View, Argo Gallery, Nicosia, 2014

The first installation entitled *LIKE ORPHANS* explores the total collapse of LAIKI, the second biggest bank in Cyprus, followed the major failure of an over-inflated banking system. It had the effects of a bland disaster. It was an awkward one: no blood was involved, no military operations took place, there were no war-sirens. Greek Cypriots, nonetheless, felt – once again – *LIKE ORPHANS*. Totally exposed to other entities, since their sovereign state had failed to protect them. The result was a controlled form of bankruptcy, with no state to back them up and no trust in their European comrades who were holding out their hands.

TWOFOURTWO's *LIKE ORPHANS* gigantic light sign installation in 2014, resurrects the actual sign age / brand logos of LAIKI Bank and ORHANIDES, one of the biggest supermarket chains that collapsed with the financial crisis of 2013. The world "Like" seems to be taking on a double meaning as "Like" refers to the social media culture as well as the word "similar", thus widening even more the work's reading.

Through a wicked gesture of anagrammatism of the names LAIKI and ORHANIDES, this textual installation not only stages the rotten flavor of the socio-political failure but raises its tensions to their most urgent state: "Where do we go from here?" In the midst of what appears to be an ongoing global crisis Cypriots have been pushed, most probably beyond their intention, to re-think and re-question their geopolitical understanding and strategies – within the wider debates and urgencies of the international bio-politics – and to re-plan their next move. A self-reflective critical position always seems to precede these sorts of disputes in order to clearly understand and assess the realities and causations that let to these dilemmas. *LIKE ORPHANS* seems to be doing that.

Beyond the state of suspension that the work indicates, it centres on the fundamental *aporia*: Who was really to be blame for this obscene state of matters and being? Were Cypriots really the victims of a major economic crime against themselves or were they the real perpetrators, who enjoyed far more than they could have ever paid back, while watching their country going down? Glen Ligon's *DOUBLE AMERICA*, 2006, (neon and paint), makes an interesting parallel on the subject and offers an interesting response while becoming itself an allegory. It is an allegory for what might be the double image of politics obscure devices and society's irregular responses. This large-scale neon sign is erratically flashing the word "America", while an inverted mirror "America" underneath also functions in the same way. Viewers become so mesmerized by the flashing spectacle that neglects its fragile mechanisms that lay bare on the floor, until it all goes off.

> The spectacle cannot be understood as an abuse of the world of vision, as a product of the techniques of mass dissemination of images. It is, rather, a *Weltanschauung*, which has become actual, materially translated. It is a world vision, which has become objectified. (Evans, Hall 96)

In today's globalized society, there is a tendency to break down barriers and merge cultures together. The ideal of "one world" has been developed to provide the notion of this "worldview". But how much of this ideal has actually been achieved? Languages still remain as cultural barriers to a global society, despite the fact that there is greater mobility across borders and cultures. And of course linked to language is the understanding of distinct cultural systems, which still remain intact and may cause difficulties as a result of errors in interpretation.

Current political systems tend to adopt a new form of language, which operates on diverse levels. It communicates through governments on one level, and among people on a different level, deliberately mixing error with manipulation in order to retain power and control. In this case, cultural errors in translation become deliberate, just as they occur in visual language. However, the result is completely contrary to that desired by government or corporate bodies, since in art a deliberate error is a prerequisite for humour, punning, and creativity, whereas in politics cultural errors are deceitful, obscuring, and manipulative.

4. Postcards from Cyprus

CAREFORU, installation view, Nicosia, 2017

The second work to be examined in this article uses tourist images from Cyprus in juxtaposition with the text "care for u", which is a pun on the Carrefour supermarket sign. Carrefour is one of the latest casualties of Cyprus' and Greece's crippling recession. The new juxtaposition of word and image smirks at the viewer and confirms that Cyprus cares for you. It is a paradox as well as a huge contrast in semiological meaning, which can extend to various other interpretations. TWOFOURTWO asked various questions through their "Postcards from Cyprus". They are loyal to their visual vocabulary, which involves interdisciplinary practices through industrialized objects and installations, and they unpack the notion of a country: is it a "patria", a home, a refuge or a holiday destination? They also offer new questions. Is the financial crisis the "New Cyprus Problem"? Are the words "occupied land" and "refugees" going to be replaced by the words "non-performing debts" and "unemployment"?

"Postcards From Cyprus", could be approached as such. It can be viewed as a staged spectacle that captures the senses before it reaches the mind. The gigantic sign stands larger than life; it attracts the gaze while intimidating the body. It shouts "CARE FOR U" out loud. Whose body is this gesture of care coming from? Whose mouth makes up the words? Whose hand reaches out to you? The sign is definitely familiar even though there is no functional mechanism, no light and no radiant identification as to where this body is coming from. It does not take long for it to become apparent. The "body" of Carrefour's sign, that of a multinational supermarket chain, is resurrected, and even though it is emptied of its contextual meaning, it performs a new gesture.

The new gesture performed by the work of art recites an anagrammatic and overpowering testimony: CARE FOR U – isn't this the most vital desire of all? Does this – new, renovated sign take on the appearance of a silenced "body" – one in a series of "bodies" of signs that TWOFOURTWO have accumulated for their practice – can it be viewed as a stage or an act of a malignant system? Are TWOFOURTWO knowingly exposing, a "cancerous body without organs" (Deleuze and Guattari 183), whose experimental practices feed and produce new forms of desires and intensities, all caught up in a vicious unbreakable circle? If so, should we ultimately examine the nature of this desire?

> Even when it falls into the void of too sudden de-stratification, or into the proliferation of a cancerous stratum, it is still desire. Desire stretches that far: desiring one's own annihilation, or desiring the power to annihilate everything. Money, army, police, and State: desire, fascist desire, even fascism is desire … (the problem is) to distinguish the BwO (Body without Organs) from its doubles: empty vitreous bodies, cancerous bodies, totalitarian and fascist. (Deleuze, Guattari 183)

Could this be one out of many possible re-appearances and gestures of a system that is unpredictable and altogether unapproachable, open to endless forms and presences? One that performs practices that are constantly re-invented, and which are precarious, both in their perception and in the potential for being controlled? TWO-FOURTWO's own art-gesture comes back as a warning.

On the other side of the room, TWOFOURTWO displayed postcards of beloved idyllic places, Mediterranean vistas, which stood as a representation of Cypriotness. The images' emblematic landscapes and the cultural mnemonics they carried along with them constitute the sense of a *topos*. The landscape itself became a signifier of a treasured "Patria", which as the phrase indicates, provides Care For U. The phrase, a smaller scale reproduction of the anagrammatic Carrefour sign, appears to be growing as it moves from the Cypriot terrain to conquer the space beyond. In all the images, the visual representations, which come in the form of collages, "Patria" seems once again to be overshadowed and overpowered by the intensity of this testimony. And so too is the viewer as s/he contemplates the phrase's contextual connotations and origins. *Wonder Beirut, the Story of a Pyromaniac Photographer*, 1997-2006, (mixed media, dimensions variable), a work by Joana Hadjithomas and Khalil Joreige, offers an interesting paradigm to talk about relevant practices and to reflect critical processes for exposing and negotiating drama.

The work presents postcards of an idealized Lebanon in the sixties, where the Lebanese Riviera and its luxury hotels are burned by the fictional figure of a photographer, who goes by the name of Abdallah Farah. Farah burns the negatives of these romanticized postcards and makes them correspond to the actual damage caused by the fighting that took place in Lebanon's recent history. The specific postcards like the Cypriot 70s postcards – which have shaped collective narratives towards notions of "Patria" – are still on sale, reproducing an idealized image of Lebanon before the recent war. That series of images communicate the completely opposite notion of the country and in a sense they can also be seen as a cultural error in pictorial translation. Art can manipulate understanding, just as the media can, via the reproduction of images in current affairs. It represents a kind of "political art" or rather "art in politics", which allows for various interpretations. Visual language is so complex that it can actually transform situations from positive to negative and vice versa without any guilt about misguidance or misinformation.

An electric blue line permeates the space. Is this where the sky and sea meet or where they fall apart? The suggestion of the horizon seems to complete the installation. TWOFOURTWO move our gaze where the local and the global intersect, using the Mediterranean horizon as the highest metaphor. The work's representation, cannot but bring to mind, under the light of the current crisis, the work by The Atlas Group/Walid Raad's *Secrets in the Open Sea*, 1994-2004, (inkjet print), where various shades of Mediterranean blue are capturing the viewer's senses. However, they discover on closer inspection, a small black and white image of people, revealed to be portraits of men and women who drowned and died in the Mediterranean between 1975 and 1991.

TWOFOURTWO's minimal gesture, engages also in an interesting dialogue with notions of Runo Lacomarcino's work "Mare Nostrum", 2016. A neon sign work that refers to the cultural complexities and multiplicity of perceptions of the Mediterranean, "a space that must be spoken of in the plural" (from the text written by Alberto Salvatori in the context of Runo Lagomarsino's exhibition: "West is everywhere you look", Francesca Minini Gallery, Milan, March-May 2016). This textual work which cites the Roman name for the Mediterranean sea – translated from the Latin as "Our Sea" – reflects on its (Mediterranean's) paradoxical nature: "… from the Balkans to Asia Minor, and from the Iberian Peninsula to North Africa, mare nostrum has always been a boundary that is both obstacle and bridge".

If the metaphorically burdened representation of the Mediterranean and its shifting territories, borders and population becomes the distillation of the current geopolitical debate, its horizon becomes its critical point, where the most profound drama is played out. Should the – Mediterranean – horizon become a space to encounter shared hopes or should it become the border to differentiates us from the "Other"? Is this the highpoint of this spectacle?

The exhibition could be perceived as a staged *Weltanschauung*, a vision of worlds in constant flow, that appear to be shaken, overpowered and overshadowed by conflicting histories and practices beyond reach. The viewer while leaving the exhibition space is offered a postcard, a memoir of this *Weltanschauung*. A long with it, TWOFOURTWO, offer the suggestion that images – as language – are no longer, transparent. But images, unlike language, can afford to make mistakes and have no consequences when translated across cultures.

5. *Kalos Kakos Ilthate (Welcome, Welcome Not)*

KALOS KAKOS ILTHATE, A2 Printed Giveaway,
Petah Tikva Museum of Art, Tel Aviv, Israel

TWOFOURTWO art group's investigative look at immigration and the subject of refugees is communicated via the imagery of their landscape photographs, which focus on the sea and the shoreline, as in UN_P1 (2015). The viewer's mind drifts towards the current international *lingua franca* used to communicate these images, for example "flow of refugees", "uprooting" and the haunting "human cargo". A double-faced sign reading "καλώς/κακώς ήλθατε" reminds us that the journey leads to a precarious future. A deliberate addition of a letter from L to K results in manifold meanings. From welcome to welcome NOT or even "good or bad you may as well be welcome".

The actual sign, which comprises the work, came to the group from the "Orphanides" chain of supermarkets when this chain financially collapsed in 2013. Although at first, the sign only served as a word twister between the meanings of good and bad when it was initially presented in a gallery space in Nicosia in 2015. However, in the following years the actual translation of the work took on a different cause. This cause was mainly affected by the dislocation of the work from the gallery space and its relocation to various other spots by the shoreline. While in spoken language, where culture plays an important role in translation, in visual language, space plays an important role in the understanding of its messages. Just as it happened in some of the earlier works, the change of concept became the translation and "the translation" became the new space allowing a "deliberate cultural error" to spark a new meaning!

Conclusion

Although visual language is gaining currency as a form of communication in today's world, it has not yet been formalized as written language has. The grammar of visual language still is not as structured as spoken language, and still relies on an individual's visual intelligence. And visual intelligence, which is not as easily assimilated as oral and written intelligence, is viewed as the acquisition of critical and intuitive visual discrimination in the process of mark making and the construction of imagery, the delivery of words and the underlying understanding of icons, symbols and visual triggers. Visual lateral thinking and appreciation of subliminal elements in art interpretation is seen in relation to how all forms of imagery are delivered, received, deciphered and understood by appropriate audiences and viewers.

This article has attempted to provide a new insight into the translation of visual language as this may occur in relation to the cultural error in translation of a language. Cultural errors in translation are not the norm, and are usually never deliberate. Errors in translation usually occur because of the lack of cultural awareness of the translators. Often trained translators tend to work on literal rather than cultural meaning and this is when errors appear because the aim of every translator is not only to make sense in the target language but also to make sense in the context of the target culture.

In visual language the above-mentioned definitions of cultural errors may not apply, since visual language is not only defined by culture but also by personal understanding and appreciation. And as the art world is mainly an expressive and creative activity, sometimes a strictly defined translation is not a prerequisite for the cognitive process of comprehension, since the desirable goal of art is to communicate to the viewer such emotions and sentiments as can be translated into personal and individual meanings.

When experiencing a cultural error in the translation of written language, this can cause an embarrassing and negative experience. In the case of visual language though and specifically in the oeuvre of the TWOFOURTWO art group, the "error" becomes the source of a new meaning, offering an insight and a new dimension of a different reality. Visual language in the meta-postmodern period has become synonymous with multi-disciplinarity and plurality. Cultural errors have been associated with the notion of free expression, and have provided a new level of conceptual and contextual creativity.

Works cited

Certoma, Chiara. *The Politics of Space and Place.* Cambridge Scholars, 2012.

Deleuze, Gilles and Guattari, Felix. *A Thousand Plateaus: Capitalism and Schizophrenia.* University of Minnesota Press, 1987.

Eleftheriadou, Artemis. *Espace Blanc.* 242 Art Group, 2011.

Eleftheriadou, Artemis. *Publish Me!* 242 Art Group, 2005.

Eleftheriadou, Artemis. *Grids.* 242 Art Group, 2004.

Eleftheriadou, Artemis. *Reaction.* 242 Art Group, 2002.

Eleftheriadou, Artemis. *Solvent.* 242 Art Group, 2001.

Evans, Jessica and Hall, Stuart. *Visual Culture: the Reader.* SAGE Publications in association with the Open University, 2013.

Hughes, Glyn. "Shared Experiences". *Cyprus Weekly* [Nicosia, CY], 24 Sep. 1999, pp. 35-36.

McLuhan, Marshall. *Understanding Media; the Extensions of Man.* MIT Press, 1964

Wittgenstein, Ludwig. *Tractatus Logico – Philosophicus.* Keagan Paul, 1922.

Wolfe, Tom. "The 'Me' Decade and the Third Great Awakening". *New York Magazine*, 23 Aug. 1976, pp. 27-48

Translation and Tragic Error: Culture, Conflict, and Northern Irish Translations of Sophocles' *Antigone*

Charles Ivan Amstrong

Introduction

Just as it is popular to compare, say, interpretation or intermedial adaptation to translation, translation itself is typically understood through comparison with other activities. Perhaps due to the complexity, variety and elusiveness of translation, it lends itself to being likened with any number of objects and pursuits. In a study of poetic translation, Matthew Reynolds has scrutinized some of these comparisons, writing that through

> the centuries, translation has been said to give a work new clothes or place a jewel in a different casket; to conquer, or enfranchise or bring home. It has infused, transfused, refined; and mirrored, and copied, and opened the window. It has been thought of as preserving fire, or suffering from disease, or bringing the dead to life. (39)

Reynolds's list goes on, but in this chapter, I want to approach a metaphor unmentioned by him. It is a metaphor that relates to the topic of cultural error in translation. Such errors can be understood as intended or unintended deformations of the source text, based upon presuppositions about the cultural context in which the translation is situated and speaks to. It can be hard to avoid deformations of this kind, and the possible inevitability at play suggests another parallel to translation, especially relevant to the tragic plays at which I am going to look. For a form of "error" – often of a fated or ineluctable kind – is at the heart of classical tragedy.

More specifically, Greek tragedy typically features a protagonist or hero who commits a tragic error. This feature is mentioned in Aristotle's treatment of the tragedy in the *Poetics*, where he writes the following of the tragic hero:

> Such a person is someone not preeminent in virtue and justice, and one who falls into adversity not through evil and depravity, but through some kind of error [*Hamartia*]; and one belonging to the class of those who enjoy a great renown and prosperity, such as Oedipus, Thyestes, and eminent men from such lineages. The well-made plot, then, ought to be single rather than double, as some maintain, with a change not to prosperity from adversity, but on the contrary from prosperity to adversity, caused not by depravity but by a great error of a character either like that stated, or better rather than worse. (71)

The Greek word for error is *Hamartia*, which has also been translated as "mistake" or "fault"[1]. Can the translator be said to be akin to a tragic hero? This presupposes, perhaps, an understanding of translation that is especially relevant to *literary* translation – or perhaps even the translation of poetry – where it has been thought of as vital to create something approaching a correspondence not only in content, but also in form, with the original. This has proverbially been seen as impossible – as a Babelian project in the sense Jacques Derrida conjures up when referring to "the necessary and impossible task of translation, its necessity *as* impossibility" (223). In his monograph *Poetry & Translation: The Art of the Impossible*, Peter Robinson claims that the impossibility in question is caused by poetry being a "synthesized meeting point" of "different aspects of uniqueness" (80-81). Faced with the challenge of trying to construct a verbal artifact

---

[1] For discussions about the virtues of the differing translations of this term, see Hyde and Dyer.

of such uniqueness, the translator might seem – like the tragic hero – fated to go wrong.

Although Robinson's argument deals with poetry, one could venture that other literary modes present a similar case. In dramatic verse, for instance, much of the same challenge inheres. In classical verse drama, the challenge of historical distance is especially acute. Recent decades have nevertheless seen a flourishing of Irish translations of classical Greek drama, with writers such as Desmond Egan, Seamus Heaney, Brendan Kennelly, Frank McGuinness, Derek Mahon, Aidan Carl Mathews, and Tom Paulin, all presenting new versions. A large proportion of these have resonated with the conflict in Northern Ireland.

The austere but bloody conflicts of classical playwrights have been approached as presenting something like an objective correlative, or a sounding board, with which to compare and (sometimes) universalize the Troubles in the north. In this chapter, I will look at two specific examples, both involving Northern Irish poets translating Sophocles' tragedy, *Antigone*. The oldest work of the two is Tom Paulin's *The Riot Act*, first staged by the Field Day Theatre company in 1984 and published the next year[2]. The later play is Seamus Heaney's *The Burial at Thebes*, commissioned by the Abbey Theatre to be performed in 2004 as part of its centenary celebrations, completing the translation of the Theban trio of plays begun by William Butler Yeats's versions of *King* Oedipus and *Oedipus at Colonus* first staged in the 1920s.

1. The rebellious idiom

Although Heaney knew Latin, and has for instance made acclaimed translations of Virgil, neither he nor Paulin could read Sophocles in

---

[2] The same author would later make a translation of Aeschylus' *Prometheus Bound*, published as *Seize the Fire: A Version of Aeschylus' 'Prometheus Bound'*. Faber and Faber, 1990.

the original Greek[3]. While Paulin has acknowledged that he based his version on the translation of the Victorian classicist R. C. Jebb, Heaney has referred to not only Jebb, but also to the Loeb edition of Hugh Lloyd-Jones as an important reference point for his work with the play. In both cases, then, we have a complex negotiation with the Greek classic via the cribs of more recent English renderings of the original. Both Heaney and Paulin follow the basic plot of Sophocles' play, which takes place in the Greek city-state of Thebes just after a war with the rivaling city of Argos.

The brothers Polyneices and Eteocles have killed each other while fighting on opposite sides, and the new king Creon decides to prohibit the burial of the rebel, Polyneices. Antigone, the sister of the two brothers, chooses to nevertheless go ahead with Polyneices' last rites. Creon has force of the city-state on his side – and declares that Antigone is to be buried alive as punishment for her transgression. When Creon hears that his son, Haemon – who is engaged to Antigone – has decided to follow his bride into the death, he regrets. But it is too late. Soon Creon's wife Eurydice also kills herself, and at the end of the play, Creon is led out of Thebes, repentant but ruined.

The play's stand-off between the laws of the state, on the one hand, and the laws of the family and the gods, on the other, has been much admired. Hegel deemed it to be the highest dramatic accomplishment of the Greeks, and based an important section of his *Phenomenology of the Spirit* upon it, while George Steiner has described *Antigone* as the only literary text "to express all the principal constants of conflict in the condition of man" (*Antigones* 231). Early on during the Northern Irish Troubles, the Irish cultural commentator Conor Cruise O'Brien argued that the character of Antigone represented a rebelliousness that was akin to that of Northern Irish civil rights protestors such as Bernadette Devlin. Such lack of compliance could only lead to uncontrolled bloodshed, O'Brien claimed, and was therefore a dangerous and unjustified line of action (148-153).

---

[3] For readings of how Heaney and Paulin respond to issues of translation and linguistic difference in relation to Russian literature, see Schwerter.

Tom Paulin has written of how he wanted "to take on O'Brien's unionist position and to suggest that the contradictions within the state meant that its politics would always be unstable, violent, tragic, until the border disappeared" ("Ireland – just the place for classical tragedy"). Thus, Paulin's translation was from the very beginning motivated by a desire to bend the original, one might say, into a new cultural context. This is perhaps particularly evident in the treatment of Creon, whose voice is transformed into rather wordy, windy and self-righteous prose.

In Paulin's version, Creon is found claiming early on that he has "always held that one of the soundest maxims of good government is *always listen to the very best advice*" (*The Riot Act* 16). There is no clear parallel to this claim in the original materials, and Paulin himself cites this as "the usual cliché" that even was used by Douglas Hurd, when he took over as Northern Ireland Secretary in September later the same year. Relatedly, Paulin's version tends to tone down the personal aspects of the interaction of the characters, in particular making Creon into a representative of the State with a capital "S".

Are such departures from the original evidence of "cultural error"? One could claim that they simplify the character of Creon, reducing the balance of the conflict of the play by making Antigone's main opponent into little more than a straw man. This movement goes together with what is a "cultural" turn in Paulin's interpretation, whereby Creon's tendency towards a rather bombastic version of correct English is contrasted with more down-to-earth language in the other characters. The latter is evident in Paulin's characteristic use of idiomatic phrases, often characteristic of the North of Ireland, ranging from "eejit", "bairns" and "ould bugger" to turns of phrase such as "carry the can" and "bet your boots." The opposition between different registers is related to Paulin's distinction, in his editorial introduction to *The Faber Book of Vernacular Verse*, between warring literary discourses in English: "Against that Parnassian official order, the springy, irreverent, chanting, quartzy, often tender and intimate, vernacular voice speaks for an alternative community that is mostly powerless and invisible. This oral community voices itself in a gestural, tactile language" (qtd. in Ó Seaghdha).

Should one read *The Riot Act* as imposing this binary – which might be construed as overly simplistic and related to a different cultural context – upon Sophocles' original? Peter McDonald has taken to task both this play and Seamus Heaney's *The Cure at Troy* for being overly domesticating, accusing them of "taking an ultimately opportunistic attitude" towards their material, which results in the translated text not only being "relevant to its present context, but also [seeking] to minister to that context, to reassure and confirm" (196)[4]. Paulin's own comments on the 1999 production at the Oxford Playhouse suggest an alternative appraisal, which would valorize precisely those elements in the text that might seem like willed deviations from the original. He was obviously only moderately happy with the Oxford Playhouse production, claiming that its denial of the "topical" set "the play in a kind of rational abstract space," communicating "the eternal conflict of principle in a formal and elegant manner" ("Ireland – just the place for classical tragedy").

2. Beyond warfare: Heaney's classicism

For Paulin, it would seem, *The Riot Act* shows that resisting cultural contextualization is itself an error. Given that there is no vantage point outside the given values and concerns of real, historical cultures, the attempt to construct English-language, literary versions of timeless classics is an impossible one. The act of translation necessarily involves muddying one's hands, adjusting the text in one way or another to the target culture. This stance finds something of a counterpoint in Heaney's version of *Antigone*, titled *The Burial at Thebes*, staged twenty years later. Writing his version, Heaney was familiar with Paulin's precedent[5].

---

[4] For the distinction between domesticating and foreignizing forms of translation, see Venuti, 19-20.

[5] See for instance the reference to *The Riot Act* as a precedent for Heaney's earlier play, *The Cure at Troy* in O'Driscoll, 420.

To a certain degree, one might see this as implying an agonistic context of competition and counter-statement: as George Steiner points out, "the translator translates after and against his predecessors almost as much as he translates his source" (*After Babel* 412). Heaney was however familiar with several versions – i.e., not only Paulin's – and was also building on the experience of writing his own version of Sophocles *Philoctetes*, *The Cure at Troy*, in 1991. Like Paulin, Heaney has spoken of the importance of Conor Cruise O'Brien's interpretation of *Antigone*. But where O'Brien provoked Paulin to an oppositional, Republican stance, Heaney's response was different. In an interview with Lorna Hardwick from 2007, he speaks of being "kind of tired" of how "the play was hijacked into, if you like, a discourse around the issues, into the cultural wars of the seventies and eighties and early nineties" (Hardwick 3). The disillusionment with "cultural wars" is striking for a translation of a play that takes place in the immediate aftermath of a harrowing war. It would suggest that Heaney is eager to find a vantage point outside of warfare *per se*.

Heaney's use of the chorus can be interpreted as an important part of his attempt to attain a voice for this position. Interestingly, Heaney is far more thorough than Paulin in following the traditional, Greek choruses of the play. Paulin remembers being advised by Stephen Rea, when accepting the Field commission, to "go easy on the choruses," since "they can be a bit of a bore" ("Ireland – just the place for classical tragedy"). Paulin shortens – and, in some cases, even omits – the choruses for the sake of dramatic tension, whereas Heaney tends to utilize them for a heightened lyrical voice that will transcend the dramatic conflict. This connects with Heaney's understanding of Sophocles' plays as classics that transcend cultural and historical specificity, rather than merely embody a transhistorical force. In the interview with Lorna Hardwick, he speaks of how "the classics" represent a kind of text that "can be travestied, if you like and mocked but they can't be outstripped or diminished or dodged" (Hardwick 1). This explains why Heaney keeps long choruses devoted to fate, love and glory. In Sophocles' work these ideas are rooted in an elaborate and vigorous

Greek mythology, but it is arguably hard to keep them from degenerating into vague abstractions in a contemporary context.

Yet, at the same time as Heaney keeps faith with this general, classical dimension in Sophocles, there are aspects in his version that also enter the cultural fray. In Heaney's poetry, continuity and fidelity are traits that not only accompany the notion of the classic but also characterize the idea of family. Both classics and family relations are carriers of a valued heritage. These concerns are linked together in Heaney's reflection, in an interview with Rui Carvalho Homem, on the humanist responsibility for preserving our shared cultural heritage:

> I can see that the cultural heritage has been the possession of an elite, and no document of civilisation is not a document of barbarism. But I'm afraid I believe in the future, and that for the sake of the future I believe we must carry our possessions, we must do Aeneas's job and, you know, get Daddy on our back, and get the household materials together and carry them along. (Homem 29)

Thus, in *The Burial at Thebes*, Heaney is attracted to the solidarity shown by Antigone not only to her brother Polyneices, but also to the tragic heritage of her father, Oedipus. Antigone's banishment and rejection echo that of her father before her, and she attains a certain dignity by grimly facing this repetition of history:

> Over and over again / Because I am who I am / I retrace that fatal line," she says in his version (*The Burial at Thebes* 39). This can be construed, as the chorus states, as her continued paying back for her father's transgressions: "Paying, perhaps, in your life / For the past life of your father. (38)

Matthew Reynolds has pointed out how poetic translations tend to grasp after self-reflective metaphors that describe their relationship to the author of the original text. The idea of a kind of economic payback for classical fathers, retracing their fatal "lines" of verse, provides a fair encapsulation of Heaney's understanding of his vocation as a translator and mediator of the classics[6]. In *The Burial at Thebes*, the conflict between Antigone's family and King Creon is not simply an instance of intercultural friction but also represents a clash between a form of dignified speech and action, on the one hand, and a political regime that has no respect for such things on the other. This is where Heaney allows himself some political satire, aligning Creon most obviously not with British rule in Northern Ireland, as in Paulin's case, but rather with the post 9/11 politics of the United States. Creon is reported as stating "I'll flush them out" and "Whoever isn't for us / Is against us in this case" (*The Burial at Thebes* 3).

Heaney has referred to this as a "faint vulgarity" in his text, and it demonstrates how his text is not consistent in avoiding "cultural wars" (Hardwick 7). He is not completely consistent, though, in identifying the cultural context of this intervention: even while unabashedly alluding to George W. Bush and the aftermath of 9/11, he has also stated that "the conditions we were living in, and have lived in Northern Ireland" led him to his choice of Sophoclean drama (Hardwick 2). When Creon, early in Heaney's text, counters Antigone's plea that Polyneices is "no common criminal" with the claim that he "terrorised us", we can see how the post 9/11 discourse around terror is being folded over into that of the Northern Irish Troubles in a complex but interesting way (*The Burial at Thebes* 23-24).

---

[6] Heaney's repeated use of the word "line" can be interpreted as drawing attention to the self-reflective undercurrent of his version's verse. Thus, when Ismene states she wants to throw herself "Like a lifeline" to his sister, Antigone quips that Ismene "chose a safe line first" (*The Burial at Thebes* 25). Earlier in the play, Ismene asks her thinker to consider "the line we come from: / We're children of Oedipus" (4). For an earlier self-conscious meditation on the metaphoric resonance of the verse line, see Heaney's *Preoccupations*, 65.

Other aspects of his version might be taken as alluding more exclusively to the situation in Northern Ireland. When for instance Creon suspects that the burial of Polyneices is tied to "disaffected elements" representing what he calls a "certain poisonous minority" in Thebes (14), this unmistakably evokes – in a Troubles context – the Catholic minority's "alienation" that became especially marked after the introduction of internment and Bloody Sunday (McKittrick and McVea 72)[7]. These elements may be read as a form of cultural error, since there is no corresponding identification of minority factions in the original and the language of terrorism has no precise parallel in ancient Greece. Seen from another perspective, though, Heaney's interventions here have the virtue of making the plot of Sophocles' play engaging to a modern audience.

Clíona Ní Ríordáin has written of how Heaney's version of *Philoctetes*, *The Cure of Troy*, is "characterized by a fidelity and respect for the original text" one finds in most of his translations (175)[8]. The previously mentioned interview with Rui Carvalho Homem, conducted after *The Cure at Troy* but three years in advance of the publication of *The Burial at Thebes*, shows Heaney fretting at the leash of this stance:

> What I learnt through doing Sophocles was that, if I had to do it again, it would have to be done freely. Obedience is all very well, but it ends up being upholstery, as Pound called it. I remember opening Shakespeare's *Tempest* and thinking "Oh my God!": the opening scene of that play is just a set of shouts, but it's a dramatist at full tilt, with a cast of

---

[7] In Heaney's version, Antigone's pronouncement that Polyneices deserves a burial because he is "no common criminal" (*The Burial at Thebes* 23) might also be linked to the question – key during the Hunger Strikes – of whether prisoners during the conflict were to be categorized as criminals or political prisoners.

[8] A significant exception, addressed at length by Ní Ríordáin, is Heaney's poem "Mycenae Lookout", a very free rendering of Aeschylus' *Agamemnon*.

characters, with a company of actors in mind, with the stage in mind... That taught me that, if ever I was going to approach the drama again, I would have to somehow get reckless, you know. Maybe that will happen. (Homem 26)

The final pronouncement here is less than adamant, and later Heaney would characterize *The Burial at Thebes* as effectively seeking a "balance" between "textual strictness" and "contemporary significance" (O'Driscoll 423)[9]. The latter play's negotiation of opposing strategies of translation entails that the poet finds himself, behind the scenes, implicated in the dramatic conflict on stage. The very language of Heaney's interview – referring to "obedience" and "recklessness" – thus reappears. On the one hand, he as a translator is drawn to the uncompromising stance of Antigone, who in Heaney's version questions whether she is "a reckless woman" or whether rather Creon is "the reckless one" (*The Burial at Thebes* 21). At the same time, Creon's autocratic demand for "Obedience / And respect" from his son, Haemon, reflects the kind of classicist deference Heaney cannot quite eschew (30-31)[10].

3. Translating *hamartia*

Ultimately, both Heaney and Paulin face up to Sophocles' central theme of error. In the original, the first explicit uses of *hamartia* – Aristotle's term for the tragic error – pertain to Antigone. In the Loeb edition, Hugh Lloyd-Jones renders the relevant line from Antigone

---

[9] In a note prefacing his posthumously published translation of the sixth book of Vergil's *Aeneid*, Heaney similarly refers to his search for "a diction decorous enough for Virgil but no so antique as to sound out of tune with a more contemporary idiom" ("Translator's Note" xiii).

[10] One might however note that the positions of Creon and Antigone are reversible, if one looks at their relationship to the gods rather than the law of the state. For Antigone, Creon shows a reckless lack of deference to the gods, while her own burying of her brother amounted to – in her final line in Heaney's version of the play – "a reverence that was right" (*The Burial at Thebes* 41).

as: "to Creon I seemed to do wrong and to show shocking recklessness" (Sophocles, *Antigone, Women of Thracis, Philoctetes, Oedipus at Colonus*, trans. Lloyd-Jones 87-89). "Wrong" is here a translation of *hamartia*. Although neither Heaney nor Paulin include this passage directly in their text, they both return to – and circle around – the alleged errors of both Antigone and Creon. In *The Burial at Thebes*, a crucial instance is the encounter between the prophet Tiresias and Creon, where Tiresias seeks to make the king change his mind. In Jebb's version, Tiresias provides the following advice:

> All men are liable to err, but when an error hath been made, that man is no longer witless or unblest who heals the ill into which he hath fallen, and remains not stubborn. (Sophocles, *Antigone*, trans. Jebb)

Whereas Paulin ignores this passage, Heaney renders it as follows: "All men make mistakes. / But mistakes don't have to be forever, / They can be admitted and atoned for. / It's the overbearing man who is to blame" (*The Burial at Thebes* 44). This passage bears a typical signature effect of Heaney's, in how it roots a desire for reconciliation in a generalized humanism that – in the word "atonement" – uneasily blurs into a religious register.

Paulin's response to the theme of error is different. A characteristic stance can be identified in his translation of the anguished debate between Creon and his son, Haemon. In Jebb's translation, Haemon claims to

> hear these murmurs in the dark, these moanings of the city for this maiden; "no woman", they say, "ever merited her doom less, – none ever was to die so shamefully for deeds so glorious as hers; who, when her own brother had fallen in bloody strife, would not leave him unburied, to be devoured by carrion dogs, or by any bird: – deserves not she the meed of golden honour?" Such is the darkling

rumour that spreads in secret. (Sophocles, *Antigone*, trans. Jebb).

In this passage, Paulin follows Jebb quite closely, but adds unmistakable, idiomatic touches of his own:

> listen, listen, please,
> to what's going [to] happen
> if you stick firm.
> would I be your son
> if I never heeded
> what's yacking in the streets?
> [...]
>
> "Thon girl did right,"
> "What wrong's she done? –
> it's what they're saying.
> 'If there was justice here,
> she'd get praise then –
> she'd be honoured for it".
> That's the whisper
> and it's catching on
> like sticky fire.
> (*The Riot Act* 37-38)

Here the vernacular flourishes of "yacking" and "thon" are typical, but I want to focus on the peculiar use of the word "stick": if Creon "stick[s] firm", Haemon claims, the insurrectionary rumours will spread "like sticky fire".

The use of "stick" and "sticky" echoes with other passages in *The Riot Act*. For instance, early in the play, Creon insists Antigone will relent her opposition to him since she is a woman, while "if she were a man, now, / she'd maybe stick" (*The Riot Act* 27). When Antigone's sister Ismene changes her mind, and wants to stand by her rebellious sibling, she declares: "I'm sticking with you" (31). Similarly, Creon asks Haemon to "stick with me / no matter" (36), and later insists that he himself will be "sticking by" the law he himself has made (40). To this Haemon responds: "There's a higher law – / aye, a deeper one – / and that you stuck a hole in" (40). This motif might seem arbitrary, as these passages have no obvious parallel in Jebb or Sophocles. Yet, even if it constitutes a kind of signature-effect in Paulin's case, it is not without any precedent in his sources. This becomes clear in the debate between Creon and Tiresias, where Paulin has Creon lamenting that "They all pick faults in me. / What we don't want, / that's easy said – / not what we'd stick to" (51). This is a response to Jebb's lines: "Old Man, ye all shoot your shafts at me, as archers at the butts; – Ye must needs practice on me with seer-craft also" (Sophocles, *Antigone*, trans. Jebb).

Heaney would appear to cleave closer to the original here, with the lines: "Why am I standing here like a target? / Why is every arrow aimed at me?" (*The Burial at Thebes* 44) Yet, one can see how Paulin's "stick" derives from the arrows of the original. In Sophocles, this imagery is based upon wordplay on the term *hamartia*: for the literal meaning of this "error" is a missing of the mark in archery. After accusing Antigone of *hamartia* for much of the play, Creon becomes the target for the arrows of his accusers at the end – as he himself becomes identified as the one being in "error".

Effectively, Paulin has created an associative force field out of the missed shafts of *hamartia*, combining the purported errors of the protagonists with both headstrongness and principled behavior – "sticking" to their allegiances and views – but also to destructiveness, as in the "sticky fire" referred to earlier. The "sticky fire" is connotatively linked with the "right blood-mess" Creon admits to having caused by the end of the play (*The Riot Act* 62). Where Paulin is expansive upon such violence, Heaney tends to be more restrained, and takes a position closer to Creon's wife, Eurydice. Facing the "mortal cost of ill-judged words and deeds," she refrains from voicing her grief in public (*The Burial at Thebes* 52). While the Messenger in Paulin's version is preoccupied with Eurydice's need for "peace", Heaney gives due weight to the tactfulness of the grieving mother: "Maybe now / She needs her privacy inside the house. / Maybe she can't give vent to grief in public" (52).

Conclusion: Translation's double bind

In conclusion, Eurydice's withdrawal from the fray can be taken as illustrating Heaney's dignified classicism. Although his *The Burial at Thebes* cannot escape from the violent territory inherent in the "cultural wars" of 9/11 and the Northern Irish Troubles, his verse struggles to find a place of remove. This would be a place for a voice transcending error to unfold. Yet the classical is, in tragedy, inextricably bonded with a fateful family history of violence. Paulin's alternative, in *The Riot Act*, is to more forcefully enter the conflict of the play, taking sides. He more clearly twists the play into a new shape, removing the generality and neutrality of the chorus with a call for insurrection.

The two Northern Irish poets exemplify contrastive stances, whereby the translator's taking of sides either represents a mistake or the remedy for false neutrality. The resulting cultural error can be read as either a vulgar lack of cultivation or, on the contrary, as a desiccated classicism that lacks cultural vitality. But how to choose one of these options without feeling the pull of the other? It is perhaps the resulting double bind that damns the translator with an impossible choice, resulting either way in a kind of *hamartia* of translation.

Works cited

Aristotle. *Poetics*, translated by Stephen Halliwell, W. H. Fyfe and Doreen C. Innes. Harvard University Press, 1995.

Derrida, Jacques. "From Des Tours de Babel", translated by Joseph F. Graham. *Theories of Translation: An Anthology*, edited by Rainer Schulte and John Biguenet. The University of Chicago Press, 1992.

Dyer, Robert R. "'Hamartia' in the 'Poetics' and Aristotle's Model of Failure". *Arion: A Journal of Humanities and the Classics*, vol. 4, no. 4, Winter 1965, pp. 658-664.

Heaney, Seamus. *Preoccupations: Selected Prose 1968-1978*. Faber and Faber, 1980.

Heaney, Seamus. *The Burial at Thebes: Sophocles 'Antigone'*. Faber and Faber, 2004.

Heaney, Seamus. "Translator's Note". Virgil, *Aeneid: Book VI*, translated by Seamus Heaney. Faber and Faber, 2016.

Homem, Rui Carvalho. "On Elegies, Eclogues, Translations, Transfusions: an interview with Seamus Heaney". *The European English* Messenger, vol. 10, no. 2, Autumn 2001.

Hyde, Isabel. "The Tragic Flaw: Is it Tragic Error?" *The Modern Language Review*, vol. 58, no. 3, July 1963, pp. 321-325.

McDonald, Peter. "The Greeks in Ireland: Irish Poets and Greek Tragedy" *Translation and Literature*, vol. 4, no. 2, 1995.

McKittrick, David, and McVea, David. *Making Sense of the Troubles: The Story of the Northern Ireland Conflict*. New Amsterdam Books, 2002.

Ní Ríordáin, Clíona. "'Puddling at the Source': Seamus Heaney and the Classical Text". *Études anglaises*, vol. 56, no. 2, volume 56, 2003, pp. 173-184.

O'Brien, Conor Cruise. *States of Ireland*. Hutchinson, 1972.

O'Driscoll, Dennis. *Stepping Stones: Interviews with Seamus Heaney*. Faber and Faber, 2008.

Paulin, Tom. *The Riot Act: A Version of "Antigone" by Sophocles*. Faber and Faber, 1985.

Paulin, Tom. *Seize the Fire: A Version of Aeschylus' "Prometheus Bound"*. Faber and Faber, 1990.

Reynolds, Matthew. *The Poetry of Translation: From Chaucer & Petrarch to Homer and Logue*. Oxford University Press, 2011.

Robinson, Peter. *Poetry and Translation: The Art of the Impossible*. Liverpool University Press, 2010.

Schwerter, Stephanie. *Northern Irish Poetry and the Russian Turn: Intertextuality in the Work of Seamus Heaney, Tom Paulin and Medbh McGuckian*. Palgrave Macmillan, 2013.

Steiner, George. *Antigones: The Antigone Myth in Western Literature, Art, and Thought*. Oxford University Press, 1984.

Steiner, George. *After Babel: Aspects of Language and Translation*, third edition. Oxford University Sophocles. *Antigone, Women of Thracis, Philoctetes, Oedipus at Colonus*, edited and translated by Hugh Lloyd-Jones. Harvard University Press, 1994.

Venuti, Lawrence. *The Translator's Invisibility: A History of Translation*. Routledge, 1995.

Webography

Hardwick, Lorna. "Interview with Seamus Heaney (recorded September 2007)". *Practitioners' Voices in Classical Reception Studies*, issue 7, 2016 http://www.open.ac. uk/ arts/ research/pvcrs/2016/heaney-interview. Accessed 17 March 2018.

Ó Seaghdha, Barra. "A Sentimental Dissenter". *Dublin Review of Books*, Issue 103, September 2018, http://www.drb.ie/essays/a-sentimental-dissenter. Accessed 16 September 2018.

Paulin, Tom. "Ireland – just the place for classical tragedy." *The Observer*, 24 October 1999, https://www.theguardian.com/theobserver/1999/oct/24/featuresreview.review9. Accessed 17 March 2018.

Sophocles, *Antigone*, translated by R. C. Jebb. Internet Classics Archive. http://classics.mit.edu/Sophocles/antigone.html. Accessed 16 March 2018.

The Farmer, the French Translator and the Travelling Salesman: Cultural Errors in Bob Dylan's Satirical Songs

Jean-Charles Meunier

Introduction

"Motorpsycho Nitemare", which was written by Bob Dylan in 1964, is a narrative song that features a succession of 9 verses, with no chorus. From a musical point of view, it is very basic, with only an acoustic guitar accompanying Bob Dylan's voice, allowing the listener to focus on the lyrics. There are few melodic variations, hence the tendency to liken it to a form of Talking blues (Margotin and Guesdon 124), which is defined as "a style of blues music in which the lyrics are more or less spoken rather than sung" (Stevenson). In his article "Nothing's Been Changed, Except the Words: Some Faithful Attempts at Covering Bob Dylan Songs in French", written in 2007, Nicolas Froeliger mentions "Motorpsycho Nitemare" and concludes that "the plot of the song simply does not work in French" (184). With this claim, he seems to imply that the translators did not overlook or misunderstand some cultural aspects of the song, but rather deliberately modified the elements in the source text which could not be understood by a French audience because of a lack of cultural "shared knowledge", a notion which I shall develop later.

Froelinger alludes to Dylan's references to the feature film *Psycho*, released four years before the song, in 1960 (Hitchcock). He may be right in contending that some of the cultural errors in this translation are present by design, yet the references to *Psycho* are only one facet of this song, as I shall show in this chapter. Within the framework of this study, I shall consider cultural errors to be those elements of translation that cause the target audience to have a perception of the song that differs from the effect Dylan originally intended the song to have on his American listeners. I am aware that this implies a bias, as the original song was not necessarily intended to be heard only by American listeners, but comparing the effect on a French audience of the translation and the original song would be beyond the scope of this article. As I shall demonstrate, the analysis of cultural errors within a song involves exploring not only the text, but also the music and the performance, which are equally important (Sylvanise 3).

In the present study, I explore how the references to the cultural context in which the song was written – the USA in the 1960s – were transferred into a different cultural environment (Dylan, "Motorpsycho Nitemare"). To this end, two French versions will be compared. The first one was translated by Hugues Aufray, a popular French performer, who began his career in 1959 and is famous for singing Dylan's work in French, and Pierre Delanoë, a French lyricist, who wrote a great number of popular hits. The song was performed by Aufray and released only one year after the original, in 1965 (Aufray, "Cauchemar psychomoteur"). The second version was translated by Sarclo, a French-speaking songwriter from Switzerland, who started singing at the end of the 1970s, performing Dylan's songs in English before writing his own songs. He appreciated the translation by Aufray and Delanoë, and in 2017, decided to record a version of his own, which will be compared in this article with Aufray's. It was performed live in 2017 in a trio (Sarclo, *Cauchemar psychomoteur*). Aufray recorded the song again in 1995 for his second album of Dylan covers, *Aufray Trans Dylan* (Aufray, "Cauchemar psychomoteur"), but as the second version is very similar to the first, I make few references to it.

In the title of the song, "Motorpsycho Nitemare", Dylan refers to the three major elements in the composition of the song. "Motorpsycho" is a portmanteau word created by Dylan following the model of another portmanteau word: motorcycle (motor + bicycle). These two portmanteau words form a minimal pair, as they only differ by one sound: /ˈməʊtəsaɪkl/ ≠ /ˈməʊtəsaɪkəʊ /. Using a word that sounds like "motorcycle" may be a way for Dylan to establish an alter ego via the main character of the song, since he himself rode a Triumph motorcycle at the time this song was released, and did so until his accident in 1966 (Shelton, chap. 11). In verse 2, the speaker is mistaken for a travelling salesman by the farmer, whereby Dylan introduces the first reference in the song: the travelling salesman jokes. The second part of the portmanteau word is an allusion to Alfred Hitchcock's film *Psycho*, as is made clear by the reference to "Tony Perkins". Finally, the word "Nitemare" is used by Dylan to make a statement about the anti-communist paranoia of the Cold War in the USA. The author implicitly compares the horror of Hitchcock's movie with the nightmare of living in the USA in the context of the 60s, and at the same time draws an analogy between madness, that is the theme of Hitchcock's film, and the paranoia of anti-communist America.

1. The Travelling salesman jokes and the Talking blues

1.1 The structure of the song: metatextuality and parody

The storyline proposed by the song is a parody of a type of jokes, which were popular in the USA from the 1920s to the 1960s (*Motorpsycho Nightmare, Untold Dylan*). In the standard joke, the travelling salesman always arrives near an isolated farm and asks for shelter. He then discovers that the farmer's daughter is very attractive and he wants to have sex with her. The farmer agrees to allow the travelling salesman stay under one condition: he is not allowed to touch his daughter. At the end of the story, the traveling salesman manages to make love to the daughter. The humour of the joke always revolves around how the travelling salesman manages to trick the farmer, and this is revealed in the punch line.

In the song, the farmer is suspicious from the beginning, as he suspects the speaker of being the legendary travelling salesman: "Are you that travelin' salesman / That I have heard about?" (verse 2). This metatextual comment, which introduces the parodic element in the song, can only be understood if the listener knows the original joke, which was probably true of most listeners in the USA at the time Dylan wrote the song. However, this was not the case in France in 1965, much less in 2017, when it is unsure if even a younger American listener would understand the parodic value of the song. Perhaps Aufray and Delanoë did not know of these jokes or perhaps they chose to adopt a domesticating approach, which, as Lawrence Venuti explains in *The Translator's Invisibility: A History of Translation*, involves "an ethnocentric reduction of the foreign text to target-language cultural values" (20). In other words, they preferred not to make any reference to a travelling salesman, and chose instead to introduce a character which a French farmer could be wary of, translating "C'est vous l'espèce de **vagabond** / Qui vient pour mendier" (verse 2) [aren't you that vagrant who has come to beg ?][1].

The reference to the travelling salesman – which could be translated "voyageur de commerce" or "commis voyageur" in French – is lost, which is problematic, as it is not just a passing reference but is a major structuring device in the original song. As a result, the French text makes it appear as if it were an original storyline created by Bob Dylan, while the original text was recognised by the listener as a parody of an existing work. This has important consequences for the interpretation of the target text. For example, when Dylan presents us with a reversal of the joke, in which the farmer's daughter Rita tries to seduce the speaker. This aspect cannot be perceived without referencing the original Travelling salesman joke. In addition, within the context of this song, in which Dylan uses humour to deal with the subject of anti-communism, the farmer's suspicious inclination suggests that the expression "travelling salesman" could hide another suspicion: that of the speaker being a "fellow-traveller", i.e. a communist sympathiser.

---

1 Unless otherwise noted, all translations of works in languages other than English are my own.

1.2 Telling Tall tales: from Cowboy jokes to Woody Guthrie's Talking Blues

In "Jake Thackray, Translator and Interpreter of Brassens", Colin Evans refers to the notion of "shared knowledge" (81). In the case of Georges Brassens, the French singer takes for granted that Aragon, Villon, Hugo and Verlaine are known to the audience, so that he can use them as bricks to build his song on and expect to be understood (79). In the case of Bob Dylan, one of the key elements to reaching an understanding of his songs deep enough to grasp its subtleties, and to perceive the humour in particular, is to be found in the songs of Woody Guthrie.

One of the characteristics of the travelling salesman jokes is the obvious exaggeration they contain, which makes them akin to Guthrie's Talking blues ("Mean Talking Blues"; "Talking Hard Work"; "Talking Columbia"). Guthrie wrote them under the influence of the Tall tales[2] common in the cowboy humour he undoubtedly heard in his childhood (Klein 1). There are a number of such exaggerations in "Motorpsycho Nitemare": outrageously excessive figures, but also hyperbolic adjectives and adverbs. Some were transferred in the target text, therefore keeping this cultural aspect of the work, such as the narrator crashing through the window "at a hundred miles an hour" (verse 8), the speaker's claim that he "was born at the bottom of a wishing well" (verse 3) and the narrator's amplified appraisal of the farmer's daughter, who "looked like she stepped out of *La Dolce Vita*" (verse 3), a reference to the Hollywood feature film (Fellini).

Some of this hyperbole, however, seems to have been overlooked, causing the listener to lose sight of this specific cultural form. For example, at the beginning of the song, Dylan sets the tone, with the speaker declaring that he was "mighty mighty tired" as he "had come a long long way" (verse 1). Despite the repetition of both the already hyperbolic adverb "mighty" and the adjective "long", Aufray

---

[2] The Oxford Advanced Learner's Dictionary of Current English defines a tall tale / tall story as a "story that is difficult to believe" (Hornby and Cowie 1313).

translated "j'étais fatigué" [I was tired], an understatement which was corrected in his second version to "j'étais très très fatigué" [I was very very tired]. Sarclo sings "J'étais carrément crevé" [I was totally wiped out], which reveals a subtle perception, not only of the exaggeration, but also of the informal register of the text, with the use of "mighty" as an adverb.

Another exaggeration is the number of miles that the speaker claims to have driven in verse 4: "ten thousand miles / Today I drove". Aufray sings "j'ai **fait** huit cent bornes" [I have walked? / driven? 500 miles], with the verb "faire" in French remaining vague as to how that distance was covered. In the first verse, the translation of "I'd **come** a long long way": is given as "comme j'avais beaucoup **marché**" [As I had **walked** a lot]. As I have already mentioned, the speaker in Aufray's song is a vagrant, which is consistent with him being on foot – but in blatant contradiction with the portmanteau word in the song title, "psychomoteur" [motorpsycho], which indicates that he is on a motorcycle.

In his desire to bring the translation closer to the original text, Sarclo changed the translation in verse 1 to "j'avais **roulé** toute la journée" [I had driven all day], thus creating a discrepancy, since the speaker is still a vagrant in his translation. More importantly, he keeps the distance of "huit cent bornes" [500 miles] in verse 4, so he loses the overstatement that Dylan used to generate humour. This could be interpreted as a cultural error, as hyperbole is one of the main characteristics of Talking blues and Travelling salesman jokes.

1.3 Between talking and singing: imitating Dylan's conversational style

In *Classic Bob Dylan, 1962-1969: My Back Pages*, Andy Gill acknowledges the legacy of Woody Guthrie's Talking blues in "Motorpsycho Nitemare" (60). The cultural specificity of the song lies as much in its form as in its content. In addition to the exaggerations, another important element of the **Talking** blues is that, as its name suggests, it is not sung. Dylan borrows his conversational style from this form, keeping part of his song spoken, so that the melody does not interfere with the message delivered. As Sarclo explains, the scansion in Bob Dylan's songs is very different from what he refers to as "la chanson française de qualité" [quality French chanson] (Personal Interview in Lyon). What he is addressing is a cultural error that consists in trying to perform a Dylan cover within the canon of the French chanson when Dylan's performance is a legacy of the folk and blues genre, and more specifically the Talking blues, in the case of "Motorpsycho Nitemare". For that reason, it could be said that the main cultural error in Aufray's first version lies in the way he performs it, that is with a very rhythmical scansion.

By declaiming each line as if it were the words of a Victor Hugo poem, Aufray is losing some of the effect of the original song on the listener. In particular, part of the humour is lost in Aufray's version for that reason. When Dylan sings this song, he makes it sound as if he were himself telling a joke to his listener, and the tone used to tell a joke is at least as important as its content in order to prompt laughter. Making the audience laugh, in the manner of a stand-up comedian, requires a subtle combination of performance skills, which the French performer would be wise to emulate so as to produce the same effect on the target audience. Shelton refers to Dylan's "control of humor and timing" (chap. 3).

When Aufray recorded a second version of the song 30 years later for the album *Aufray Trans Dylan* ("Cauchemar psychomoteur" 95), he seems to have been aware of the discrepancy between his rendition of the song, as characterised by the regular pace of the scansion in the French chanson tradition, and Dylan's original conversational performance. While, as I mentioned in the introduction, he hardly changed any words in his text, the performance sounds as if he tried to rectify this cultural error. His singing is closer to talking. However, as this is not part of his usual performing style, it does not come naturally, at times he gives the impression that he is shouting out the last word of the line in order to break the melody. His attempt to infuse some talking in the singing does not add anything in terms of expressivity, and the result sounds less like Bob Dylan than it sounds like Jean-Patrick Capdevielle, a French singer known for songs such as "Quand t'es dans le desert", which reveals his rock music influences.

Sarclo, on the other hand, who began his career singing Dylan – in English – in the bars of Lausanne when he was a student, has adopted this conversational style in his personal work. This explains why this mode of performance sounds so natural in his version of "Motorpsycho Nitemare" (*Cauchemar psychomoteur*). He explains how he perceives this difference between Dylan's conversational style, borrowed from the Talking blues, and the more regulated rhythm of the French chanson:

> Il y a quelque chose d'une liberté de rythme qui fait que tout d'un coup les mots prennent une liberté intérieure, prennent un poids, prennent une signification plus lourde, plus ample, plus à la hauteur de la dignité des mots, parce que, quand on parle, toi et moi, on crée l'emphase en faisant traîner sur une syllabe, en précipitant trois mots ici, en en ralentissant deux là.
>
> [There is something like a freedom in rhythm that makes the word suddenly take on an inner freedom, a weight, a deeper and wider meaning... a meaning that is closer to the dignity of words, because when you and I speak, we create emphasis by lingering on a syllable, by accelerating three words here, by slowing down two others there.]
>
> (*Personal Interview in Lyon*)

In his performance, Sarclo emulates this form, speaking rather than singing so as to leave room for the "dignity" of words, as he calls it. This gives the listener a completely different impression, i.e. that he is creating an intimate space of conversation with his audience, within which he can communicate the humour of the text. Proximity between performer and audience – audience participation being only one aspect of it – is one of the main stakes of the American folk revival, as Pete Seeger explains in his autobiography (252-53). The bottom line of these attempts is to transfer onto the listener the impact of a musical form – i.e. the Talking blues – which is culturally anchored in American culture and takes its source in the 1930s, particularly with the contributions of Woody Guthrie (Shelton, chap. 3).

2. From Hitchcock to Dylan: parody of a motel horror film

2.1 The topos of the road in American culture

In the last verse of the song, Dylan tells the audience that Rita has "moved away / And got a job at a motel", which makes Dylan's song a prequel to the film *Psycho*. The word "motel", like the word "motorcycle", is a portmanteau word (motor + hotel), and designates a hotel for motorists. Due to the size of the country and the overwhelming presence of automobiles in the USA, the road movie has become a topos in American literature, especially since Jack Kerouac's novel *On the Road*. The same topos is omnipresent in cinema, including scenes of horror on the road. A few examples include Steven Spielberg's first feature film *Duel*, released in 1968, as well as George Miller's *Mad Max* film, which was followed by other episodes. This genre is linked with another one, which is the motel horror film, with examples such as *The Shining* by Stanley Kubrick and, more recently, the *Hostel* trilogy, by Eli Roth, which began in 2005. The graphic violence and the sexual content in *Psycho* played a very important role in the development of these two genres (*How Psycho Changed Cinema*).

Even though the reference to the motel is very important, both for these cultural reasons and more specifically because of the intertextual humour with *Psycho*, it is absent in both French versions. In Aufray's version, Rita has not found a job at all – it is the speaker who has found a job in between (verse 9). This significantly changes the meaning of the sentence, as in the original text, the fact that Rita has left the farm is mentioned because, as Froeliger explains, "the narrator [sic] is more afraid of the daughter than of the gun-wielding father" (184). Surprisingly, this mistake was not corrected in the revised version on *Aufray Trans Dylan* (Aufray, "Cauchemar psychomoteur"). Sarclo rectifies the error, translating "Même si Rita est partie /Qu'elle a trouvé un boulot" [Even if Rita is gone / And she has found a job], but he makes no reference to a motel either (*Cauchemar psychomoteur*).

Madness is a recurrent theme in this type of films. Thus, the sentence "He must have thought that I was **nuts**" in verse 1 could be seen as a first allusion to *Psycho*. It is used primarily to oppose the two characters ,who symbolise urban and rural America, the speaker seeing the farmer as a "hillbilly" while he himself is probably regarded as a "city slacker" by the farmer. The latter is a stereotypical right-wing conservative who reads *The Reader's Digest* (verse 8), which is also a way of saying that he is not educated, since he only reads digests instead of full books.

The spelling "nitemare" in the title of the song may be construed as a reference to illiteracy. Dylan's rhetorical strategy consists in blending together into his parody of a joke multiple references to *Psycho*, thus creating a situation in which the speaker is violently driven out for his communist sympathies: "You unpatriotic / Rotten doctor, Commie rat" (verse 7). This allows Dylan to draw a parallel between the nightmarish story of Psycho and the rampant anti-communist paranoia of the Cold War era (Rezé and Bowen 101; Nevins and Commager 498), all the while using the channel of humour.

This parallel is downplayed in the French translations, as the sentence about the speaker being "nuts" is not translated. In addition, another allusion to the farmer's entrenched conservatism is also absent: "Well, by the dirt 'neath my nails / I guess he knew I wouldn't lie". The speaker expects the farmer to equate the quality of being hard-working with that of being honest, so he is defending himself against the potential accusation of being a "city-slacker", an expression commonly used in rural America to refer to city dwellers. The French translations, "En voyant mes ongles sales / Il sut que je travaillais" [When he saw my dirty nails / He understood that I was a hard worker], do not refer at all to the idea of being honest. In order to translate Dylan's mockery of the conservative farmer equating hard work with honesty, the translator in 2018 could use an expression such as "l'Amérique qui se lève tôt" [that America who gets up early], in reference to Nicolas Sarkozy's speech in Périgueux on 12 October 2006. In a similar rhetoric, he referred to "la France qui se lève tôt" [that France who gets up early] in order to oppose honest hard-working taxpayers and dishonest freeloaders living on welfare. The expression is probably still in the minds of many French listeners and would probably cause them to smile at this intrusion of French politics in a song originally by Bob Dylan. The disadvantage of such a translation, though, is that it might be quickly outdated, as Sarkozy's speech might not be remembered forever.

2.2 Psycho, gender and reversal

Rita coming in the middle of the night and inviting the speaker to take a shower is a reversal of the situation in the famous shower scene. The humour in the song thus comes from the parodic effect, but it could be argued that the reference is not necessary and that humour can still function without that parodic effect, as stereotypically gender relationships between men and women, both in the USA and in France, make it unlikely for Rita to make sexual advances towards the stranger. The opposite would be expected, especially following the speaker's acknowledgement of her looks in verse 3 when he refers to Federico Fellini's *La Dolce Vita*. To reinforce this expectation, he adds that he "immediately tried to cool it with her dad" (verse 3), which seems to betray his intentions to appease him so that he can sleep with his daughter, as in the travelling salesman jokes.

The speaker gives up this pursuit when he understands that the farmer is "sly" and tells him not to touch his daughter (verse 4). The reference to the shower is present in both songs. The way it is *performed*, though, is very different, giving us another example of the importance of speaking the lyrics instead of singing them in order to give each word its full effect. Where Dylan sings "I'll show you up to the door", Sarclo sings "Je vais te montrer où **c'est**" [I will show you where it is], insisting on the last word, with a salacious tone, which invariably prompts laughter in the audience.

When Rita appears, the speaker says that she is "lookin' just like Tony Perkins" (verse 5), an explicit reference to the actor who plays the role of Norman Bates in *Psycho*. Rita is seen by the speaker as a female version of Hitchcock's insane character. Aufray and Delanoë translated "Elle me faisait de l'œil / Comme Tony Perkins" [She was making eyes at me / Like Tony Perkins], which is surprising as it gives the impression that they misinterpreted the meaning of the word "look", as if Dylan had written that she was looking at the speaker in the same way as Tony Perkins would. Their interpretation is probably induced by the sexual connotation of Rita's invitation to take a shower, but it seems to imply that, in *Psycho*, Perkins makes eyes at Janet Leigh / Marion Crane, which is not the case. Sarclo's translation is surprising too: he translates "Elle souriait dans le noir / Comme Tony Perkins" [She was smiling in the dark / Like Tony Perkins].

Apparently, he wanted to stress the creepy analogy with Perkins rather than the sexual connotation, probably because the speaker mentions that he "was sleepin'", which implies that she arrives in the middle of the night. In reference to the film, the vision of Rita smiling is much closer to the image that viewers will have kept of Tony Perkins, especially his disturbing grin on the very last image – coinciding with the voice of his mother in his mind, saying "she wouldn't even harm a fly" –, which fades with the macabre image of the car containing his victim.

Both these translations involve Rita *doing* something (making eyes / smiling), when the expression in the source text only refers to her looks. This means that it involves the speaker's perception of Rita and not what she is doing. The fact that she looks like Tony Perkins is only in the speaker's imagination. Rita's attitude can be understood as a sexual invitation, but only the speaker sees it as a threat to his life, because he has seen the film *Psycho*. Dylan may be mocking the influence of America's culture of violence on the minds of American citizens, who are getting more and more paranoid as a result.

2.3 Making parody explicit

Obviously the speaker has seen the movie *Psycho*, since he compares Rita with Tony Perkins. The expression "I've been through this movie before" (verse 5) contains a double entendre. It could simply mean "you can't fool me", but could also be read as an intertextual reference, the speaker telling Rita that he has seen the movie *Psycho* – which was released four years before the song – and he knows how it ends for him.

We can draw a parallel between this double entendre and the farmer's first question to the speaker at the beginning of the story, "Are you that travelin' salesman / That I have heard about?", which also implies that he knows about travelling salesman jokes and knows how they invariably end, i.e., he knows that the farmer is always fooled in the punch line. In both cases, Dylan is explicitly making the listener aware of the parodic aspect of his text, thus asserting the centrality of parody in his song and the importance of interpreting it in this light. In *A Theory of Parody*, Linda Hutcheon speaks of "the intertextual dialogue ... between the reader and his or her memory of other texts, as provoked by the text in question" (87). She then goes on to discuss reader competence in decoding the elements of parody, using the example of Italo Calvino's *If on a Winter's Night a Traveler*, in which "the didactic narrative voice is careful to ensure their comprehension" (Hutcheon 90). There is a parallel to be drawn here with the song under scrutiny, as Dylan, with both the examples mentioned above, is drawing the listener's attention to the intertextuality in the song.

As a result, the translators would be making a capital cultural error if they ignored these references. They are confronted with a double difficulty. If they adopt what Venuti calls a "foreignizing method" (20), that is if they preserve the foreign elements in their translation, they run the risk that the French listener might not understand most of the song, as the references

Dylan makes will probably be foreign to them, or sound only vaguely familiar. For example, the listeners may be familiar with the film as the famous scene from the film *Psycho*, where a woman is murdered in a shower, has become part of popular culture both in France and in the USA.

However, they may not understand the reference to the swamp at the end of the song, which coincides with the very last image of the film, when the car containing the body of Marion Crane is fished out of the swamp. Likewise, they may not grasp the allusion made by Rita, when mumbling something about "her mother on the hill" (verse 7), a reference to the Hopperesque mansion overlooking the Bates motel.

If the translation takes the form of domestication, on the other hand, the translator will have to find equivalences for the references in French, which could be very complicated. The exaggerations in the Travelling salesman jokes can be found in the French "blagues de Marseillais", jokes about the inhabitants of the town of Marseilles, in the south of France, who are made fun of because they have the reputation of exaggerating everything (Gasquet-Cyrus 582). But these same jokes might not be an exact equivalent, as they might not necessarily include the sexual connotations of the traditional Travelling salesman jokes. Concerning the reference to *Psycho*, it is an impossible task to find a French film, which would contain the same six references mentioned in the song.

However, while the French listeners are extremely unlikely to know the travelling salesman jokes, there is a fair chance that they will know about *Psycho*, so this is probably less of an obstacle for the translator. Given the globalisation of the cinema industry, we can speculate whether the French and American listeners are on equal footing when it comes to their interpretative competence in that matter. This is difficult to assess, and the answer to this question might probably be different in 1964-1965 and today. On the one hand, the effect of globalisation is much more significant nowadays. On the other hand, the time gap since the release of the film is also much wider. As a result, it may well be that the contemporary French listener is as competent to detect the references to *Psycho* as the American listener, if not more.

Conclusion

"Motorpsycho Nitemare", although not one of the most famous of Bob Dylan's songs, is representative of the difficulties that translators have to overcome when translating his songs. The intertextuality is usually very rich, but also very diverse, ranging from what is considered highbrow literature to Abraham Lincoln to pop culture and sometimes other songs, including his own. The song "Po' Boy", for example, which appears on the album *Love and Theft* in 2001 (Dylan, "Po' Boy") includes what could be an intertextual reference to his own song *Motorpsycho Nitemare*, written 37 years earlier: "My mother was a daughter of a wealthy farmer / My father was a traveling salesman, I never met him". This extract seems to reveal that, even in 2001, Dylan is still counting on at least some of his listeners to know about the Travelling salesman joke. Dylan concludes "Motorpsycho Nitemare" with an ironic reflection to express the fact that freedom of speech is threatened by anticommunism: "Without freedom of speech / I might be in the swamp" (verse 9).

The way he draws elements from the shared cultural knowledge of his audience, interlacing the madness of *Psycho* with the licentious humour of the Travelling salesman jokes and the hyperboles of the Talking blues form finds its climax in the farmer's excessive reaction to the speaker's preposterous declaration – "I like Fidel Castro **and his beard**" (verse 6) –, which is precisely designed to get him expelled from the farm. The way it is translated in French, "Fidel Castro / C'est un bon **copain**" [Fidel Castro, he's a good pal of mine], relies on a discrepancy between the word "copain" [pal] and what would usually be expected in a political statement, in order to generate humour. The way this line is translated epitomises a hallmark of the original song, i.e. the interpenetration of heterogeneous ingredients contained in the original song, which makes it very difficult for the translator to incorporate all of them and avoid cultural errors.

As we have seen, beyond the difficulties of translating the text, it is also very important to examine the style of the performance if the singer wants to create a similar effect as the original song. What Bob Dylan has kept from his early confrontations with the audience in the 1960s is that the strength of the spoken message does not just depend on the choice of words, but also on the way they are pronounced (emphasis, delay...). This is particularly true of humour. Dylan quickly discovered that humour was a potent way to relate to his audience. Shelton declares: "The audience responded more to Dylan's wit than to his slow, serious, intense material. Audience reaction led him to play Chaplinesque clown" (chap. 3). Whether some of Aufray's early performances of Dylan's songs, including "Motorpsycho Nitemare", are cultural errors, or whether they are adaptation choices remains open to debate but it seems to me that, over the years, Aufray's tendency is to bring the songs closer to the original works, in particular in his choice of instruments.

Works cited

Calvino, Italo. *If on a Winter's Night a Traveler*. Translated by William Weaver. Harcourt Brace & Company, 1999.

Evans, Colin. "Jake Thackray, Translator and Interpreter of Brassens". *Équivalences*, vol. 22, no. 1, 1992, pp. 73-90. *Crossref*, doi:10.3406/equiv.1992.1153.

Froeliger, Nicolas. "Nothing's Been Changed, Except the Words: Some Faithful Attempts at Covering Bob Dylan Songs in French". *Oral Tradition*, vol. 22, no. 1, 2007, pp. 175-96. *Crossref*, doi: 10.1353/ort.2007.0008.

Gill, Andy. *Classic Bob Dylan, 1962-1969: My Back Pages*. Sevenoaks, 1998.

Hornby, Albert S., and Anthony P. Cowie. *Oxford Advanced Learner's Dictionary of Current English*. 4. ed., 6. Impr. Oxford Univ. Press, 1993.

Hutcheon, Linda. *A Theory of Parody: The Teachings of Twentieth-Century Art Forms*. University of Illinois Press, 2000.

Kerouac, Jack. *On the Road*. Viking Press, 1957.

Klein, Joe. *Woody Guthrie: A Life*. A.A. Knopf. Random House, 1980.

Margotin, Philippe, and Jean-Michel Guesdon. *Bob Dylan: All the Songs: The Story behind Every Track*. First edition, Black Dog & Leventhal Publishers, 2015.

Nevins, Allan, and Henry Steele Commager. *A Pocket History of the United States*. 8. revised and enl. ed., [5. Dr.]. Washington Square Press [u.a.], 1986.

Rezé, Michel, and Ralph Henry Bowen. *Key Words in American Life*. Masson, 1979.

Seeger, Pete, et al. *Pete Seeger: His Life in His Own Words*. Paradigm Publishers, 2012.

Shelton, Robert. *No Direction Home: The Life and Music of Bob Dylan*. Epub file. Omnibus Press, 2011.

Sylvanise, Frédéric. "À la recherche d'une poétique ou comment lire une chanson populaire américaine". *Itinéraires*, no. 2014-2, July 2015. *Crossref*, doi: 10.4000/itineraires.2486.

Venuti, Lawrence. *The Translator's Invisibility: A History of Translation*. Routledge, 1995. *Open WorldCat*, http://site. ebrary. com/id/10097452.

Discography

Aufray, Hugues. "Cauchemar psychomoteur". *Aufray chante Dylan*. Barclay, 1965.

Aufray, Hugues. "Cauchemar psychomoteur". *Aufray trans Dylan*. Arcade, 1995.

Capdevielle, Jean-Patrick. "Quand t'es dans le désert". *Les enfants des ténèbres et les anges de la rue*. CBS, 1979.

Dylan, Bob. "Motorpsycho Nitemare." *Another Side of Bob Dylan*. CBS, 1964.

Dylan, Bob. "Po' Boy". *Love and Theft*. Columbia, 2001.

Guthrie, Woody. "Mean Talking Blues". *Hard Travelin' (The Asch Recordings Vol. 3)*. Smithsonian Folkways, 1998.

Guthrie, Woody. "Talking Columbia". *Hard Travelin' (The Asch Recordings Vol. 3)*. Smithsonian Folkways, 1998.

Guthrie, Woody. "Talking Hard Work". *This Land Is Your Land (The Asch Recordings, Vol. 1)*. Smithsonian Folkways, 1997.

Filmography

Fellini, Federico. *La Dolce Vita*. 1960.

Hitchcock, Alfred. *Psycho*. 1960.

Kubrick, Stanley. *The Shining*. Warner Bros. 1980.

Miller, George. *Mad Max*. Roadshow Film Distributors, 1979.

Roth, Eli. *Hostel*. Lionsgate, 2005.

Spielberg, Steven. *Duel*. Universal Pictures, 1971.

Webography

Gasquet-Cyrus, Mederic. *Pratiques et Représentations de l'humour Verbal: Étude Sociolinguistique Du Cas Marseillais*. www.academia.edu. Accessed 19 December 2018.

https://www.academia.edu/1976689/Pratiques_et_repr%C3%A9sentations_de_lhumour_verbal_%C3%A9tude_sociolinguistique_du_cas_marseillais. Accessed 19 December 2018.

How Psycho Changed Cinema. 1 Apr. 2010. *news.bbc.co.uk*, http://news.bbc.co.uk/2/hi/uk_news/magazine/8593508.stm. Accessed 19 Dec. 2018.

Motorpsycho Nightmare: The Meaning of the Song and the Lyrics | Untold Dylan. https://bob-dylan.org.uk/archives/1805. Accessed 28 August 2018.

Sarclo. *Cauchemar psychomoteur*. 2017. YouTube, https://www.youtube.com/watch?v=E1N85lYy72I. Accessed 28 August 2018.

Additional Sources Cited

Sarclo. Personal Interview in Lyon. 19 Jan. 2018.

Stevenson, Angus, editor. "Talking Blues". *Oxford Dictionary of English*, 3rd ed. Oxford University Press, 2010. Mac Dictionary, Version 2.2.2 (203).

The Vanishing of Verlaine: Cultural Error in Translations of Gainsbourg's "Je suis venu te dire que je m'en vais"

Paul Grundy

Introduction

While musicians who have conquered international audiences need not dwell unduly on the cultural errors they may have produced, certain translated songs are worthy of attention if only because of the chasm they expose between the priorities of lyric-based song and the commercial expectations of the pop industry at large. Translation can play a significant role in either widening or reducing this chasm. Serge Gainsbourg's famous ballad "Je suis venu te dire que je m'en vais" (1973), which, in recent decades has been re-released in English, Italian and Flemish, is a case in point.

Translating Gainsbourg implies the refusal to take any song at face value, given not only the artist's humour, but also his love of reprise and reinvention. Musically, it is well known that Gainsbourg unabashedly recycled famous themes. As his longtime partner Jane Birkin explains: "Often Serge used classical music like Chopin or Brahms for people he loved. He wanted to give us the very best although he was perfectly capable of writing himself"[1]. Gainsbourg's ode to Brigitte Bardot, "Initials B.B." (1968), relied heavily on a theme from Antonín Dvořák's 9th Symphony (1893), while "Jane B" (1969), written for Birkin herself, borrowed from Chopin's Prelude Op. 28, No. 4 (1839).

Textual recycling in Gainsbourg's work is just as unavoidable. Not content with writing music to existing texts, he clearly loved to adapt well-known lyrics. "La Chanson de Prévert" (Bouvier,

---

[1] Pound, Cath. "The Erotic Songs Lost in Translation". *BBC Culture*, 10 August 2017.

Vincendet 114) famously refers back to Prévert and Kosma's song, "Les Feuilles mortes," which was released a decade earlier in 1950 (Odéon). Both songs begin, "Oh je voudrais tant que tu te souviennes" [Oh, how I'd love you to remember][2], and evoke a lost love, the Gainsbourg character's memories revived through a *mise en abîme* of the Prévert work.

In "Je suis venu te dire que je m'en vais", the use of reprise is even more extensive, which explains why the song is referred to by Serge Vincendet (477) as a collage[3] of barely modified passages of Paul Verlaine's "Chanson d'automne" (*Œuvres* 21), a timeless poem known in English as "Autumn Song". Gainsbourg's listener is alerted to this intertextual game by the recurring line, "Comme dit si bien Verlaine 'au vent mauvais'" [As Verlaine, swept away by "the evil wind", so aptly puts it]. Here Gainsbourg refers to the "evil wind" of the last strophe of Verlaine's poem (22). The latter reads: "Je m'en vais / Au vent mauvais" [Away I go / In an evil wind].

Given Verlaine's status as a French cultural icon, an internationally renowned poet and a source of inspiration for Gainsbourg (factors which will be considered), one might expect any meaningful translation of "Je suis venu te dire que je m'en vais" to embrace Verlaine's name, language and imagery. In practice, however, this is clearly not the case. As we will see, Jarvis Cocker and Jo Lemaire erase him from their interpretations.

Such a discovery raises questions about song translation. To what extent should a debt towards an earlier work be accounted for? Are we not faced with the most glaring of cultural errors when the translation of a song based on another text simply disregards the primary source? Given the importance of Verlaine's carefully crafted lines to the outcome of Gainsbourg's song (see 1.2), does one have to be a purist to expect a translation to follow the songwriter's foot-

---

2 Hereafter, the translations in square brackets are my translations.
3 "Ce texte est un collage de passages à peine modifiés du poème de Paul Verlaine 'Chanson d'automne'" [This text is a collage of barely modified passages of Paul Verlaine's "Autumn Song"].

steps back to the source, and take into account the mood and register of a plundered text?

One answer to this question could be resoundingly negative: the average pop listener is far less preoccupied with intertextuality than with instant pleasure. However, even an outlook based purely on pleasure could just as easily fall in favour of the inclusion of Verlaine's name, as one may well wonder what is disturbing about the presence of the noun "Verlaine" in an English song. "Verlaine" presents no great challenge to a non-French speaker. Far from sounding clumsy, the name trips off the tongue.

Looking beyond the mere sound of the name, the present study reviews four translations of "Je suis venu te dire que je m'en vais" (by Jarvis Cocker, Mick Harvey, Giangilberto Monti and Jo Lemaire) and argues that the varying degrees of indifference towards Verlaine's poem adversely affects the quality of these works. While two of them do mention Verlaine, might all these translated versions have benefited from further engagement with Verlaine's renowned text? At the end of this study, an alternative translation, inspired by English translations of "Chanson d'automne" and therefore in tune with Gainsbourg's cultural gesturing, is proposed, in an attempt to provide the concrete example, which these questions demand. Is the vanishing of Verlaine a cultural error, the sign of a dumbing down process and a predatory approach towards a musical masterpiece, or a perfectly understandable, albeit commercial, process of simplification for the benefit of listeners from other cultures?

1. A neglected source: "Chanson d'automne"

1.1 Translating parody songs

From a literary viewpoint, the jettisoning of Verlaine is an error for the simple reason that "parody songs absolutely depend on allusion to earlier texts" (Low 30). Although Gainsbourg's song is not a parody in the most common sense of the word, it can easily be seen as such according to Linda Hutcheon's etymological analysis[4] of the term: parody is not only a mocking "counter-song", but also, in keeping with the second meaning of the Greek prefix "para" ("besides" rather than "counter"), a "beside song", a knowing, consenting discourse which reveals an "intimacy" with, rather than an opposition to, another text. "Je suis venu te dire que je m'en vais" is precisely that: a Gainsbourg song set beside Verlaine's "Chanson d'automne", the latter offering the former its famous autumnal melancholy and imagery of crying and separation.

1.2 The two texts side by side

"Chanson d'automne" is evoked in the third line of the refrain: "Comme dit si bien Verlaine, 'au vent mauvais'". This refrain, which reproduces the key phrases "je m'en v*ais*" [I am leaving], and "au vent mauvais" [caught in an evil wind], occurs four times. Verlaine's name and poem are therefore an integral part of a haunting loop, which precedes and follows all the verses. Regarding the overall song, the quickest of glances at the respective texts reveals its origins.

---

[4] "Most theorists of parody go back to the etymological root of the term in the Greek noun *parodia*, meaning 'counter-song,' and stop there. A closer look at that root offers more information, however. The textual or discursive nature of parody (as opposed to satire) is clear from the *odos* part of the word, meaning song. The prefix *para* has two meanings, only one of which is usually mentioned – that of 'counter' or 'against'. Thus, parody becomes an opposition or contrast between texts. One text is set against another with the intent of mocking it or making it ludicrous. However, *para* in Greek can also mean 'beside', and therefore there is a suggestion of an accord or intimacy instead of a contrast. It is this second, neglected meaning of the prefix that broadens the pragmatic scope of parody in a way most helpful to discussions of modern art forms" (32).

"Chanson d'Automne"	"Je suis venu te dire que je m'en vais"
Les sanglots longs Des violons De l'automne Blessent mon cœur D'une langueur Monotone.	Je suis venu te dire que je m'en vais Et tes larmes n'y pourront rien changer Comme dit si bien Verlaine "au vent mauvais," Je suis venu te dire que je m'en vais.
Tout suffocant Et blême, quand Sonne l'heure, Je me souviens Des jours anciens Et je pleure.	Tu te souviens des jours anciens et tu pleures Tu suffoques, tu blêmis à présent qu'a sonné l'heure. Des adieux à jamais (ouais), Je suis au regret de te dire que je m'en vais Je t'aimais, oui, mais
Et je m'en vais Au vent mauvais Qui m'emporte Deçà, delà, Pareil à la Feuille morte.	Je suis venu te dire que je m'en vais Tes sanglots longs n'y pourront rien changer Comme dit si bien Verlaine "au vent mauvais," Je suis venu te dire que je m'en vais. Tu te souviens des jours heureux et tu pleures Tu sanglotes, tu gémis

	à présent qu'a sonné l'heure. Des adieux à jamais (ouais) Je suis au regret de te dire que je m'en vais Car tu m'en as trop fait.

Gainsbourg creates variations in his refrains by alternating "larmes" [tears] and "sanglots longs" [long sobs], a key image from Verlaine's famous opening line. "Sanglots" [sobs] later turns into a verb: "tu sanglotes" [you sob]. In Gainsbourg's verses, Verlaine's image of time passing, "quand l'heure sonne" [when the hour tolls], is adapted to "à présent que l'heure a sonné" [now that the hour has tolled]. The adjectives from the seventh and eighth line, "suffocant" and "blême" [choking and pallid], are changed to verbs: "tu suffoques", "tu blemish" [you choke and turn pale], and conjugated in the second-person rather than the first. The line "Je me souviens / Des jours anciens / Et je pleure" [I remember the long gone days and I cry] is also changed to a second-person phrase. This intertextual gesturing offers two readings. Those who know "Chanson d'automne" may interpret Gainsbourg's playful *manœuvres* as an implicit response to the speaker of Verlaine's poem as well as Gainsbourg's narrator announcing his imminent departure.

What options does the translator have? On the one hand, Verlaine's work dates back to the nineteenth century and, despite gaining widespread recognition, is not as well known outside France. On the other, transmission combats ignorance. Furthermore, "Chanson d'automne" contains no historical information. It is minimalist, timeless poetry. There is, above all, a mood to be captured. Just as Gainsbourg's song is given gravitas and grace by the lines of poetry it borrows, a translation of "Je suis venu te dire que je m'en vais" could draw on translations of Verlaine's text. This solution, if singable, might yet satisfy Gainsbourg's own literary aspirations, which are discussed here.

2. Reasons to include Verlaine

2.1 Gainsbourg's literary aspirations and Verlaine

Despite his extraordinary songwriting skills, Gainsbourg claimed to be incapable of the pure description of feelings at which the likes of Charles Aznavour excelled (Bouvier, Vincendet 26)[5]. Suggesting that his talent lay more in wordplay, he went as far as saying that if he did not play with words, he did not know what to say[6]. This comment was far from flippant. Along with anglicisms, neologisms and alliteration, collage was a way of producing meaning.

Herein lies the danger for the translator. While "Je suis venu te dire que je m'en vais" can function as a sentimental song without the listener knowing anything about the intertextual game it is based on (the original music is so sensuous that many listeners around the world probably enjoy the song without even understanding the lyrics), the translator who disregards the song's playful literary dimension is likely to reduce it to the platitudinous account of a departure and a goodbye. Add to that the problem of re-recording, which, by plunging a song into a more modern-day sound, may also deprive it of its singular charm, and a masterpiece like "Je suis venu te dire que je m'en vais" can be left with little to distinguish it from the infinite number of vacuous, commercial songs about parting lovers.

Gainsbourg's determination to rise above the mediocrity of pop song lyrics is worth taking into account[7], not least because this literary ambition ties in with an affinity with 19th-century literature. Vincendet proclaims that Gainsbourg is to be considered as a

---

[5] "Je suis incapable de décrire des sentiments comme Aznavour." ["I am incapable of describing feelings as well as Aznavour"].

[6] "Les paroles me prennent du temps, si je ne joue pas avec les mots, je ne sais pas quoi dire" [Lyrics take me a long time. If I do not play around with words, I do not know what to say] (26).

[7] "Je veux lutter contre la pauvreté des textes de chansons" ["I wish to combat the mediocrity of song lyrics"] (24).

"passeur culturel" from that age[8], which spawned a host of provocative literary personalities such as Léon Bloy, Barbey d'Aurevilly and Huysmans. All of them, claims Vincendet, were precursors to Gainsbourg's cynical dandy persona (40).

Verlaine's embodiment of poetry and decadence is fully in tune with that persona. Not surprisingly, Verlaine also features in two other Gainsbourg songs. He is referred to in "Rues de Paris" (161) alongside Rimbaud: "Boulevard du Montparnasse / Val de Grâce / Plein d'oiseaux / On se croit dans un poème / Du pauvre Verlaine / Ou d'Arthur Rimbaud" [Walking along Montparnasse and Val de Grâce, with birds everywhere I go, it's like being in a poem by poor old Verlaine or Arthur Rimbaud]. In "Hmm hmm hmm" (818), Verlaine also appears, this time being alluded to as "l'autre" [that other fellow], as Gainsbourg pretends to forget his name: "Je suis pas non plus Arthur Rimbault / Celui-là il devait faire un beau couple avec l'autre, là, merde j'ai beau / Chercher j'trouve pas boh" [I'm no Arthur Rimbaud / He sure must have made a nice couple with that other fellow, damn it, I can't remember, let me see...]. With a strong touch of self-derision, Gainsbourg uses Verlaine, Rimbaud and Poe to evaluate his own standing as a poet.

2.2 Verlaine as both a French and international cultural phenomenon

The reasons for not jettisoning Verlaine are multiplied when one considers Verlaine's standing both as a French cultural phenomenon and an international icon. In "Art poétique" (*Œuvres* 150), a poem which many singers, including Léo Ferré (Barclay-Universal), have performed, Verlaine proclaimed that poetry should be music first and foremost ("de la musique avant toute chose"), and that there should always be more of it: "de la musique encore et toujours"

---

[8] "Il faut considérer Serge Gainsbourg comme un passeur. Il vient d'une autre époque, le XIXᵉ siècle, comme il s'en réclame lui-même" (40). ["Serge Gainsbourg should be seen as a cultural *passeur*. He comes from another era, the nineteenth century, as he himself declares"].

(*Œuvres* 150-151). His wishes have literally come true, as the sheer quantity of musical adaptations of his work demonstrates. According to Philippe Jaroussky, a prominent singer of Verlaine works, the number of Verlaine adaptations surpasses that of any other French poet[9]. Léo Ferré, Charles Trenet, and George Brassens all sang his texts, while Claude Debussy, Gabriel Fauré and Camille Saint-Saëns composed music for his poetry. It is not unduly bold to state that works like "Chanson d'automne" and "Art poétique" are national treasures and a permanent feature of the French artistic and educational landscape. The expulsion of Verlaine from the translation of a song based on a Verlaine text might therefore be seen as a rejection of French cultural heritage. It also flies in the face of critical recognition in the English-speaking world of Verlaine's "melodious genius" (Shapiro xvi) and "singing voice", which "can be confused with no other" (Sorrell xxvii).

2.3 Dylan and the allure of the decadent French poet

The disappearance of Verlaine also equates to a missed opportunity. Long before Cocker and Lemaire released their versions of Gainsbourg's song, Verlaine's name had helped to inject the mystique of an alluring episode of French poetry into an English-language song. Bob Dylan used it to good effect in "You're Gonna Make Me Lonesome When You Go" (Columbia): "Situations have ended sad / Relationships have all been bad / Mine have been like Verlaine's and Rimbaud / But there's no way I can compare / All them scenes to this affair / You're gonna make me lonesome when you go".

Dylan's strategy enriches his song. The anecdote of Verlaine's passionate relationship with Rimbaud, which brings homosexuality and French decadence to the fore, invites listeners to consider a culture and a lifestyle, which might be far removed from their own. The reference is also an effective and original way of dramatizing a separation, especially for those listeners who might have heard about the incredible "bungled attempt to shoot Rimbaud" by

---

[9]   Interview on the "Classique mais pas has been" website, 28 Feb. 2015.

Verlaine (Sorrell xiv). It is noteworthy that these French references have had no adverse effect on Dylan's non-French audiences. On the contrary, the song has caught on admirably, with cover versions by a host of artists in recent decades[10]. As a result, Verlaine's name has been appearing in English-language songs all around the world for decades.

2.4 A historical angle: the joining of nations

The omission of Verlaine becomes a more significant error when seen in the light of the "Verlaine message", Britain's famous acknowledgment of the French poet. On June 1st 1944, a message was broadcast by the BBC to inform the Resistance of the imminent invasion of Normandy. It consisted of the first three lines of "Chanson d'automne", and was followed on June 5th by a second message, containing the next three lines of the poem. The Verlaine Message Museum, in Tourcoing, France, bears witness to these events[11].

It is poignantly ironic that Jarvis Cocker, an enlightened and cultured British celebrity who, through his francophilia, Parisian residence and French wife, was considered ideal for a Gainsbourg project (he is presented as by the BBC as "a great admirer of Gainsbourg who certainly appreciates the difficulty of translation", and "an obvious choice to interpret Gainsbourg")[12], should remove the reference to a poem which symbolizes the collaboration of two great nations at a critical moment of World War Two. If the aims behind an album of classic French songs reinterpreted in English can be any-

---

[10] Miley Cyrus and Johnzo West covered the song for Amnesty International on *Chimes of Freedom: Songs of Bob Dylan Honoring 50 Years of Amnesty International* (Fontana, 2012). Elvis Costello covered it on the bonus disk for his album *Kojak Variety* (Rhino, 2004). Other artists who have covered the song include Madeleine Peyroux (2004), Shawn Colvin (1991), Raul Malo (2004) and Mary Lou Lord (2000), to name but a few.

[11] "Ce dimanche, le musée Message Verlaine est à redécouvrir." *La Voix du Nord*, 3 February 2018.

[12] Pound, Cath. "The Erotic Songs Lost in Translation". *BBC Culture*, 10 August 2017.

thing other than commercial, surely they should have something to do with the development of intercultural understanding.

Low's thoughts about the importance of songs and their translations tie in with this curious vanishing trick: "One of the continuing problems facing humanity in the twenty-first century is animosity between nations, always compounded by cultural ignorance and usually linked to language differences. Empathy needs to be strengthened, everywhere. Perhaps we need to listen to each other's songs more, both music and words" (2). Far more than an old poem in a book, "Chanson d'automne" is now a popular song, which carries with it the very value of intercultural bridge-building Low refers to. How can this potential be exploited if our cultural protagonists, those very celebrities who enjoy media exposure (Jarvis Cocker has his own BBC radio programme)[13], do not pass the message on in translation?

3. Four commercial versions

3.1 "I just came to tell you that I'm going" by Jarvis Cocker

In his version, "I just came to tell you that I'm going" (Verve Records), Cocker's preferred strategy is to introduce an unnamed poet: "As the poet said, 'an ill wind is blowing' / I just came to tell you that I'm going". This choice seems to be situated somewhere between, on the one hand, the error of underestimating the aforementioned importance of Verlaine to Gainsbourg, and on the other, the more calculated, commercial strategy of avoiding, within a three-minute product, any unnecessary literary baggage.

The album the song appears on, *Monsieur Gainsbourg Revisited* (Verve), is a homage to Gainsbourg, and so, presumably, to the latter's poetic sensitivity, which, after all, was celebrated by François Mitterrand in eulogistic terms. When Gainsbourg died, in 1991, France's then-president referred, in his condolences, to the loss of "our Baudelaire, our Apollinaire", the man who had "elevated song to

---

[13] Jarvis Cocker's Sunday Service on BBC Radio 6.

the level of art"[14]. Surely, therefore, Gainsbourg's choice, which consisted in drawing his listener's attention to a particular text, "Chanson d'automne", was worthy of greater attention. Verlaine was Gainsbourg's means of evoking a separation. To later remove Verlaine points to an English complacency which seems to say, "We know how pop works. We don't burden listeners with cultural baggage. Some sort of 'poet' will do".

There are lessons for the British pop industry here. While, as Low states, "the genre of song requires language that is easily processed" (71), what he stresses above all is that the principle of easy reception was never "intended to produce song-translations with no foreign elements: on the contrary, one reason for translating songs is precisely the fact that good songs are produced by cultures other than yours" (71).

Furthermore, the result of Verlaine's omission from Cocker's version is arguably more confusing than any text containing a reference would have been. Who or what is meant by "the poet"? The appearance of this non-committal term in alliance with the typically English saying, "it's an ill wind" (a bad situation), points to a covert approach, the decision that a target text should "conceal its linguistic character as a translation" (Low 70). By associating an unnamed "poet" with the well known expression "an ill wind" (this sometimes extends to "it's an ill wind that blows nobody any good", meaning that even misfortune can benefit someone), Cocker's line implies that the "poet" in question is not foreign, but from the English-speaking world. Low's criticism of domestication, which he calls a "reluctance to present anything strange or foreign, for people that people might dislike it or not cope with it – a reluctance that misjudges people generally and children in particular", seems apt here (70).

Cocker explains to the BBC that he can only sing lyrics, which work for him personally. He translated the song himself after receiving a version which he found poor because, "if you're going to

---

[14] François Mitterand's telegram of condolences relating to Gainsbourg's death on 2nd March 1991.

sing a song you have to be able to put some of yourself into it"[15]. Somehow, as Cocker fashioned a version of the song which suited him, Verlaine vanished. This omission was apparently seen as an error by fellow music professional Marianne Faithful, who, when singing a text almost identical to Cocker's on French television[16], restored Verlaine to the refrain through the albeit uninspiring line, "As Verlaine said, the wind is blowing".

3.2 "Ik kom je zeggen" by Jo Lemaire

Jo Lemaire's Flemish translation, "Ik kom je zeggen" (Mercury), is even more radical in terms of cultural erasure. It removes the reference to Verlaine and indeed to any sort of poet, as if the whole idea of poetry was a mere inconvenience[17]. Instead, Lemaire sings a line, which is puzzlingly evasive: "Woorden van spijt komen te laat" [Words of regret come too late]. The result is an over-simplified refrain with a redundant observation. Gainsbourg's song focuses on the act of crying (weeping, sobbing, choking, suffocating). The theme is even reinforced by the addition to the music of a recording of Jane Birkin sobbing. Within the song's story of parting lovers, which takes place *after* a declaration, words of any sort, late or not, are of course notable by their absence.

Is Lemaire guilty of a naive error or a calculated attempt to have the best of both worlds? That is to say, in the latter case, an attempt to enjoy pop success through the cover of a tried and tested classic while conveniently removing all traces of Frenchness? Throwing away the principal reference of the song, Verlaine's "Autumn Song", was a choice which enacted, whether consciously or not,

---

[15] Pound, Cath. *The Erotic Songs Lost in Translation*, BBC Culture, 10th August 2017.

[16] "Taratata's Gainsbourg Special". *Taratata*, 25 Sep. 2011.

[17] "Ik kom je zeggen dat ik je verlaat / En je tranen veranderen daar niets aan / Woorden van spijt komen te laat / Ik kom je zeggen dat ik je verlaat" [I have come to say that I'm leaving you / And your tears won't change anything / Words of regret come too late / I have come to say that I'm leaving you].

a resistance to the gems of French culture, and arguably, by extension, to French cultural hegemony.

3.3 "Sono venuto a dirti che vado via" by Giangilberto Monti

By way of contrast, an Italian version by Giangilberto Monti, "Sono venuto a dirti che vado via" (*Carosello Records*), which probably offers the most fluid of the four translations mentioned here, does reference Verlaine. The refrain ends on "come dice Verlaine al vento malvaggio / sono venuto a dirti che me ne vado" [as Verlaine says with the evil wind blowing, I have come to tell you that I'm going].

The inclusion of the name, however, rather flatters to deceive. The rest of the text consists of simplified language designed to rhyme and remain as immediately accessible as the sugary pop arrangements and backing voices which accompany it. Hence "les jours anciens" [the days of old] are reformulated as "notre passato" [our past] or "bei giorni" [beautiful days], whereas, by way of comparison, the "jours anciens" of Verlaine's poem have been translated into Italian more imaginatively as "giorni in fuga" (Bajini 22) or "antichi giorni" (Frezza 34), solutions which mean "fleeing days" or "olden days." Gainsbourg's playful line "à présent que l'heure a sonné" [now that the hour has tolled], which cleverly fuses the past and the present, probably merits a more creative solution than "adesso è tardi" [now it is late].

3.4 "I have come to tell you I'm going" by Mick Harvey

A second English translation, "I have come to tell you I'm going" by Mick Harvey (*Intoxicated Man*), also includes Verlaine. Harvey uses the following refrain: "I have come to tell you that it's goodbye / All your tears couldn't change the reason why / As Verlaine's evil wind blows up on high / I have come to tell you that it's goodbye". His version displays a certain elegance, and the will to formulate an atmospheric melancholy which seems to come from times past. Expressions like "the bell will toll" and "the hour is nigh" are employed in relation to the imminent end of romance. At these moments, Harvey's words are in tune with Norman Shapiro's translation of "Chanson d'automne", which, for "Quand sonne l'heure", proposes "When tolls the hour" (16). One may also be reminded of Poe's "The Bells" (23-27), which chimed only a few years before Verlaine's: "Hear the tolling of the bells ... "tolling, tolling, tolling" (23).

Nevertheless, the consistency of Harvey's attempt is debatable. The tone leaps jarringly, sometimes within the same line, from the poetic to the prosaic. This is noticeable in evocations of the central act of crying, which demands considerable care in translation. While Harvey tries to make some improvements (he actually avoids "you cry" as a translation for "tu pleures", preferring "tears roll" and "tears flow"), lines like "You sob and you groan when you realize I'll really go", or "Sobbing cannot change the reason why", stand out as run-of-the-mill. The relatively poor alliterative and rhythmical potential of the word "sob" compared to "sanglot" probably has something to do with this.

To put these criticisms into perspective, Harvey's work is far more convincing than the other versions, taking into account the well-crafted music, consideration for the influence of Verlaine and aversion to simplistic pop lyrics. Nevertheless, a more consistent translation of "Je suis venu te dire que je m'en vais" can still be envisaged, one which, informed by some of the many available translations of Verlaine's "Chanson d'automne", would take Harvey's attempt to its logical poetic conclusion.

4. Towards an alternative translation: "My last goodbye"

4.1 Coming and going

One of the first problems to solve for any translator of this song is linguistic, rather than cultural. Ironically, it concerns the song's most straightforward statement: "je m'en vais" (I am leaving). Listeners – especially those who are accustomed to the original version – may well be left perplexed by the loss in translation, at critical points of the song, of Gainsbourg's incisive meter, and in particular, of the punchy, monosyllabic end to the first and last lines of the refrain "que je m'en vais".

These words, which immediately allow the listener to identify the song, are too important to be left in a floating, approximate meter. They do, after all, sum up the narrator's romantic tribulations. Within the melody we know so well, the "ing" ending of "I'm go<u>ing</u>" (used by Cocker) simply sticks out, adding an extra syllable, which only serves a grammatical purpose. By way of comparison, let us now consider the refrain of the English rendering of Brel's "Ne me quitte pas" (Philips). Translated as "If you go away", the song was performed, among many others, by Frank Sinatra (Re-prise). Although this translation of Brel's dramatic refrain is less forceful than the imperative form Brel chose ("Don't leave me," Brel implores), it undeniably fulfills the requirements of meter. Together, these four simple words ("If you go away") reproduce the dynamics of the most important phrase of the French song. Although comparatively bland in semantic terms, this musical choice cutely takes into account the liaison which arises on the "e" of "quitte" to produce three syllables instead of two ("quitt<u>e</u> pas": "go away").

In contrast, Jarvis Cocker begins with the ill-fitting "I just came to tell you that I'm going" and compounds its jarring effect by making the second line rhyme with the already problematic "ing": "And all your tears won't change anything". This choice neither helps the flow of Cocker's text or reproduces Gainsbourg's fluidity. The delivery of these words is hurried, as if they were to be gotten out of the way rather than dwelled upon.

Would an English version be better served by "on my way"? This alternative ("I just came to tell you I'm on my way") would have a similar meaning to "I'm going", but the same meter, vowel sound and length as Gainsbourg's end to the first line: "je m'en **vais**"/"on my **way**". It is noticeable that when Jarvis Cocker uses the expression "on my way" in a verse, it immediately fits. In the first line of the song, "on my way" could be followed by a close [eɪ] rhyme such as "you can save your tears for another **day**"). Hence the seductive vowel sound in Gainsbourg's oft-repeated refrain ("vais/changer

/mauvais/vais") would be reproduced, along with the reply ("rien changer"/"another day").

Mick Harvey avoids these problems by moving away from the verb "go" to the impersonal "It's goodbye," a choice which produces "I have come to tell you that it's goodbye / All your tears couldn't change the reason why". In terms of meter, there is a greater concern for the original than in Cocker's version. "It's goodbye" is singable at the end of the line. However, there is still a nagging doubt about the credibility of the expression. Would anyone ever say "I have come to tell you that it's goodbye"? Furthermore, "it's goodbye" is much more abrupt than "je m'en vais", which is sung to a lilting, descending melody.

These problems may well be related to the paradox, which lies at the heart of Gainsbourg's opening line, which simultaneously presents the idea of coming and going. As a speech act, "Je suis venu te dire que je m'en vais" is not logical, but poetic, and therefore requires care. In French, the paradox is made seamless by the alliteration of "venu" and "vais". The two verbs echo each other, as they do in the Italian version ("venuto" / "vado via"). In English, however, although one may recall the expression "I don't know whether I'm coming or going", the simple past "came" and the continuous form "going" can easily seem dissociated.

The options in English are therefore limited. "On my way", however, is an expression, which, as discussed, has an appropriate meter and allows the departing character's voice to fade away. It can also be reinforced later by a more categorical statement: "Je m'en vais" is repeated in Gainsbourg's refrain, but there is nothing to prevent a variation at the end of the English refrain, such as "I'm just here to say my last goodbye". Such a strategy is used by Monti ("vado via" changes to "me ne vado" in the last line of his refrain), and keeps the translated refrain engaging. The phrase "my last goodbye" also offers the possibility of a title.

4.2 The Verlainian world of windswept weeping and tolling bells

The following version of "Je suis venu te dire que je m'en vais" draws on translations of "Chanson d'automne", the most helpful of which were found to be those of Elie Siegel (Aesthetic Realism), Norman Shapiro (17) and Martin Sorrell (27). These texts conjure up a rich variety of English-language options for the windswept evocations of autumnal melancholy, striking clocks and weeping which originally inspired Gainsbourg. Hence we retrace Gainsbourg's footsteps back to Verlaine's poem.

"Je suis venu te dire que je m'en vais"	My Last Goodbye (Grundy)
1. Je suis venu te dire que je m'en vais	I just came to tell you I'm on my way.
2. Et tes larmes n'y pourront rien changer	You can save those tears for another day.
3. Comme dit si bien Verlaine "au vent mauvais,"	As Verlaine's evil wind heaves a final sigh,
4. Je suis venu te dire que je m'en vais.	I'm just here to say my last goodbye.
5. Tu te souviens des jours anciens et tu pleures	You remember the long gone days and you cry.
6. Tu suffoques, tu blêmis	As pale as death, you gasp for breath now
7. à présent qu'a sonné l'heure.	the hour's already nigh.
8. Des adieux à jamais (ouais),	A final farewell and the toll of a bell,
9. Je suis au regret de te dire que	I'm sorry to say my last

je m'en vais	goodbye.
10. Je t'aimais, oui, mais	Yes, I loved you but, I...
11. Je suis venu te dire que je m'en vais	just came to tell you I'm on my way.
12. Tes sanglots longs n'y pourront rien changer	That long-drawn sobbing sound won't make me stay.
13. Comme dit si bien Verlaine "au vent mauvais,"	As Verlaine's evil wind heaves a final sigh,
14. Je suis venu te dire que je m'en vais.	I'm just here to say my last goodbye.
15. Tu te souviens des jours heureux et tu pleures	You remember the good times and you cry.
16. Tu sanglotes, tu gémis	You weep and whine and whimper now
17. à présent qu'a sonné l'heure.	the hour's already nigh.
18. Des adieux à jamais (ouais)	A final farewell and the toll of a bell,
19. Je suis au regret de te dire que je m'en vais	I'm sorry to say my last goodbye.
20. Car tu m'en as trop fait.	Well, you've put me through

One unavoidable problem Gainsbourg's song poses comes via its imagery of blowing wind, which is a cliché. Elie Siegel's image of the "long sighs / Of the violins / Of autumn" is a welcome reminder that wind does not only blow – it also sighs. Sighing can easily find its place within the images of sobbing and weeping which permeate the song. "As Verlaine's evil wind heaves a final sigh" is therefore proposed here, the aim of this line being to bind together the ominous wind, ending romance and regretted departure, while renewing Verlaine's relevance to the story.

The evocations of crying and its variations (weeping, sobbing, choking and suffocating) are equally problematic, especially as Gainsbourg playfully switches between verbs and nouns throughout, conveying a sense of derision regarding the crying character, which the recorded sobs serve to enhance. The famously alliterative "sanglots longs" (borrowed from Verlaine), clearly call out for a play on sound of some sort, one which the literal translation "long sobs" does not provide. Harvey's offering, "sobbing cannot change the reason why", neglects the length of the sobs and sounds rather like a telling-off. The direction Shapiro's opening takes is therefore a tempting one: Shapiro enriches the sobbing by introducing a rhyme: "The Autumn's throbbing / Strings moan, sobbing" (17). However, there is no obvious place for the extra action of throbbing in the Gainsbourg song. On the other hand, Shapiro's subsequent description of Autumn's moaning violins ("Long-drawn and low") does seem helpful (17). It provided the basis for "That long-drawn sobbing sound won't make me stay" in "My Last Goodbye".

The incisive "tu suffoques, tu blémis" [you suffocate, you go pale], with its punchy repetition of the second person pronoun, can easily become unwieldy in English. The three syllables of "suffocate" and, worse still, the four of "suffocating" are hard to fit in, although Cocker tries, by accelerating his chosen line ("Suffocating, your face so pale"). While Harvey justifiably uses the simpler "You choke and grow pale", both solutions sound like compromises when sung. It seems that some form of symmetry, to reflect the repetition of "tu" and the close connection between the two actions, is desirable. In Shapiro's "Autumn Song", the elegant, rhyming phrase "Pallid as death, I gasp for breath" has that very virtue (17). In "My Last Goodbye", this idea is simplified to "As pale as death, you gasp for breath," for greater singability. Gainsbourg's later variations on the act of weeping at line 16 ("tu sanglotes, tu gémis," meaning "you sob, you groan"), which are disregarded by Cocker (he simply sings his first verse and refrain four times), are accounted for by the alliterative and slightly mocking "You weep and whine and whimper" (l. 16).

Finally, the farewell scenes of "Chanson d'automne" and "Je suis venu te dire que je m'en vais" are dramatized by the imagery of the hour striking or sounding. The lines "quand sonne l'heure" (Verlaine) and "à présent qu'a sonné l'heure" (Gainsbourg) evoke an impact, such as the toll of a bell. Shapiro's "When tolls the hour" (17) and Sorrell's "The hour strikes" (27) reflect this. While "the end is nigh" is also a useful expression, its association with a tolling bell fully takes into account the physicality of the sound. In Gainsbourg's line, "à présent qu'a sonné l'heure", there is also a fusion of the past and the present to consider. Taking into account these observations, "A Final Farewell" uses "the hour's already nigh" and follows up with a tolling bell: "A final farewell and the toll of a bell".

Conclusion

"My Last Goodbye" is a test translation provided in tandem with the following question regarding pop song translation. Given the importance of immediate accessibility for the listener, what place is there for the preservation of a songwriter's cultural references and sources of inspiration?

This no doubt depends on the amount, and the complexity, in any given song. In the case of "Je suis venu te dire que je m'en vais" and its clear focus on Verlaine, there seems to be little justification for erasure. Surely Gainsbourg, despite his keenness for English versions of his songs, would not have approved of the dumbing down of his own masterpieces, which, within the confines of song, merit their full literary dimension wherever possible.

"My Last Goodbye" was written without consultation with the Verlaine translators it (occasionally) borrows from (one of them, Siegel, died in 1978). In that sense, it is simultaneously authentic (it retraces Gainsbourg's footsteps, and by consequence, relives the act of borrowing) and unoriginal (it involves borrowing). One way of steering well clear of plagiarism, and, in the process, resolving the cultural error of Verlaine's disappearance, might have been to ask a specialist Verlaine translator such as Sorrell or Shapiro to work on the Gainsbourg song. However, even such fine minds would still have been challenged by the demands made by music. As for "My Last Goodbye", no sung version of the text is available to the public, as things stand. The proof will only ever be in the music.

Works cited

Bajini, Sandro. "Canzone d'autunno". *Paul Verlaine, Poemi saturnini, 1866*. Mondadori, 1992, pp. 21-22.

Bouvier, Yves-Ferdinand ; Vincendet, Serge. *L'Intégrale et cætera – les paroles 1950-1991*. Bartillat, 2009.

Frezza, Luciana. "Canzone d'autunno". *Poesie*. Rizzoli, 1974, p. 34.

Hutcheon, Linda. *A Theory of Parody: the Teachings of Twentieth-Century Art Forms*. Methuen, 1985.

Low, Peter. *Translating Song*. Routledge, 2017.

Poe, Allen Edgar. "The Bells". *Poetry for Young People – Edgar Allen Poe*. Sterling, 1995, pp. 23-27.

Shapiro, Norman. *One Hundred and One Poems by Paul Verlaine: A Bilingual Edition*. University of Chicago and London Press, 1999.

Sorrell, Martin. *Paul Verlaine – Selected Poems*. Oxford World's Classics, 2009.

Verlaine, Paul. "Art Poétique". *Œuvres poétiques complètes*. Laffont, 1992, p. 150.

Verlaine, Paul. "Chanson d'automne". *Œuvres poétiques complètes*. Laffont, 1992, p. 21.

Songs

Brel, Jacques. "Ne me quitte pas". Philips, 1959.

Cocker, Jarvis. "I Just Came to Tell You that I'm Going". Monsieur Gainsbourg Revisited, Verve Records, 2006.

Costello, Elvis. "You're Gonna Make Me Lonesome When You Go". Kojak Variety, Rhino, 2004.

Cyrus, Miley and West, Johnzo. "You're Gonna Make Me Lonesome When You Go". *Chimes of Freedom: Songs of Bob Dylan Honoring 50 Years of Amnesty International.* Fontana, 2012.

Lemaire, Jo. "Ik kom je zeggen". *Enkelvoud.* Mercury, 1998.

Monti, Giangilberto, featuring Carrieri, Roberta. "Sono venuto a dirti che vado via". *Maledette canzoni.* Carosello Records, 2006.

Prévert, Jacques and Kosma, Joseph. "Les Feuilles mortes". Disques Odéon, 1950.

Dylan, Bob. "You're Gonna Make Me Lonesome When You Go". Blood on the Tracks. Columbia, 1975.

Ferré, Léo. "Art Poétique." *Verlaine et Rimbaud chantés par Léo Ferré.* Barclay-Universal, 1964.

Gainsbourg, Serge. "Initials B.B.". *Initials B.B.* Philips Phonografic Industries, 1968.

Gainsbourg, Serge. "Je suis venu te dire que je m'en vais". *Vu de l'extérieur.* Fontana, Philips, 1973.

Gainsbourg, Serge. "La Chanson de Prévert". *L'Étonnant Serge Gainsbourg*, Mercury, 1961.

Harvey, Mick. "I Have Come to Tell You I'm Going". Intoxicated Man, Mute, 1995.

Sinatra, Frank. "If you go away". *My Way.* Reprise, 1969.

Webography

Cocker, Jarvis. Jarvis Cocker's Sunday Service, https://www.bbc.co.uk/programmes/b00ptsjd. Accessed 4 Jan. 2019.

Pound, Cath. "The Erotic Songs Lost in Translation". *BBC Culture.* Accessed 10 August 2017 http://www.bbc.com/culture/story/20170810-jane-birkin-reinvents-serge-gainsbourg-songs. Accessed 4 January 2019.

Jaroussky, Philippe. "Philippe Jaroussky et les chansons douces de Paul Verlaine." Classique mais pas has been, 28 Feb. 2015, http://classiquemaispashasbeen.fr/2015/02/28/philippe-jaroussky-et-les-chansons-douces-de-paul-verlaine. Accessed 4 January 2019.

Mitterand, François. Telegramme of condolences relating to Gainsbourg's death on 2 Mar. 1991, http://discours.vie-publique.fr/notices/917004600.html. Accessed 4 January 2019.

Siegel, Elie. "Autumn Song," https://aestheticrealism.net/poetry/Autumn-Verlaine.htm. Accessed 4 January 2019.

Faithful, Marianne. "Taratata's Gainsbourg special," 25 Sept. 2011, https://www.facebook.com/mariannefaithfullofficial/videos/marianne-performing-i-just-came-to-tell-you-that-im-going/10150150610940802/. Accessed 4 January 2019.

"Ce dimanche, le musée Message Verlaine est à redécouvrir." La Voix du Nord, 3 February 2018 http://www.lavoixdunord.fr/310734/article/2018-02-03/ce-dimanche-le-musee-message-verlaine-est-redecouvrir. Accessed 4 January 2019.

Edward Filmer's *French Court Airs Englished*

Chantal Schütz

Introduction

In 1629, Edward Filmer (1589-1650), the younger brother of the philosopher and politician Sir Robert Filmer – a well-known royalist author, best known as an opponent of both Hobbes and Locke – published, a book of *French court-aires, with their ditties Englished,* which he introduced with the following statement:

> Out of a Civill regard and speciall care not to wrong Strangers, I have attempted to furnish these Forraine Compositions with a fortune equall to what they had at Home. (Filmer, *To the queene*)

Filmer's declaration of intent managed to encapsulate, in an emblematic fashion, the most salient issues at stake: the extreme popularity of *Airs de cour* in France, his wish not to ruin them through translation, and his confident belief, that he would be able to generate as much enthusiasm for them in England as in France. A close examination of the collection reveals that while Filmer's translations capture the gist of the French lyrics, he made several errors that go well beyond the issue of meaning. In this respect, the applicability of the concept of cultural error is threefold.

First of all, Filmer was trying to import not only texts but a musical format that was deeply embedded in a foreign culture, since court airs rely heavily on the elegant diction of the performers, and the very value of the airs has more to do with their texts than with their music. The reception of French vocal music in the English-speaking world has remained fraught with such cultural misunderstandings, as for instance in the case of Debussy's opera *Pelléas et Mélisande* or Ravel's *L'Enfant et les sortilèges*, which are far more rarely performed outside France than one might expect, due to their resistance to translation and their reliance on textual comprehension.

The basic cultural error in Filmer's case seems therefore to apply to the very idea of transposing French songs into English and voicing the hope that they would be appreciated in England, where the emphasis was placed more on expressivity through contrapuntal writing, or on theatricality. Beyond the error of appreciation in terms of potential reception, Filmer committed errors as a result of his lack of knowledge of court procedures (he refers to his book as "this my first Court-sute"), and this, in turn, generated various *faux pas*. Finally, relatively faithful translations can nevertheless engender mismatches if the level of language and the imagery chosen to transpose the original texts are shocking to the intended audience or too remote from the aesthetic of the model text. This is precisely the miscalculation that dominates Filmer's collection.

1. Why translate French court airs?

The book is dedicated to the queen of England, Henrietta-Maria, daughter of Henri IV of France and wife to Charles I. It collects 19 *Airs de cour* (court airs) written in the first decades of the 17th century by the noted composers Pierre Guédron (1560?-1620?) and Antoine Boësset (1586?-1643). All of these songs were published in France by the holders of the exclusive royal privilege for music printing who dominated the French market for over two centuries, the printers Adrian Le Roy and Robert Ballard (Boorman et al.).

Written by the finest court poets and composers, court airs are secular, strophic songs usually dealing with love, mostly against the backdrop of pastoral settings, that were performed both at court and in aristocratic circles, where they were appreciated for their simple lyrical nature. While the rate at which these books were published over the period reveals both a keen appetite for the songs and their widespread consumption, it also indicates the fast pace of renewal and innovation – the *Airs de différent autheurs avec la table-*

ture de luth (i.e. the version for solo voice and lute) proved so popular that Ballard had to issue it a second time to meet the demand. Many airs were also reprinted in a large number of derivative collections (Durosoir 9).

Throughout the early modern period, instrumental music circulated extensively across Europe, and cross-fertilization flourished between Italy, France, England, Germany, Spain and the Netherlands. The English lute-song would not have developed its idiosyncrasies had not its main proponent, John Dowland, first worked in Paris and then travelled to Italy (Poulton 26-27 and 194-199; Fischlin, 274).

Filmer's collection stands out because of its careful presentation and because translation, as he understood it, was not purely instrumental, a mere technique destined to give access to music lovers beyond linguistic borders, it took on the pathos of an explicit, almost political duty. In his preface, the author-translator expresses a hope that further (and better) translations might appear in the wake of his own:

> Having hazarded to breake the yce to abler pennes, whose happier faculties in this kind may hereafter incite them, with some more rich *English* lining of other *French* pieces of this Musicall stuffe, to venture-for and winne the applause of my indegenerating[1] Countriemen. (Filmer, *Preface*)[2]

Yet, although the period was propitious to translations of all kinds, no other such collections of French songs appeared in pre-Civil War England. Two of the songs selected by Filmer had however already appeared in England in 1610 with the original French text, in Robert

---

[1] This word does not figure in the OED, but presumably has the same meaning as "undegenerating", ie., those who "maintain the qualities proper to the race or kind"; who do not "fall away from ancestral virtue or excellence".

[2] All references to Filmer's collection are by titles of sections or songs, as the pages are not numbered.

Dowland's *A Musical Banquet*, a collection aimed at familiarizing the English public with works from the continent. Yet Filmer's wish to emulate the success of the books of translated Italian madrigals that launched the fashion for English madrigals in the 1590s remained a wish.

Nicholas Yonge's *Musica Transalpina* (1588 and 1597) and Thomas Watson's *First Set of Italian Madrigals Englished* (1590) had succeeded in "englishing" Italian madrigals. While Yonge had remained quite close to the Italian text, Watson emphasized that he had translated the lyrics "not to the sense of the originall dittie, but after the affection of the Noate", allowing himself more freedom in order to fit the words to the musical effect (Macy 2). I contend that Filmer followed Watson's example because of the particular difficulties of translating from French with the intent of musical performance, as he states unambiguously:

> where Lines are not so much turned into another Language for their owne, as for the Musickes sake that they belong-to and (in a manner) serve, I cannot absolutely conclude, but that the Translater may, without the blot of insolence, carrie himselfe with a Looser regard to those Pieces of his Patterne that hee shall judge himselfe least Obliged unto. (Filmer, *Preface*)

That such translations can result in a plethora of "cultural errors" is not a surprise. But does this explain why the book did not unleash the craze for French court airs the translator seemed to have hoped for when he stated that he had "attempted to furnish these Forraine Compositions with a fortune equall to what they had at Home"? Could the decision to give precedence to the music over the spirit of the text have been a miscalculation in terms of potential reception, given that this forced the translator to complexify the texts in order to fit them to the music (Sullivan 97)?

2. Strategic errors

Filmer's book was published only four years after the formation of a Franco-English alliance embodied by Henrietta-Maria and Charles I – a match that was not without crises in the early years of their marriage, involving the exclusion from court of a large part of Henrietta's French-speaking Catholic retinue (Griffey 10-15). By 1629, however, the strained relationship between the spouses had started to ease. Filmer was obviously trying to capitalize both on the fashion for French artistic productions that accompanied Henrietta's establishment in London, and on his friendship with the playwright Ben Jonson, the preeminent author of court masques dedicated to celebrations of royal power and representation.

One of Jonson's works, *The Fortunate Isles and Their Union,* a masque performed at court in 1625, referred to the Franco-English alliance as the union of the Rose and the Lily, a trope used again in the commendatory poem Jonson provided for Filmer's book (Jacquot, 132). The poem hints that the translated songs will be an incentive for the queen to improve her English:

> They are a Schoole to win
> The faire *French* Daughter to learne *English* in;
> And, graced with her song,
> To make the Language sweet upon her tongue.
> (Filmer, *To my worthy Friend)*

In the dedication, Filmer underlines that Henrietta's supposed familiarity with the songs, all published between 1602 and 1617, should help them find a place at the English court while making it easier for her to learn the new words:

> I have thought meet to Arme them with the Maiesticke Patronage of a Queene of their former Acquaintance, and of a fortune somewhat resembling their owne; who having nobly Favoured them in the time of their greatest Securitie amongst their Naturall and Potent friends at home, will, as

is humbly hoped, resolutely undertake to Protect them now, in the time of Need, from the Affronts and Dangers incident to the life of Aliens, and vouchsafe them (being now as it were Naturaliz'd for her owne Subjects, and taught the Language wherein by her nearest People shee is pray'd for) a more Princely measure of Countenance and Affection, then formely, when shee could not call them hers by so Soveraine an interest. (Filmer, *To the queene*)

Given the critical juncture at which the book was offered to the queen, Jonson and Filmer may well have committed their first error by underlining the insufficient effort Henrietta had made to adapt to her new environment, or on the contrary, by painting an overly rosy picture of the harmony between the two countries.

There may well have been a strategic error in Filmer's decision to request an endorsement from Ben Jonson, whose favor with the royal couple was beginning to wane. In addition, Henrietta never really gained complete mastery of English, and she is noted as still having trouble speaking and writing English in the 1640s (White 21). Conversely, her entourage mastered French sufficiently for her not to really need to exert herself – and as a consequence, they probably did not require French lyrics to be translated for them (Griffey, 22-23).

One might thus have doubts as to whether Filmer's candid suggestion that all he wanted was to provide the French-born queen with English-speaking articulacy and grace – and find it hard to see in these declarations anything more than the discreet *langue de bois* of official, if not officious, self-ingratiation. However, on another level, some genuine issues with the linguistic incapacity of the English would-be singers of French music are undeniable. Filmer explains that the fashion for all things French was already quite strong, but that his ears smarted from the terrible pronunciation of singers, who attempted to perform the airs in the original language:

my moderate desires are, that my Home-hearted unaffecting Countrie-men, Favourers and Practizers of Musicke, would courteously entertaine this Recopilation[3] as a Worke naturaliz'd chiefly for their sakes; and, whereas our Tailors Shops and Dancing-schooles have bee'n so employ'd in *French* Imitations, that our more deserving Masters of Musicke might sometimes, for pleasing Novelties sake, daigne to repair hither for Life of Aire worthy of their more noble Arts Emulation. And, as for some Roving Spirits, whose Transitorie View of *France* may have magnified them with the Scumme onely and Froathie top of the *French* Tongue, without diving into the substantiall Depth by a more piercing diligence therein, I am patiently provided to heare them Counterblast these my Endeavours with this Airie Position: That it is impossible that any Words but *French* should ever Become the *Loover*[4] Aires (though they themselves, besides understanding them but to halves, pronounce them to a natural *French* Eare as Misbecomingly as ever Crude Forrainer was heard to sing an *English* Ballet)[5] such is the aptnesse of halfe-digested Noveltie to breed in the Stomackes of our yong Countrie-men a Queasie despising of the, almost-matchlesse, Abilities of their owne Language. (Filmer, *Preface*)

Controversies about Englishmen's attraction to foreign forms or fashions are a constant of the period: as early as 1613, Thomas Campion had complained that "some there are who admit only French or Italian ayres, as if every country had not his proper ayre, which the people thereof naturally usurp in their Musicke" (42), while scholars and writers parried and debated about "inkhorn" terms borrowed from French, Italian or Latin to supplement English (Crystal 292).

---

[3] A new or subsequent compilation.
[4] Louvre.
[5] A ballad.

Filmer's comments on this are ambiguous since he both panders to that taste by publishing French songs and yet criticizes it by intoning a paean to the "matchless" abilities of the English language. However, they are particularly instructive in mapping the possible, and perhaps successful, arguments of that time.

But, whether knowingly or unwittingly, Filmer misjudged another point. Could Henrietta really have been familiar with the chosen airs? Born in 1609, she arrived in England at the age of 15. There is no doubt that she was a proficient singer and dancer, and also a lover of lyric and pastoral poetry (Griffey 116). What seems unlikely is that the songs chosen by Filmer would have figured in her repertoire, since many of them were composed while she was an infant (Till). By the time, she began to learn to sing, musical fashions had already changed and Guédron, who authored most of the songs in the Filmer collection, had been replaced as royal chamber composer by his son-in-law Boësset. The considerable output of court airs over the period and the fact that only a few songs remained favorites beyond their publication period leave no doubt that audiences expected steady renewal.

The songs could easily have been taken up by Henrietta Maria's lavish musical establishment, which included about 15 men and 2 or 3 singing boys (who came from France with her). She herself could have sung them to the accompaniment of her private lutenist and teacher Jacques Gaultier. But since all of these potential performers were French-speaking, there would have been little incentive to do so. Be that as it may, so little is known about the actual repertoire of secular music that was performed in the private setting of the queen's apartments that the question remains open (Griffey 196).

The way in which the songs in Filmer's collection are printed suggests that he had private performance in mind, and that the dedication to the queen was perhaps a way of using her patronage to promote sales. Filmer chose to organize the book in the native English manner that had proved extremely popular since Dowland had published his *First booke of songes* in 1597 with a "table" layout.

Until that publication, vocal ensemble music had normally been published in sets of small part-books, but Dowland opted for a single large volume with all the parts for each song distributed around the sides of a single page. This allows for joint performance by four singers or instruments from the same score as well as for performance by a solo singer and lutenist.

This practical aspect was certainly one of the reasons for the huge success of Dowland's book (which went through five editions between 1597 and 1613) – and the model was adopted by all later publications of lute-songs in England, up until Attey's *First Book of Ayres* in 1622 (Holman 8). On the contrary, Le Roy and Ballard usually issued the polyphonic songs first, then a version with a lute accompaniment in a separate book. Filmer conflated these two editions in his collection, combining the polyphonic and solo versions. He also made the unusual step of including the original French lyrics (the "ditties") at the end of the book, as a legitimation of his efforts to be faithful to the originals: "by the same meanes testifying, to the skilfull in both Tongues, my integritie (as farre as is formerly professed) in their Translations" (Filmer, *Preface*).

3. Cultural gaps in translation

Filmer's volume however is mainly of interest for its quaint treatment of the transposition into English of the elegant, abstract French lyrics of the early 17th century, including a poem by François de Malherbe (1555–1628), the great reformer of French poetry, who defined the rules of classicism, seeking to impose greater simplicity and purity in vocabulary and versification.

Many of Filmer's translations turn the spare French lyrics into heavily metaphorical English texts – his style is notable for lavish use of rhetorical devices, including allegory, ampliation/ amplification and transposition. Maybe the sovereign error in the seventeenth century context of the cultural heterogenesis of French and English was Filmer's repeated reintroduction of the realities of bodily function into the songs. The poems that were set as court airs all belonged to the *précieux* style that had become dominant in early seventeenth century France. This involved a refined approach to language, a limited lexical range and the use of stock imagery, all in the service of good taste and decorum (Durosoir 44). The codes of *bienséance*, or propriety, involved avoiding all reference to corporeal terms and the language of physical love, as Malherbe made it clear in the corrections he brought to the texts of his contemporaries, and as French classical theatre would later demonstrate.

Filmer's translations suffer from these aesthetic choices, but also pose problems because they turn out to be rather awkward *contrafacta*. *Contrafactum*, which consists in fitting new word to an extant tune, was widespread in early modern Europe, both in popular music (eg. in broadside ballads) and in more sophisticated circles. Masses were made to fit folk songs or successful polyphonic Chansons (eg. Janequin's *Missa super La Bataille*, 1532), while court airs were reused as spiritual songs (as in the collections *La Pieuse alouette*, 1621 or *La Philomèle séraphique*, 1640).

The same issues arise both with the new words of *contrafacta* and in airs that use strophic structures: the tune and rhythm are usually written to match the first verse, and as soon as the poet deviates from the syntactic structure of that verse, which is almost inevitable, textual and musical rhythms diverge (Maynard 102-3). While changes in the character of the lyric in subsequent verses can be addressed by the performer through expression or ornamentation, and were a mark of the art of said performer, mismatches in meter / rhythm and number of syllables are more difficult to accommodate (Walker 22-23). Filmer acknowledges that he had to grapple with this difficulty, but he mostly focuses on the challenge posed by the passage from French accentuation to English:

> Now, because translated Ditties and originals differ chiefly in this Preposterous Point, that, whereas the Musicall Notes are fitted to the Originals, the translations are, contrarily, to be fitted to the Musicall Notes, I have bee'n forced, by this new Taske, for the more even Accord with the Musicke, in

divers Aires, to alter the naturall first Cast of the Verse, and to ordaine, in the proper place of an *Iambicke* Foot, a dissonant *Trochaicke*, as more sutable to the nature of the Note. (Filmer, *Preface*)

As a translator, Filmer's task was to make sure note values were altered as little as possible, in order to achieve the kind of reception Yonge describes: "many skilfull Gentlemen and other great Musiciens, [...] affirmed the accent of the words to be well mainteined, the descant not hindred, (though some fewe notes altred) and in euerie place the due decorum kept" (Yonge 1588, *The epistle dedicatory*). Thomas Watson evaded the difficulty by translating "after the affection of the Noate", making his English versions more directly dependent on the rhythm of the musical phrase.

Filmer was very much aware of the influence of the rhythms of French diction on the fashioning of tunes for court airs – the form's very success relied on a certain formal freedom inherited from the efforts of Lejeune and Baïf to create *musique mesurée* (Walker 159, Durosoir 135-6). Filmer underlines the total disregard of French authors for scansion:

being led rather by their free Fant'sie of Aire (wherein many of them doe naturally excell) then by any Strict and Artificiall scanning of the Line, by which they Build, doe often, by disproportion'd Musicall Quantities, invert the naturall Stroke of a Verse, applying to the place of an *Iambicke* Foot, such Modulation as Jumps rather with a *Trochay*. (Filmer, *Preface*)

Filmer's mastery of French also extends to an understanding of the lack of accents in Gallic diction, to the point that he even makes fun of native speakers' inability to pronounce foreign languages any differently:

French syllables, as well in Verse as Prose, are pronounced with a more Continu'd Equalitie of sound, then ours. For that Tongue admits seldome of any Tones or Intentions of the Voice (by Grammarians called Accents) unlesse at the End of the Clause, or in the *penultims* of words ending in their e *fœminine*. And this their Mother-pronunciation they often apply even to the Latine, and other *acquired* Tongues. (Filmer, *Preface*)

Filmer's efforts sometimes resulted in changing the spirit of the original pieces, either because of some excessive attention to get the words to fit to the music, or because he chose to remain more faithful to the original and ended up with musical accents placed on the wrong syllables. For instance in "Las! pourquoy ne suis-je née", the English iambic pentameter inevitably shifts the accents of the French decasyllable that the music beautifully espouses, in spite of its irregularity. This is most notable in the line "Que pour souff**rir** mile & **mi**le **tourments** ?", rendered as "To breake my **pea**cefull sleepe **of** in**nocence**?", which results in the musical accents falling on the unstressed preposition "of", and the additional indignity of the trochaic pattern on the final French word resulting in "innocence" having accents on both its unstressed syllables and none on the first syllable.

Filmer's awareness of the difficulties brought him to favor the musical phrasing over English poetic rules, which he summarizes by stating that he has "chosen rather, wittingly, to tolerate a little roughnesse in the Fluencie of some of the Verses, thereby the lesse to disrellish the Musicke" (Filmer, *Preface*). What he does not recognize, however, is how much his English complicates the style of the original text, in order to make it fit the musical phrase. This is a major cultural error, since the general trend in French poetry of the early seventeenth century was to move away from complexity and rhetorical excess towards clarity and simplicity. Filmer's aesthetic, on the contrary, seems to hark back to that of Elizabethan diction, which had been fashionable two decades before his translation, but was no longer seen as appropriate in the 1620s (Sullivan 133).

What is striking when the French and English texts are set side by side is that, contrary to what is usual in translation, the English lines are systematically longer than the French ones. This is due to the fact that the translator is obliged to replace all the feminine endings of the French lyric with full syllables in English. These word endings that normally go unpronounced correspond to an unaccentuated note in the music, not only on feminine rhymes but also within the lines. For example, in "Je voudrais bien; O Cloris", the sleek French line "Arreste toy, retarde ta Lumiere" is expanded into "Controll thy race, keepe backe thy beamie quiver".

The method used to extend the fairly straightforward French sentence is representative of Filmer's system: adding adjectives, replacing a simple concept by a weighty metaphor ("beamy quiver" for light), transposing a relatively light alliteration in "t" by a more ponderous one in "p" and "b". Similarly, in "Adorable princesse", the line "O beauté sans exemple" becomes "Thou, unmatch'd *Beauties Treasure*". In "Enfin la voici" the simple words "Une si douce majesté" are turned into "High state with so meeke graces mix'd" and a little further in the same song "Le respect & l'amour" becomes "True respect and chast fires". Amplification sometimes requires adding verbs too, as when "Et montres à la Guerre / Au centre de la Terre / Ses Demons enchaînés" becomes the almost grotesque "And mak'st Bellona grumble /To see her Demons tumble/In chaines with Hellish Fiends".

The English version thus generally appears to be both more florid and more specific, thanks to this almost systematic addition of adjectives. However, beyond simple amplification, it also complicates the French, making it sometimes impossible to understand the meaning of the lyrics without referring to the original, as in "Las! pourquoy ne suis-je née":

> Que me sert-il d'estre belle,
> Que mile amans me viennent rechercher :
> S'il faut que moy-mesme, cruelle,
> Je feigne estre un rocher ?
> (Filmer, *Las! pourquoy ne suis-je née*)

which becomes :

> What availe my bankes of Roses,
> Whose blushes make my Wooers red with fire,
> If, forc'd to wound with sharpe opposes,
> I prove to them all-Bry'r[6]?
> (Filmer, *Why, alas! cri'd-out my Mother*)

This tortuous metaphor runs counter to the aesthetic of the "simple style". A collateral effect of this method is having to spread the meaning of sentences over two or more lines, where the French usually tries to provide autonomous lines, in order to facilitate the composer's work. Thus, in "Arme-toi, ma raison", the metaphor is drawn-out so much that the meaning only emerges by the end of the verse:

> Je souffre tant de maux
> En l'amoureux servage,
> Que si les animaux
> Parloyent nostre langage,
> Ils viendroyent à mes cris de pitié requerir
> Le bel œil qui me fait mourir.
> (Filmer, *Arme-toi, ma raison*)

> With so strong gall doth Love
> My deserv'd Nectar season,
> That, if brute mouthes could move

---

[6] Briar.

Tongues of discursive Reason,
My cries would make them plead for remorse, which is fled
The bright Eie that would shine mee dead.
(Filmer, *Reason arme thy wrong'd hands*)

The most striking shift between the original songs and their English version, however, is the way Filmer transposes abstract notions into concrete instances that illustrate them: in Malherbe's "Que n'êtes vous lassées", good and evil ("de mal en bien") are turned into "nettle" and "balm-leaf", while "la violence que me fait ce Malheur" has "my heart lie breaking/ In conflict with this Hell", and the absolute arbiters of the state of mortals ("absolus arbitres/ De l'estat des mortels") are styled "free judges / of all wrongs and grudges, / That earthly stomackes feele".

Malherbe's poetical rules were designed among other goals to help fit poetry to music: for example, they prohibit enjambments in order to favour strophic settings. Paradoxically, though, it is in the translation of the short clear hexasyllabic lines of this highly expressive French poem that Filmer has recourse to polysyllabic English equivalents that convey the rhetoric of excess demanded by the passion of king Henri IV for Charlotte-Marguerite de Montmorency (Verchaly 42-3). Knowing little about or simply ignoring the precepts of the French reformer of poetry, Filmer reconstructs an inflamed discourse in a contrafactum that matches the accents of the tune while perhaps offering a substitute to the ornamentation that professional singers were expected to add to the piece. Yet the major cultural error in this song is the intrusion of corporal functions suggested by the relatively worn metaphor of disease used by Malherbe in the first verse, which, in accordance with *bienséance*, carefully avoided anything too precise about the nature of the lover's sickness:

Que n'estes vous lassées
Mes tristes pensées
De troubler ma raison ?

Et faire avecque blâme
Rebeller mon ame
Contre sa guarison.
(Filmer, *Que n'estes vous lassées*)

Thus, "Aussi suis-je un squellette" is rendered far more descriptively as "My bones of flesh are stripped", "ma peau meurtrie" as "my skinne blew-striped", and the polite discourse centered around the noble sense of vision and the aspiration to see is transposed into the realm of food, famine and appetite, albeit for the heavenly food Ambrosia:

Deux beaux yeux sont l'empire
Pour qui je soupire,
Sans eux rien ne m'est doux:
Donnés moy cette joye
Que je les revoye,
(Filmer, *Que n'estes vous lassées*)

Two sweete Eies are my wishes;
Feasts, without these dishes,
Rellish of nought but rue:
Do but, yer Famine end mee, [sic]
This *Ambrosia* send mee,
(Filmer, *Why have my Thoughts conspired*)

The metaphor of disease governs the whole of the English version of "Quel espoir de guérir", in which the decorous "amoureux martire" becomes "a Love-kindled fever" that provokes thirst and swelling to the point of bursting, and "la mort" is amplified to "death's cooling cup". The most telling case of medicalizing the French text is "Las! pourquoi ne suis-je née", where the mild metaphor of unfortunate birth is extended into a conceit that runs through the whole song, involving the cries induced by the pains of childbirth, the interrupted sleep of the newborn child, the eyes of the narrator that are in turn made pregnant by light and then brought into labor. The disease metaphor continues around the image of blood (the "red fountain of my vaines") that begets the "canker" of envy and makes it "ranker" than an "ulcer" – all images that are blatantly absent from the French text.

Another cultural gap illustrated by Filmer's translations is the transposition of the fairly bland and predictable metaphors of French pastoral poetry into quasi-scientific explorations. Thus in "Où luis-tu soleil de mon âme", the image of the marigold ("soucy") suggests an extended investigation of the "dark riddle" posed by the narrator's dependence on the sun of his beloved's eyes: "Thy effects have draw'n mee to thinking / How I, like the Marigold, live!" (for "C'est donc vous agreable veuë,/ Qui me faict semblable au soucy"). In "O ! Grands Dieux que de charmes", the same metaphor makes the text take on the format of a scientifically informed voyage to an exotic country where the narrator must avoid getting lost in a maze or being reduced to "ashes": "In this Maze, to conduct us,/ The Skie doth instruct us / With directive light" (for "Donc pour nous mieux conduire / Le Ciel fait reluire / Des feux nompareils").

Generally speaking, Filmer's translations tend to pull urbane expressions of gallant love towards mannerist and strongly contrasted outbursts of despair, involving furious sounds and potent images grounded in corporeal semantics, as when "ma triste voix" is rendered as "my blazing dints" (in "Arme toy ma raison" – "Reason! arme thy wrong'd hands"). The governing rhetoric is that of excess, as in the powerful alliterations of one of the verses of "Vous que le Bonheur r'appelle" ("Thou, whome Fortune, now turn'd tender"):

> Thralldome stands on happie pillres,
> Whose Frame, Fate-proofe, feares no powres
> Of, her ruines strongest willers,
> Shakes of *Death* and *Lethe's* showres,
> (Filmer, *Reason ! arme thy wrong'd hands*)

Bien heureuse servitude
Dont le genereux effort,
Peut vaincre l'ingratitude
De l'oubli & de la mort.
(Filmer, *Arme toy ma raison*)

This rhetoric of excess and *copia* is in complete contrast to the conceit of inexpressibility that underpins the aesthetic of the English lute-song, a genre that resisted outward show and favoured concision (Fischlin 51). Filmer was in effect neither conforming to the aesthetic of the French court airs he was seeking to import, nor to that of the English songs his compatriots were accustomed to. His attempt to force the one into the mould of the other is perhaps best epitomized by a strange typographical quirk in the complaint "Las! pourquoi ne suis-je née". In the ninth of twelve verses, the narrator states that "My affections tongued measure/ in silence speaks alowd" (translating the three lines "C'est qu'il ne peut, ny ne doit ignorer, / L'affection que je luy porte,/ Qu'on ne peut mesurer").

The two capitalized lines self-referentially convey the desperate efforts of the translator to fit the words to the measures of the music, to the measure of French prosody and to the measure of good taste. The lines seem to shout out to the reader and to apologize for the errors of the translator. It is all the more ironic that the French text of that song hints that it was written to be read ("Vous qui lirés cette plainte") whereas Filmer brings us back to the aural world of song: "Friend! whose Eares this plaint shall swallow", but also to the bodily metaphor of the gluttonous ear.

Conclusion

The notion of a cultural error is, of course, not part of early modern language: it was invented 400 years after the events, by retrospectively-minded literary critics. Errors can be dangerous, but "cultural errors", that are revealed centuries after they were committed, involve as little danger as culture itself. In hindsight, Filmer's insistence on forcing abstract polite French poetry into expressionistic English verse looks like an anticipation of Voltaire's well-known demoting of Shakespeare's drama as brutal, savage and barbaric.

We know what followed: eighteenth century Shakespeare translations into French bear the mark of an attempt to evacuate the language of the body, of contrasts and of excess. Going in the opposite direction, Filmer's translations of *poésie galante* did come at a time when English verse was moving toward the more polished and elegant lyrics of the cavalier poets, and yet, being above all destined for musical performance, their "rough" quality was not an error: it was a technique of metamorphosis that allowed poetic nuance to sustain the sounds of musical performance, in whose service Filmer, of his own avail, wished to put the words of poetry.

Works cited

Attey, John. *The first booke of ayres of foure parts with tableture for the lute.* Thomas Snodham, 1622.

Bataille, Gabriel. *Airs de Différents Autheurs, Mis en Tablature de Luth par eux Mesmes.* Pierre Ballard, 1612.

Boorman, Stanley, Eleanor Selfridge-Field, and Donald W. Krummel. "Printing and publishing of music". *Grove Music Online.* January 01, 2001. Oxford University Press. http://// www.o xfordmusiconline.com/grovemusic/view/10.1093/gmo/97 81561592630.001.0001/omo9781561592630-e- 0000040101, accessed on 12 of December 2018

Brooks, Jeanice. *Courtly Song in Late Sixteenth-Century France.* University of Chicago Press, 2000.

Campion, Thomas. *Tvvo bookes of ayres.* Thomas Snodham, 1613.

Crystal, David. *The Stories of English.* Penguin Books, 2004.

Durosoir, Georgie. *L'air de cour en France: 1571-1655.* Editions Mardaga, 1991.

Filmer, Edward. *French court-aires, vvith their ditties Englished, of foure and fiue parts Together with that of the lute.* William Stansby, 1629.

Fischlin, Daniel. *In Small Proportions: A Poetics of the English Ayre, 1596-1622.* Wayne State University Press, 1998.

Griffey, Erin. *Henrietta Maria: Piety, Politics and Patronage.* Ashgate, 2008.

Holman, Peter, *Dowland: Lachrimae (1604).* Cambridge University Press, 1999.

Jacquot, Jean. "La reine Henriette-Marie et l'influence française dans les spectacles à la cour de Charles Ier". *Cahiers de l'Association internationale des études françaises*, 1957, n° 9. pp. 128-160.

Leconte, Thomas. *Catalogue de l'air de cour en France (1602-ca 1660)*. [En ligne], mis en ligne en décembre 2005. http://philidor.cmbv.fr/ark:/13681/rvpuxaxf0asmzsrfdbyw

Macy, Laura. "The Due Decorum Kept: Elizabethan Translation and the Madrigals Englished of Nicholas Yonge and Thomas Watson". *Journal of Musicological Research*, vol.17: 1, pp. 1-21, DOI: 10.1080/01411899708574736. Accessed 2 Sep. 2018.

Maynard, Winifred. *Elizabethan Lyric Poetry and Its Music*. Clarendon, 1986.

Sullivan, Kathryn Jane. *French Court-Aires, with Their Ditties Englished: How Language Influences Text Settings in the 17th Century French Air de Cour*. Monash, 2018, https://aueast.erc.monash.edu.au/fpfiles/12011603/ThesisJune2018.pdf.

Till, David, and Robert Ford. "Filmer, Edward". *Grove Music Online*. January 01, 2001. Oxford University Press. Date of access 2 Sep. 2018, http:////www.oxfordmusiconline.com /grove music/view/10.1093/gmo/9781561592630.001.0001/omo-9781561592630-e-0000009646

Verchaly, André. *Airs de cour pour voix et luth (1603-1643)*. Société française de musicologie, Heugel, 1961 ; repr. SEDIM, 1989.

Watson, Thomas, 1557? *The First Sett of Italian Madrigalls Englished*. Thomas East, 1590.

Yonge, Nicholas, d. *Musica Transalpina Madrigales Translated of Foure, Fiue and Sixe Partes*. Thomas East, 1588.

Yonge, Nicholas, d. *Musica Transalpina. The Second Booke of Madrigalles, to 5. & 6. Voices*. Thomas East, 1597.

Authors

Authors

Charles Ivan Armstrong is professor of British literature in the Department of Foreign Languages and Translation at the University of Agder, Norway. He is President of the Nordic Association of English Studies and Secretary of the International Yeats Society, as well as a Visiting Fellow at Wolfson College, Cambridge. His most recent book is *Reframing Yeats: Genre, Allusion and History* (Bloomsbury Academic, 2013).

Paula Cifuentes-Férez is a lecturer at the Department of Translation and Interpreting at the University of Murcia (Spain). Her main research interests lie within the area of Cognitive Linguistics applied to translation, the impact of emotions and personality factors (especially, self-esteem and creative intelligence) in translation.

Michael Cronin is the 1776 Chair of French at TCD. He was Director of the Centre for Translation and Textual Studies at Dublin City University. He is an elected Member of the Royal Irish Academy, the Academia Europaea and is an Officer in the Ordre des Palmes Académiques. He has published extensively on language, culture, translation and travel writing. Among his works are *Across the Lines: Travel, Language, Translation* (2000), *Translation and Identity* (2006), *The Expanding Word* (2012), and *Eco–Translation: Translation and Ecology in the Age of the Anthropocene* (2017). His current interests are in developing eco-criticism in relation to modern languages and translation, exploring the notion of 'translation trauma' in relation to population displacement and investigating language identities as mediated through travel.

Ana-Isabel Foulquié-Rubio is a lecturer at the University of Murcia. She holds a PhD in Translation and Interpreting in the field of Public Service Interpreting, from the University of Murcia and a Degree in

Translation and Interpreting, from the University of Granada. In 1999, she was appointed as a Sworn Translator by the Spanish Ministry of Foreign Affairs. Since 2002, she combines her work as freelance translator and interpreter with lecturing in different universities such as University of Ulster, University of Alicante and University of Murcia.

Paul Grundy teaches in the English Department of the Université Polytechnique Hauts-de-France. His research deals with interethnic dialogues and tolerance in twentieth-century American fiction. Having recently worked on the theme of tolerance in British political discourse, he is also interested in song translation and representations of new media in science fiction.

Katja Grupp is Professor of German as a foreign Language at the University for Applied Sciences (IUBH) in Bad Honnef, Germany. After studying Slavonic Languages, Eastern European History and Economy in Potsdam and Bonn, she worked as a DAAD-Lecturer in Kaliningrad, Russia. She is the author of the *Bild Lücke Deutschland* (Image, Gap, Germany) which deals with cultural learning and understanding.

Gundula Gwenn Hiller is the Director of the Centre for Intercultural Learning at the European University Viadrina in Frankfurt (Oder). Her research and teaching area is intercultural communication and competence acquisition in the multilingual and international Higher Education context.

Terence Holden teaches in the Languages and Philosophy Departments of the University of Boğazici, Istanbul. He previously worked as a research assistant at the EHESS, Paris, and has worked extensively as a translator. He obtained his doctorate from the University of Edinburgh in 2010; his thesis was published by Bloomsbury Press under the title *Levinas, Messianism and Parody*.

Costas Mantzalos is a Professor of Fine Arts at Frederick University in Nicosia. He was trained as a visual artist and also specialized in information design in the UK. He then registered for a higher research degree and investigated the survey of postmodern graphic arts in Cyprus. Costas Mantzalos is also a design consultant for international organizations such as Hilton Hotels, Tetra Pak, Unicef, as well as the cofounder of the TWOFOURTWO art group, a two-person group working as an entity in Frankfurt, Paris and Thessaloniki.

Jean-Charles Meunier teaches English at the Université Polytechnique Hauts-de-France. His research focuses on the revival of folk music in the USA, exploring the work of Woody Guthrie, Peet Seeger among others. His current research project explores the translation of Bob Dylan's songs into French.

Bentolhoda Nakhaei is a Lecturer in Translation studies at the Université Clermont Auvergne, Clermont Ferrand. Her research interest is in the domain of translation studies in three languages, Persian, English, and French. She holds a PhD on the poetics of Omar Khayyám from the Université of Ispahan and the Sorbonne Nouvelle.

Vicky Pericleous is a visual artist and assistant professor at Frederick University, Department of Art and Communication. She holds a B. A (Hons) in Fine Art from Manchester Metropolitan University, (1995-1997), an M.A in Theatre Design / Scenography, (re-named Visual Language of Performance), from Wimbledon School of Art, London, (1997-1999) and attended the Venice Fine Art Academy, Italy, (1995-6) on an Erasmus scholarship.

Clíona Ní Ríordáin is a Professor of Translation Studies and convenes the Master's degree in Irish Studies at the Sorbonne Nouvelle, where she leads the research group ERIN (part of the PRISMES research cluster). Her most recent publication *Jeune Poésie d'Irlande: Les poètes du Munster* (Illador, 2015), was co-edited and co-translated with Paul Bensimon. The duo has completed a new volume of translations, *Plus loin encore*, a bilingual volume of Gerry Murphy's poetry, due in autumn 2019. Her seminar, "Traduction: Pouvoir et Marges", examines questions of power and marginality in a variety of intercultural contexts.

Marie Schröer is a research assistant and lecturer (French literary and cultural studies) at the University of Koblenz-Landau. Her publications focus on contemporary literature, semiotics and comics. She has earned a PhD from Potsdam University for her dissertation on autobiographical comics, co-hosts the platform *Berlin Comic-Kolloquium* (www.comic-kolloquium.de) and writes comic reviews for the German newspaper *Tagesspiegel*.

Chantal Schütz is associate professor of English at the École Polytechnique and head of the Department of Languages and Communication. Her recent work includes articles and book chapters on: Shakespeare and music; Middleton; music, musical instruments and musicians at court.

Stephanie Schwerter is professor of Anglophone literature at the Université Polytechinque Hauts-de-France. Previously, she taught Comparative Literature and Translation Studies at the École des Hautes Etudes en Sciences Sociales in Paris and worked at the University of Ulster and at Queen's University Belfast in Northern Ireland.

Marina Tsvetkova is Professor of English at the National Research University Higher School of Economics in Nizhny Novgorod, Russia. She is a graduate of Moscow Lomonossov University where she studied languages and literature. Her area of expertise is comparative studies in literature, translation studies, intercultural communication, as well as the semiotics of cinema.

Angela Vaupel is a Senior Lecturer in Cultural Studies at St Mary's University College, Queen's University Belfast, UK. Her research interests are interdisciplinary and draw on cultural and film studies, intercultural education, and (German) exile and identity studies. Angela is a founding member of the International Feuchtwanger Society and a fellow of the Higher Education Academy in the UK.

ibidem.eu